France and the Atlantic Revolution of the Eighteenth Century, 1770–1799

JACQUES GODECHOT

France and the Atlantic Revolution of the Eighteenth Century, 1770–1799

Translated by Herbert H. Rowen

THE FREE PRESS, NEW YORK
COLLIER-MACMILLAN PUBLISHERS, LONDON

Copyright © *1965* by The Free Press

a division of Macmillan Publishing Co. Inc.
New York

All rights reserved. No part of this book may be reproduced or utilized in any form or by any means, electronic or mechanical, including photocopying, recording, or by any information storage and retrieval system, without permission in writing from the Publisher.

Collier Macmillan Ltd.
Stockley Rd, West Drayton, Middx
Sydney, Auckland, Toronto, Johannesburg,
an affiliate of Macmillan Publishing Co. Inc.
New York.

First Printing in Great Britain 1971
Reprinted 1973, 1975, 1977, and 1979

ISBN 0–02–973890–3

Printed and bound in Great Britain at
The Camelot Press Ltd, Southampton

CONTENTS

chapter one

THE ATLANTIC REVOLUTION: CHARACTERISTICS AND CAUSES

General Characteristics of the Atlantic Revolution

In 1763 the era of great social movements was long past. There had been no major civil war for many decades, not since the wars of religion of the late sixteenth and early seventeenth centuries in Germany, the revolutions of 1640–1648 and 1688–1689 in England, the rebellions of the Fronde (1648–1652), and the Protestant *Camisards* in the early eighteenth century in France. These disorders ended with consolidation of the authority of the "princes"—the general name for all sovereign rulers in the early modern period. Thereafter the people lived so quietly and obediently under the rule of emperors, kings, and republics that there appeared no prospect that the social movements would be renewed. The potentates and diplomats who brought the Seven Years' War to an end by means of treaties which rewrote the map of the Western world were untroubled by threats to their authority from their own subjects. Had they not sent their subjects to war—Frenchmen against Englishmen, Prussians against Austrians, Russians against Swedes and Turks? Had they not shipped their soldiers to India and America to fight? Had they not turned their alliances topsy-turvy? Nothing had stirred the people to resistance. The cabinets, as the governments were called, ruled without thought of possible violent reaction from their subjects.

The pattern of cabinet rule may be summed up in a few phrases. Warfare was turning into an affair of daintiness and good manners; strategy and tactics into a pedantic chess game which left almost no place for battle—the confrontation of men in the supreme test of strength. Similarly, international relations were handled in secret by the kings' private diplomats. Territories changed hands thanks to wily schemes and skillful intrigues. At stake was the preservation of the balance among the great powers; yet the strength of each ruler was measured not by the industrial resources at his disposal but by the number of "souls" at his command. To be sure, there was the force of public opinion, just coming into existence. It spoke through the mouths of the *philosophes,*[1] often in sarcastic tones. But was there any danger from these men of thought, who satirized the vanity of wars and diplomatic maneuvers? Their visible influence extended no further than to a small number of "wits." Besides, they proclaimed that they were citizens of the world, not just of one country. Thus, although the philosophes made fun of the way the princes conducted foreign policy, there seemed to be no danger from their jibes.

But around 1770 a force was released which the gov-

[1] The French word for "philosopher," now used in English for social and political thinkers of the Enlightenment, as distinct from philosophers concerned with metaphysics.—*Trans.*

ernments were no longer accustomed to dealing with. This was the crowd, the mass of ordinary people. Riots and popular uprisings began to occur everywhere in the Western world from the Urals to the Alleghenies, often with very dissimilar causes and apparently very unrelated goals. These outbreaks were especially violent along the Atlantic coasts, especially in North America, France, and the Netherlands. Before we study these events in detail, their number and their significance may be briefly noted.

The revolutionary movement began in 1768 in the republic of Geneva, a tiny corner of Western Europe wedged between France, the Swiss Confederation, and the kingdom of Sardinia. Agitation arose among the poor "natives" (*natifs*), persons born in Geneva of immigrant parents of foreign nationality. Following the advice of their celebrated compatriot Jean-Jacques Rousseau in his *Social Contract,* published six years before, they demanded equality of rights with the citizens.

During 1768 agitation also began in the English colonies of North America. The colonists were aroused by measures taken by the British government regarding Canada and Louisiana, by new taxes, and by the attitude of King George III of England, who apparently wished to govern his American subjects in all things without consulting their representatives. The Boston Massacre, the first armed conflict, occurred in 1770. It was followed three years later by another popular disturbance, the Boston Tea Party. In 1775 came the battles of Lexington and Concord between colonial insurgents and His Britannic Majesty's army. Civil war was soon transformed into international war, which ended only eight years later with the recognition of the independence of the United States of America.

But 1775 was the year not only of the American uprising. During the same year two other insurrections took place, at opposite ends of Europe. Although both were peasant rebellions, there was no visible connection between them. One was the great uprising of Russian peasants known as the Pugachev Revolt, which lasted from 1773 to 1775; the other was the peasant revolt in the Paris region which has remained celebrated under the name of the Flour War (*guerre des farines*).

Three years later disorders broke out in Ireland in connection with the demands of the Irish Volunteers, a movement at first limited to Protestants but soon extended to Catholics. Like the "natives" of Geneva, the serfs of Russia, and the American colonists, the Irish demanded a change in their status in society. The agitation of the Irish caused disorders within England by contagion and by reaction. These were the Yorkshire Movement and especially the frightful Gordon Riots in London during June 1780. During the Gordon Riots, some fifty houses were burned down, more than were lost by similar violence in Paris during the entire period of the revolution. A few concessions by the British Parliament, but even more the end of the war in America, brought the agitation in Great Britain to a halt. But the revolution was rekindled in Geneva at the same moment. The "natives," unable to gain victory in 1768, seized power with the aid of the "burghers" (*bourgeois*) in April 1782 and attempted to give the old republic a new and more democratic constitution. They failed as a result of the intervention of French, Sardinian, Bernese, and Zurich troops called in by the aristocrats.

This setback did not discourage the Dutch burghers, who began an insurrection in 1783 against the stadholder, the leader of the United Provinces. Like the Genevans, they were victorious after four years of struggle, but they too had to face foreign troops. Prussian soldiers and British sailors called in by the stadholder entered the Dutch Republic in 1787 and reestablished the old regime.

In spite of what had happened in Geneva and Amsterdam, the Belgians did not hesitate to revolt against their sovereign, Emperor Joseph II, in 1787. The Belgian "Patriots" were victorious in 1789, but they unfortunately were split between liberals (Vonckists) and conservatives (Statists). They too had to accept defeat when faced by intervention of Austrian troops the following year.

In the midst of these events, revolution broke out in France. It began with a revolt of the nobility in 1787. When elections to the Estates General were held in 1789, the revolution spread to every stratum of the nation, especially to the peasantry, who constituted 90 percent of the population. In France the revolution was deeper and more violent than anywhere else in the West. This is why for so long it has been customary to speak of the "French Revolution" even when what is meant are all social and political movements which disturbed Europe from 1787 to 1815. The revolution in France not only toppled the old regime and replaced it by a new order in that country; it also rekindled and fed the flame of revolution, and bore it to other parts of the world. First was Poland, where King Stanislas Poniatowski carried through a true political revolution on May 3, 1791, with the aid of the bourgeoisie and a fraction of the "enlightened" nobility. Poland was drawn into new wars with its neighbors and a more democratic revolution in 1794, but the price it paid was defeat and the partition of the remaining Polish territory among Russia, Prussia, and Austria in 1795.

The revolution in France gave new hope to the refugee revolutionaries from Geneva, Holland, Belgium, and Ireland. In France they reasserted and strengthened their beliefs, and formed military units in preparation for resuming their interrupted work. The revolution broke out again in 1792 in Switzerland, at Geneva, and at Porrentruy, within the old bishopric of Basel. In the same year Belgian revolutionaries returning home upon the heels of the French troops renewed their attack on the old regime in the Austrian Netherlands. A revolution broke out in 1790 in the Comtat Venaissin and Avignon, papal possessions enclaved in southern France, and these territories joined France the next year. Savoy imitated them in 1792. During the same year the Rhineland also displayed its sympathies for the revolution. In 1795 Dutch revolutionaries following after invading French troops were able to return to Holland where they organized a democratic republic. The following year it was Italy which was reached by the revolution; in 1798 it was all of Switzerland; and in 1799 the revolutionary ideas were carried by French armies to Malta and Egypt. England and Ireland were not spared disorder. Only the vigorous action of the British government prevented the revolutionary movement from spreading in England and overthrowing its authority in Ireland. Although by 1799 the revolutionary ideas had gained adherents everywhere in the West, there were countries—Russia, Scandinavia, the Ottoman Empire, Spain, and Portugal—where they had very little broad influence.

The year 1799 marked a stage in the course of the revolution, not its end. The spread of revolutionary ideas did not end when a military dictator came to power in France in the person of Napoleon Bonaparte. The soldiers of the Consulate and the Empire carried the revolutionary doctrines to regions where they had as yet hardly penetrated—Hungary, Russia, the South of Spain, and Portugal. From Iberia they were carried to Spanish and Portuguese America. The war of independence of the Spanish colonies in America was an integral part of the revolutionary movement. But after 1799 a change took place in the methods by which the revolution spread. No longer was there vigorous activity by the mass of the people. We shall therefore halt this account of the Atlantic Revolution with the coup d'état of 18 Brumaire in France, which did not mark an end of the revolution but significant changes in its character.

This brief account shows that the three decades from 1770 to 1800 were marked by revolutionary disorders, in contrast to the calm and the popular submissiveness which had characterized the previous seventy years. Yet it is possible to hold that all these revolutionary disorders were the result only of mere coincidence. To prove that they actually belonged to a single great movement and formed a single Atlantic Revolution we must prove that they arose from identical general causes.

The Causes of the Atlantic Revolution

Causes common to a revolutionary movement extending over half of Europe and the European-colonized part of America necessarily lay very deep in the character of society. In the first place, these causes were certainly bound up with transformations in the social structure itself. This was asserted in 1793 by Barnave, a French revolutionary and former member of the Constituent Assembly, who died later that year on the guillotine. In an interesting book, *Introduction to the French Revolution,* which was published for the first time in 1843 and republished in 1960, Barnave showed that everywhere in Europe society had been originally feudal, with the immense majority of inhabitants living under the domination of the landed aristocracy. Possession of the land had been the only source of wealth and the basis of power. The great discoveries of the sixteenth century and the rise of transoceanic navigation led to development of a new social class, the commercial bourgeoisie, and to the growth of great cities, in particular the ports situated on either side of the ocean—London, Paris, Rouen, Antwerp, Amsterdam, Hamburg, New York, and Philadelphia.

The commercial bourgeoisie of these great cities spurred the expansion of industry, which became very rapid after the late eighteenth century thanks to the invention of the steam engine and other machines. The labor force expanded rapidly too. The revolution originated ultimately in the desire of the new classes, especially the bourgeoisie, to come to power. Nor, declared Barnave, was the revolution limited to a single country; it was a "European revolution with France at its apex."

Present-day historians, recognizing the truth of Barnave's ideas, have also been struck by their "Marxist" formulation. They regret, however, that Barnave spoke of a purely "European" revolution, for the revolutionary movement first showed its force across the Atlantic. It would be better to speak either of the "Revolution of the West" or of the "Atlantic Revolution."

If as a whole the pattern described by Barnave is correct, it is nevertheless rather vague. It can now be made more precise as a result of the numerous studies of the social structure of the Western countries made during recent years. Although these studies bring out very noticeable regional differences, they also demonstrate incontestable similarities.

Two types of social structure can be distinguished in Europe and America. In some regions, the peasants were usually owners of the land; in other regions they worked as serfs or slaves upon lands belonging to large landowners, who were generally noblemen. Europe west of the Elbe and North America above the Potomac belonged to the first type of structure. In these countries the tiller of the soil was either its absolute owner, in the Roman sense of the word, or a manorial tenant—actually the owner of the land subject to the payment of manorial ("feudal") dues which varied in importance according to the region. Or he might be a renting farmer, paying either a money rent or a share of the crop. Of course, there were landless peasants, whom the French called *brassiers* because they had only their arms (*bras*) with which to work; but they could move about freely and take up another trade if they wished. Property in land was generally small and scattered. Although the nobility and the Church still owned an important portion of the land—in some regions as much as 30 to 40 percent of the acreage—it must not be forgotten that a large fraction of the nobles' lands and the greatest part of the clergy's lands were rented to peasantry. This was the fundamental agrarian structure of western Germany, the Low Countries, France, northern Italy, and northern Spain. In England small landed property was becoming less important, giving way to great enclosed estates which the landlords farmed with free wage-laborers. In central and southern Italy and in most of Spain large estates or *latifundia* predominated, but the agricultural workers who cultivated them—very badly, it may be added—lived in big villages of urban character and were completely free. Furthermore, the agrarian system presented significant variations. In the west and south of Western Europe, the fields were generally irregular in form and were enclosed by hedges; this system further strengthened the peasant's individualism. In the north, on the contrary, the open-field system prevailed. The parcels of land were grouped into "fields" (*soles*) or "seasons"; everyone who cultivated the same seasonal field was compelled to plant the same crop. Once the harvest was brought in all the inhabitants of the village, including those who possessed no land, were entitled to bring their livestock to graze upon the stubble. This was the system of "stubble right" (*vaine pâture*), to which the *brassiers* were strongly attached. However, the big landowners, noble and bourgeois alike, increasingly sought the abolition of stubble rights so that they could make their fields more productive.

This structure of peasant society in Western Europe forms an extraordinary contrast to the system that prevailed east of the Elbe river. While west of the Elbe serfdom remained exceptional (in France in 1789 there were less than a million serfs—more precisely *mainmortables,* peasants who could not inherit property without paying a fee to their lord), serfdom was the rule beyond the Elbe. The peasant serfs were almost never owners, tenants, renters, or even sharecroppers. They were *adscripti glebae,* bound to the soil and sold with it. The peasants of Eastern Europe, in their immense majority without any education, passively accepted the rule of the lord, who enjoyed very extensive and almost absolute powers over them. The mentality of the Prussian Junker and the Polish or Hungarian magnate was therefore very different from that of the French squire, the British landlord, or even the Neapolitan baron. South of the Potomac in the British North American colonies, and in the French, Spanish, and Portuguese colonies of Central and South America the land was tilled by black slaves imported from Africa. Conditions resembled those on the estates of Eastern Europe, although the white proprietors would have been indignant to hear themselves compared to Polish or

Russian noblemen. They considered slavery a "peculiar institution" bound up with the tropical or equatorial climate; they saw no reason whatever for it to disturb their feeling of belonging to the Western world, which they held to be the vanguard of civilization.

If we pass from the peasantry to an examination of the structure of the other social classes, the contrast between the regions of Eastern and Western Europe becomes even sharper. Everywhere in Western Europe there existed a rich and active bourgeoisie which inhabited numerous large cities. London, Paris, and Naples exceeded 500,000 inhabitants; Hamburg, Liverpool, Amsterdam, Nantes, and Bordeaux attained or passed 100,000, and it would take too much space to list the cities with more than 50,000 inhabitants. East of the Elbe it is possible to cite only Warsaw, Moscow, and St. Petersburg among cities with more than 100,000 population. In Western Europe the bourgeoisie formed a powerful class whose wealth was comparable to, and sometimes even surpassed, that of the nobility. They were in control of almost all trade and the largest part of industry. Furthermore, industry had begun a full-scale revolution in 1750. The invention of the steam engine and various other machines, especially in the textile industry, resulted in the appearance of the first large factories, most of which were in the hands of the bourgeoisie. East of the Elbe, however, the bourgeoisie was extremely small in numbers. Internal trade was almost entirely in the hands of Jews; foreign trade was conducted by the nobility or even by the state.

In Western Europe one of the principal causes of social disturbances consisted in the rise of the bourgeoisie. They possessed wealth and desired power. They did in fact participate in the exercise of power in England, the

Netherlands, and several regions of Italy but wanted to gain power in France and to have a larger share of it in Italy, Ireland, and the British colonies of America.

We thus see that the rise and ambitions of the bourgeoisie formed one of the elements of social disorder in the West. But other factors of more acute character resulted from the expansion of the population.

Nowadays sociologists agree that quantitative changes of the population structure are among the essential causes of the revolutions of the contemporary world. No one disputes that the acquisition of independence by the countries of North Africa was essentially prompted by an increase in their population at a rate so rapid that some writers have characterized it as "demented." Why should it have been otherwise in the past? More and more numerous studies of the demographic evolution of the West in the eighteenth century show that a considerable increase also occurred then. Of course it was not a new phenomenon: the population of the globe has been growing ever since the origin of mankind. But today we are quite sure that this growth was not continuous but came in spurts. Europe probably did not have many more inhabitants at the end of the seventeenth century than it had at the end of the fifteenth. During the eighteenth century, on the contrary, the population of Europe doubled on the average, although the increase varied according to the region. It was very large in England but less in France. In Venice the population actually became smaller. The figures on population in Poland and Russia are uncertain, but the fact of growth is indisputable. More important perhaps than the increase in numbers as such was the modification of the demographic pattern.

Between the fifteenth and the eighteenth centuries the failure of the European population to grow had been the consequence of a series of profound crises, epidemics (generally called "plagues"), and wars. Plagues and wars in particular resulted in catastrophic drops in the population. To be sure, the high birth rate permitted a rapid return to the previous figure, but then new crises followed which prevented any further rise. Infant mortality was considerable. More than half the newborn did not live beyond one year of age. Life expectancy was short; the average life extended little beyond twenty-four years. This whole pattern was transformed during the eighteenth century. Although infant mortality remained very high and decreased only very, very slowly, the adult mortality rate diminished considerably; thus life expectancy increased. In France the total population, which had never exceeded 18 million since the fourteenth century, passed this figure around 1730 and reached 26 million in 1789. The population of the whole of Europe passed from 100 million to about 200 million between 1700 and 1800.

This was a phenomenon of capital importance. The increase of the population created two fundamental problems. One was subsistence: would the augmentation of food production keep up with the growth in the population? The other was employment: would the surplus population be able to find work? These questions preoccupied the scientists and philosophes of the eighteenth century. They gave various and often contradictory replies. The Englishman Thomas Malthus, a pessimist, favored reducing the number of births.

In any case we are in the presence of the fact that the European population doubled. What were the consequences of this increase? Did it cause the disorders and the revolution? So far as expansion of food production is concerned, the problem is very complex. It seems well established at the present time, thanks to recent studies, that the increase in the European population was due first of all to improvement of agricultural production. The discovery of America in the late fifteenth and sixteenth centuries made available to Europeans new plants which either were more nutritious or had a bigger yield than the crops which had long been cultivated in Europe. These included maize (American corn), which had a yield of 32 to 1, while the best varieties of wheat sowed in Europe yielded only three or four to one; the potato, which grew very well in poor soils; tobacco, whose leaf was in great demand and sold at a very high price; and vegetables such as the kidney bean and the pumpkin. These plants were introduced into Europe as early as the sixteenth century but were accepted slowly, and the consequences of their cultivation only became evident in the eighteenth century. There is no doubt that they improved the diet of the European peasant and thereby contributed to increasing his resistance to disease. Hence adult mortality fell. The progress of hygiene and medicine does not seem to have played a major part in reducing mortality. But as the European population increased, the surplus in agricultural products decreased. Other ways for increasing production had to be considered. The English agronomists and the French physiocrats began scientific study of the process of cultivation of the soil. They recommended development of pasturage by means of artificial meadows, abandonment of triennial or biennial rotation of crops (which left as much as half the ground fallow each year), development of industrial crops, selection of seed, and suppression of open pasture by means of the enclosure of farmlands. These suggestions were often adopted. In France, butcher shops increased in number and had spread even to the smallest villages by the end of the eighteenth century. Nonetheless it does seem a fact that agricultural production was unable to keep up with the increase in the population. After 1770, bad crops due to weather conditions (excessive rainfall or heat) resulted in famines such as Western Europe had not seen for fifty years.

Employment was a different problem. When population began to increase, men easily found jobs in agriculture, which was developing rapidly. In certain countries of Western Europe, like France, the Netherlands, Germany and especially England, the start of the Industrial Revolution and the building of big factories resulted in the creation of new jobs. But soon there were not enough jobs, and unemployment developed. The number of jobless vagrants in France on the eve of the revolution was considerable. Here is the significant complaint made by the villagers of La Caune, near Châlons, in their grievance list (*cahier de doléances*) in 1789: "The number of our children makes us despair. We do not have the means to feed or clothe them." An inquiry conducted by the "committee on mendicancy" of the Constituent Assembly in 1790 revealed that in about half of France (44 departments out of 86) the number of the "indigent" (that is, the unemployed) was more than 10 percent; in six departments, including Haute-Garonne, Le Nord, and Pas-de-Calais, it reached one-fifth of the population. In England and Germany the employment situation was less difficult: in the former country big industry was more developed; in the latter overseas emigration was more important. However, despite the great extent of vacant land, the arrival of an increasing number of immigrants in America confronted that country with problems like those which the increase in population placed before Europe.

The considerable increase in the population of the Western world resulting from introduction of new plants of American origin into Europe must be considered incontestably one of the major causes of the revolutions of the Atlantic world. Indeed, it was from the innumerable unemployed that were recruited not the leaders, but the troops, of the revolutionary armies.

The difficulties met after 1770 by a young population in the full flood of expansion are bound up with the economic cycle. The business cycle has not been studied in its entirety for the whole of the West but only in some individual countries—England, Spain, Holland, and especially France. Tables of prices and sometimes of wages have been established and curves drawn. The examination of these curves demonstrates that in a general manner prices rose slowly from about 1730 to 1770. From 1770 to 1790 we observe a plateau marked by very accentuated sawteeth in the curves. These peaks and hollows on the graphs are the indicators of repeated economic crises, which appear to be the origins of the demographic crises revealed by the birth and death curves. Where in most cases the birth rate clearly exceeded the death rate between 1730 and 1770, from 1770 until 1790 a surplus of deaths is often observable. The demographic curves thus reproduce the sawteeth of the price curve and confirm the existence of serious and profound crises. The shape of the price curve in Western Europe has been explained by variation of the imports of precious metals. The discovery of gold in Brazil in the Minas Gerães and its introduction into European monetary circulation brought an increase in prices after 1730. The slowing of gold shipments around 1770 is one of the causes of the slackening of the increase in prices and hence of the economic stagnation.

Although wages increased, they lagged far behind prices, so that wage-earners—farm laborers, artisans, and factory hands—found themselves in a less favorable situation. In France prices increased on the average from 48 to 65 percent between 1730 and 1789, but wages rose only from 11 to 26 percent. Comparing the rise of *nominal wages* with the increase in the cost of living, we observe a fall in *real wages*. This fall was the consequence on the one hand of the rapid increase in the population of working age and on the other hand of the weak development of big industry in France. In fact, Watt's steam engine, perfected in England between 1769 and 1776, was not put to use in France until 1785 at the metallurgical factory of Le Creusot. The smelting of iron ore by means of coke instead of charcoal was practiced in England and Germany as early as 1750, but not before 1785 in France. Where the British textile industry used 20,000 jennies in 1789, France possessed only 7,000. In the last decade of the eighteenth century, England had numerous factories employing more than a hundred workers, but France had only a few—several metallurgical plants in Le Nord, Alsace, Lorraine, and Le Creusot. Western Germany and Belgium were perhaps better equipped than France, but northern Italy was definitely behind France. At the end of the eighteenth century, England had at least a twenty years' headstart over the most developed countries on the continent.

The transformation of agriculture as recommended by the English agronomists and the French and Italian physiocrats did not create new jobs for the excess population. On the contrary, extension of pasturage, development of artificial meadows, enclosures, partition of common lands, and suppression of open grazing had the inevitable consequence of reducing the number of farm jobs. Livestock raising requires fewer hands than tilling the soil. When communal lands and open grazing were abolished, the poor *brassier* could no longer keep a cow or sheep and was reduced to the status of a rural proletarian. The modernization of agriculture therefore had the result of increasing the number of available workers. In England most of them were rapidly absorbed by industry, then in the process of rapid expansion. On the continent they were driven into unemployment and destitution and became elements of social disorder.

International trade also felt the effect of these changes. England became an even more intense competitor in the great international markets, clashing sharply with France especially. French merchants hoped to find compensation in increased trade with the United States, as seemed to be promised by the treaty of 1778, but they were disappointed. Instead of opening new outlets to French trade, the Anglo-French treaty of commerce of 1787 (the "Eden treaty") merely increased English exports to France and hence the economic struggle between the two countries.

In America the situation was somewhat different. The economic cycle does not seem to have developed there as it did in Europe, although the problems of employment and economic competition were similar. In the second half of the eighteenth century the local aristocracy tended to monopolize the land and to assemble vast estates, in particular in the Hudson valley. The surplus population resulting from the excess of births and the arrival of immigrants had difficulty in finding land in already cleared regions. The land-seeker had to go West as a pioneer. As for the merchants, the numerous fiscal measures adopted by the British government after 1763, especially the tax on tea, cut into their trade and drove them into opposition. In summary, after 1770, in America as in Europe, the economic cycle was unfavorable, increasing general insecurity and encouraging social agitation.

It was in this atmosphere of uncertainty and economic and social difficulties that the ideas of the philosophes began to spread. The philosophes in the eighteenth century were recruited in various countries of the West, but they felt themselves to be cosmopolitans and wrote for the world. Of this varied group of writers, those who wrote in French—Montesquieu, Voltaire, Rousseau, D'Alembert, Diderot, and many others—were indisputably the most numerous and the most brilliant. But the British with John Locke, Adam Smith, David Hume, and Arthur Young also held a prominent place. The Italians were represented by Beccaria, Genovesi, and Pietro Verri; the Germans by Kant, Schiller, and Goethe; the Americans by Franklin—to cite only the most famous.

The philosophes of the eighteenth century were the heirs of the ideas of Francis Bacon, Descartes, and Spinoza, who had demonstrated the possibility of dominating nature by means of science and had substituted the results of experience and the conclusions of reason for the authority of tradition not only in the realm of science but also in the realms of religion, morality, economics, and politics. Yet the philosophes were not all in agreement among themselves. They formed "schools," among which three fundamental tendencies can be distinguished. The first school was linked to the ideas of John Locke and Montesquieu. It asserted that all government is based upon a treaty or contract between the sovereign and his subjects and that all good government must be composed of three separate powers—the legislative, the executive, and the judicial. Montesquieu insisted upon the role which the aristocracy and the "intermediate corporations" must play in any good government. This tendency was therefore favorable to the aristocracy. As expounded in Montesquieu's *Spirit of the Laws,* published in 1748, the doctrines of this school had extraordinary success in Europe and America. Montesquieu's concepts were taken up and developed further, notably by Réal de Curban in France in the six volumes of his *Science of Government,* and in England by William Blackstone in his *Commentaries on the Laws* (1758) and William Warburton in his *Alliance between Church and States* (1736).

The second school numbered Voltaire among its most eminent representatives. Voltaire did not attack absolute monarchy; he merely wanted it to be "enlightened" by the counsels of the philosophes. Where Montesquieu invoked "historic rights," Voltaire appealed to "natural rights," implying the equality of all persons before the monarch. He attacked the privileges of the nobility and the Church with wit and vehemence. Sometimes he fought religion as such. In the same class as Voltaire may be put the French physiocrats and their Italian emulators, who held that only a strong monarch was capable of making the indispensable economic reforms.

Jean-Jacques Rousseau, a Genevan, was the principal theoretician of the third tendency. In his *Discourse on the Sciences and the Arts* of 1750 and even more in his *Discourse on Inequality* of 1755 and his *Social Contract* of 1752, he put himself forward as the apostle of equality. Holding that civilization and luxury have perverted mankind, he called for a return to primitive simplicity and equality. The sovereignty of the people, he held, will make it possible to destroy privileges, to combat abuses, and to limit property in certain cases. Disciples of Rousseau, particularly Abbé Mably and Morelly, went even further, proposing the radical suppression of private property and outlining a communist system of society.

All these ideas were popularized by innumerable commentators, notably in the *Encyclopédie,* which began to appear in France in 1751 and was translated into the principal Western languages. They were also debated by the numerous discussion groups—academies, scholarly societies, economic societies, societies of "friends of the country," reading clubs, salons, cafés, and Masonic lodges, all of which multiplied in the eighteenth century. There has been much debate over the role of Freemasonry in the origins of the Revolution. As early as 1798 Abbé Barruel, an emigrant French priest living in Hamburg, wrote in his *Memoirs for a History of Jacobinism* that the revolution was the result of a Masonic plot. This accusation has been frequently repeated and no doubt is still to be heard. It might perhaps be possible to give some credence to this idea if the revolution had remained limited to one small country. But simple common sense does not permit us to accept this theory. How would a secret association have been able to rouse huge numbers of peasants, bourgeois, and artisans everywhere from the Alleghenies to the Vistula? It would have had to possess power and ramifications such as Freemasonry never did. Today the composition of the Masonic lodges in France on the eve of the revolution is well known. Most Masons were nobles, rich bourgeois, or clergymen; many of them were at least half committed to the counterrevolution after 1792. It is certain that the Freemasons were not the authors of the revolution. It is indisputable, however, that the lodges, like other "intellectual societies," contributed to spreading the ideas of the philosophes, and that they thereby helped to shake the prestige of the most venerable authorities and to undermine the old regime.

This intellectual movement of the second half of the eighteenth century was so unified and coherent in essentials that it has been given a characteristic name in every language: *Enlightenment* in English, *Aufklärung* in German, *Illuminismo* in Italian, *les lumières* in French. There can be no doubt that even if these ideas had been spread in a period of prosperity and tranquillity, they would have caused disturbances and had political and social repercussions. But the world after 1770 was in the full flood of change. Trying unsuccessfully to solve acute problems of poverty and unemployment, it was confronted with the spectacle of a scientific and industrial revolution and saw the appearance of new machines like the steam engine and the aeronautical balloon. In such a world the ideas of the Enlightenment could not help but have fundamental consequences. The Enlightenment is unquestionably one of the important causes of the Atlantic Revolution.

The Atlantic Revolution also had political causes. The slow but continuous rise of prices during the course of the eighteenth century affected not only individuals but also the states. The financial resources of governments, coming essentially from taxes, rapidly became insufficient to cover their expenses. This was all the more true because expenses rose considerably as a result of the great wars that disturbed the first two-thirds of the eighteenth century. From 1700 to 1783 there took place the War of the Spanish Succession, which lasted twelve years, the War of the Polish Succession, which lasted four, the War of the Austrian Succession, which lasted seven, and the Seven Years' War: in all a total of thirty years of war out of sixty-three, or almost one year out of every two. The states had to introduce new taxes in order to meet their enormous military expenses. But nowhere was it possible to demand more of the peasants and the bourgeois, who until then had borne the principal share of government expenditures. It became imperative to abolish the fiscal privileges of the nobility and the clergy. Although this meant a frontal attack on privileged institutions, most sovereigns did not hesitate to adopt this policy. To justify their conduct, they employed the theories of those philosophes who sang the praises of absolute monarchy provided it was "enlightened." Thus "enlightened despotism" was born. It was characteristic particularly of the reigns of Frederick II in Prussia, Catherine II in Russia, Maria Theresa and Joseph II in the Holy Roman Empire (Germany), and sovereigns of lesser importance in Italy and Spain.

In a majority of states the aristocracy organized (in Montesquieu's phrase) in "intermediate corporations" resisted this policy of the enlightened despots, which tended to strengthen the power of the state and to diminish or even to abolish totally the aristocrats' privileges. Russia and the Ottoman Empire were the only countries in Europe that were not the arena of such struggles. This was a consequence of the social structure of these states: the weakness of the nobility and the bourgeoisie, which were badly organized, and the huge numbers of the peasantry, who were subject to unlimited burdens of taxation and labor services. In most other countries of Europe and the European colonies of America, the privileged corporations, in the name of the "historic rights" which Montesquieu defended, resisted the demands of the state. In

Sweden it was the Riksdag, composed of the representatives of the four orders (nobility, clergy, bourgeoisie, peasantry), with the aristocracy predominant, which opposed the monarchy until the coup d'état of King Gustavus III in 1772. In Poland, Bohemia, and Hungary the diets, composed only or almost only of the nobles and the bishops, relentlessly resisted every effort to reinforce the central power, to make the executive more powerful, and to modernize the administration of the state. In Prussia there existed no national diet but only provincial assemblies (*Landtäge*), in which the nobility held the preponderant influence; they too attempted to struggle against the claims of the monarch. In Italy the aristocracy dominated most of the states. In old republics like Venice and Genoa they ruled as they pleased, but where the states were headed by princes, as in Lombardy and Tuscany, they opposed the princes' reforms. The situation was similar in most of the German principalities, in the Austrian Netherlands and in the United Provinces. In France the aristocracy was the master of the *parlements,* the courts of justice which claimed the right to present their views on all legislative enactments. They also dominated the provincial Estates which still existed in Languedoc, Brittany, and Burgundy. Even in Great Britain the aristocracy remained very powerful in Parliament. The assemblies of the English colonies of North America represented primarily the local aristocracy. The great administrative bodies of the French colonies in the Antilles were in the hands of the privileged classes, and in the Spanish colonies the *cabildos* were likewise composed of aristocrats.

In all these countries—that is, throughout the West—the aristocracy formed a front against the claims of the sovereigns. They strove not only to maintain their position but also to improve it, by obtaining confirmation of their privileges and monopolies, by having land registers brought up to date, and by more harshly than ever requiring from their vassals recognition of their privileges and payment of the feudal dues owed to them (for they too were the victims of the price rise and needed more money). This attitude of the nobility has been studied especially in France, where it has been called the "aristocratic reaction," the "reaction of the nobility," and the "feudal reaction." But the aristocratic reaction was not a specifically French phenomenon; it was a phenomenon of the West as a whole.

The sovereigns first attempted to break the aristocratic reaction by traditional means—that is, by decrees and commands and by invoking their theoretical omnipotence. But the interests at stake were such that the resistance of the privileged classes became more and more stubborn. The sovereigns then gave thought to the counsels of philosophes of the Voltairean tendency, who held all subjects to be equal before the monarch, and they sought the alliance of the Third Estate against the privileged orders. In France, Louis XV suppressed the parlements in 1771 upon the advice of his ministers Maupeou, Terray, and D'Aiguillon, and reformed the fiscal system by placing slightly greater burdens upon the privileged groups. In Sweden Gustavus III amended the constitution by his own authority in 1772; he reduced the powers of the aristocratic Riksdag and governed with the support of the bourgeoisie and the peasantry. In the Hapsburg states, Maria Theresa compelled the "constituted corporations" of Austria, Bohemia, the southern Netherlands, and Lombardy to accept heavier taxation and a new customs tariff in 1775. In 1765 the British government extended the Stamp Act to its possessions of North America without consulting the colonial assemblies. Faced by their resistance, the king withdrew the Stamp Act the next year, but he affirmed the superiority of the Crown over the colonial assemblies by the Declaratory Act. In the same period Louis XV also proclaimed his authority over the French parlements, the citadels of the aristocracy, in the famous "flagellation" session.

If sovereigns sought the support of the people, the privileged orders did not hesitate to do so too. Outbidding the rulers, the aristocrats proclaimed themselves to be the only defenders of the people. In France the members of the parlements took the name of "Fathers of the People." For a dozen years the bourgeoisie sincerely believed that they had no better defenders than the parlements; not until 1788 did the duplicity of the parlements become apparent. In the English colonies of America, the assemblies sought support against the British sovereign among the merchants, small farmers, and artisans. In general the people were encouraged not only by the philosophes but also by the privileged orders to enter into struggle against the sovereign. In most countries of the West the "aristocratic reaction" inevitably led to a revolt of the nobility and soon thereafter to a revolt of the people.

chapter two

THE REVOLUTIONS IN THE ATLANTIC WORLD, 1770–1789

The revolutions in the Atlantic world had causes which, as we have seen, were many in number and profound in character. Beyond question a given cause played a greater role in some regions than in others. Furthermore, each national revolution broke out in its own context and had its own specific causes. Nonetheless these revolutions all had a similar objective—to establish a new regime in which the citizens would enjoy greater equality and liberty and participate more fully in central government and local administration. This objective was very vague in the beginning but became more precise as time went on; how completely it was attained varied in the different countries of the West. Still, in general, the revolutions transformed the structure of the Atlantic world. By 1799 it no longer much resembled what it had been in 1770, and by 1825 it was completely transformed.

The American Revolution

It is not our purpose here to retell the history of the struggle for the independence of the United States. It is a well-known story and has been the subject of many excellent studies. However, we do propose to call attention to those facts which show that this struggle not only constituted a war for independence by colonists who wished to be free from a far-off mother country, but also that it was above all a political and social revolution, the most important in the Atlantic world before the French revolution.

At the origin of the American revolution lay a quarrel of economic and social character between the English colonies and the British government. In America the Seven Years War was a struggle between the French colonists in Canada and Louisiana and the British colonists. The Treaty of Paris which ended the war in 1763 seemed a victory for the British colonists. They looked forward to settling on the rich lands extending from the Alleghenies to the Mississippi which Great Britain had just annexed. However, the British government planned to reserve these lands to the French colonists who had just become its subjects or to immigrants from Europe, where jobs were becoming difficult to find. On October 7, 1763, the English government forbade the subjects of its older colonies to settle in the new lands. Furthermore, since the war had been extremely costly, the English government considered that it was fair that the colonies should pay a portion of its costs, since they had benefited by it. But the commercial system which bound the colonies to the mother country had become more flexible during the war. Although in normal times the colonies could not buy or sell in any other country than the mother country, the colonies in America had been authorized during the emergency to trade with the French Antilles—in particular to buy molasses, which brought them large profits. In 1763, the old commercial system was reestablished in its full rigor. But it did not provide enough revenues to refloat the British finances, and in 1765 a stamp tax was placed upon various kinds of commercial paper and newspapers in the colonies.

These measures aroused vigorous discontent. Protests came above all from the merchants of the principal ports and the great planters—the aristocracy who dominated the colonial assemblies. Like the "intermediate corporations" in Europe, these assemblies undertook a struggle against the sovereign. They declared that by virtue of the British constitutional traditions no new tax could be established without the consent of the subjects or their representatives. The Parliament in London replied that its members "virtually" represented all the subjects of the crown. The colonial assemblies did not accept this argument; they demanded not only the repeal of the new taxes but revision of the status of the British colonies. Delegates of nine colonies met together for the first time in history in a congress at Albany, New York, which rejected the principle of "taxation without representation." The assemblies worked to shore up their protests with popular support. Merchants agreed to boycott English goods and city workers joined with them in forming associations of "Sons of Liberty" to resist the arbitrary actions of the British sovereign. The English government gave in and withdrew the Stamp Act in 1766. But next year the British Parliament laid new taxes on paper, glass, lead, and tea sold in the colonies. The boycott and agitation were resumed. The custom officials who attempted to collect custom duties were beaten. Tension between American colonists and British soldiers increased. On March 5, 1770, the first shots of the Anglo-American war were fired in Boston. Three rioters were killed in this "Boston Massacre."

Again the British government gave way. It withdrew all the new taxes except that upon tea, which was kept in order to maintain the very principle of the superiority of the mother country. But it was precisely this principle which was at stake. Some American "patriots," such as Samuel Adams, began to think of independence. "Committees of Correspondence" were formed in all the colonies and spread the watchwords of the patriots.

The conflict calmed down somewhat, but surged up again in 1773. As a result of the economic crisis then raging in Europe, the English East India Company was no longer able to sell its tea in the continental market. The British government therefore granted it a monopoly of the sale of tea in the colonies. This monopoly was particularly injurious to the interests of American merchants. Where in previous years they had endeavored to calm the mass of the population, they now assumed the leadership of the opposition. When the colonists began smuggling tea, the East India Company dropped its price. The opponents of the monopoly—merchants, members of the committees of correspondence, Sons of Liberty—thereupon organized a demonstration designed to show their hostility to the British policy in dramatic fashion. On December 16, 1773, a group of men disguised as redskins boarded the ships of the East India Company in Boston harbor and threw the tea cargoes overboard.

The British government replied to this challenge by the "Coercive Acts." The port of Boston was closed and British officials were appointed in place of those who had been elected by the colonists. But at the same time (1774) the British Parliament passed the Quebec Act, which aroused discontent among the colonists for different reasons. It guaranteed to the inhabitants of French Canada their own language, religion, and institutions; any hope of absorption of Canada by the older British colonies thereby vanished.

The grievances of the English colonists in America mounted. A Continental Congress, in which representatives of all thirteen colonies sat, met at Philadelphia on September 5, 1774. It sent the British government a firm but moderate protest against the Coercive Acts, and organized a more effective boycott of all British goods by means of an "Association" which brought together all the revolutionary elements of the thirteen colonies. The chasm was growing deeper, first between the patriots and the Tories (who began to be called "Loyalists" because they supported the British government), and second between the patriots and the king of England's soldiers and officials. The war was not long in breaking out. Early in April 1775 General Gage, the British commander at Boston, was informed that patriots were collecting powder and military equipment in the little village of Concord, northwest of Boston. On April 18, a strong detachment of the Boston garrison was sent to Concord to seize the stores and arrest the patriot leaders Samuel Adams and John Hancock. After a night march, the redcoats were halted at the village of Lexington by some fifty armed patriots—the first rebels. Hesitating only a moment, the troops opened fire, and the patriots lost eight of their number. The soldiers were able to continue their advance; but at Concord they were met by sustained fire from the patriots. They had to turn back without accomplishing their mission. On the way to Boston they were harassed by the rebels and lost a tenth of their force—247 men out of 2,500, three times as many as the patriots lost. We have placed some stress upon this incident, for it was the first time in the history of the revolutions of the late eighteenth century that armed revolutionaries compelled troops of the regular army to retreat. The event was to be repeated many times, notably in Paris on July 14, 1789, when the armed people seized the fortress of the Bastille.

Lexington and Concord were the first battles in a war which began as a civil conflict—that is, a clash between rebels and a professional army—but soon became an international war when the United States obtained the alliance of France, Spain, and the United Provinces. It is not our purpose here to tell the entire story of this war, but it is enough to indicate its principal stages. In May 1775 a second Continental Congress called the citizenry to arms and organized an army under the command of General George Washington. For some time the patriots hoped that they could win concessions which would permit them to remain a part of Great Britain, but it soon became apparent that the positions of the colonies and Great Britain were irreconcilable. The English writer Thomas Paine, in a vigorous pamphlet entitled *Common Sense,* urged the colonies not only to declare their independence but also to become a republic. On June 7, 1776, Richard Henry Lee, a deputy from Virginia at the Continental Congress, proposed the formation of an independent American federation. A committee of five members under the chairmanship of Thomas Jefferson prepared a declaration of independence, which was adopted by the Congress on July 4, 1776.

For more than two years the rebels had to fight almost alone against the British armies, aided only by enthusiastic volunteers from Europe, including the Prussian von Steuben, the Pole Kosciuszko, and the Frenchman Lafayette. Only after the British army under General Burgoyne was forced to capitulate on the battlefield at Saratoga, on October 17, 1777, was the young United States able to gain the alliance of France (February 6, 1778). By this treaty France promised not only to obtain recognition of the independence of the United States from England but also not to reconquer Canada. The treaty also contained economic and commercial clauses. The United States negotiated an alliance with Spain in 1779 and with the United Provinces in 1780. The neutrals, led by Tsarina Catherine II of Russia, thereupon formed a league of armed neutrality designed to compel the English to respect freedom of the seas. Thus Great Britain was isolated; her communications in the Atlantic, under attack by French, Spanish, and Dutch fleets, became difficult; and she could no longer send reinforcements and supplies to her armies in America. France, on the contrary, was able to transport an expeditionary force of 8,000 men under the command of Rochambeau to the United States, and she also furnished arms and ammunition to the rebels. In 1780 the rebels began to win on the battlefield. The last British army surrendered at Yorktown on October 19, 1781. On November 30, 1782, the United States signed peace preliminaries with England; the Anglo-French treaty of Versailles, concluded in 1783, recognized the independence of the United States south of the Great Lakes and to the Mississippi.

Was the struggle of the United States against England only a war of independence? Or was it also at the same time a revolution? The problem has been vigorously debated, especially by American historians, who are deeply divided on this question. Some of them have seen in the American war of independence a revolution perhaps more radical than the French revolution. Others have denied that it brought about profound economic and social transformations in the former English colonies. The middle opinion now seems to be prevailing. It is that the American war of independence was indeed also a political, economic, and social revolution, but that as an economic and social revolution it was moderate in character. In any case it must be noted that the revolution was decisive and triumphant; it was not followed sooner or later by a counter-revolution, as happened in Europe.

The war in America was beyond dispute a great political revolution. The American patriots were the first who attempted to apply in practice the ideas of the philosophes, notably Locke, Montesquieu, and Rousseau, who had written that all government should be based upon a treaty or "social contract." First the new American states and then the federation which they formed adopted constitutions; these were generally preceded by declarations of rights. To be sure, the constitutions and the declarations were more easily accepted by the American citizens than they were later by the inhabitants of Europe because the notions of constitutions, individual freedom, and equality before the law were more familiar in the English colonies of America than in continental Europe. It remains true nonetheless that the practical measures adopted for writing the constitutions and declarations of rights achieved the status of a kind of higher law in Europe. The use of constitutional conventions was imitated, especially in France, as were such other institutions as the committees of correspondence, the committees of public safety and surveillance, clubs, representatives on mission, price controls, paper money, oaths of obedience to the law, and imprisonment of subjects.

In North Carolina it was the colonial legislative assembly which adopted the new constitution. But the deputies were provided by each county with instructions that resembled the grievance lists (*cahiers*) which the French deputies carried in 1789. These instructions urged the deputies to make a distinction between fundamental laws and ordinary laws, to consider the question of the number of houses in the new government (some called for two chambers, others wanted only a single chamber), and to assure the "separation of powers" as Locke and Montesquieu had recommended.

In Pennsylvania, it was a convention which was instructed to draft a constitution. The convention was elected in highly irregular circumstances. The western part of the state, which had been settled more recently and was more democratic, named a larger percentage of deputies in proportion to its population than the older eastern part. The Pennsylvania convention drafted a constitution in 1776 which was probably the most democratic of any adopted anywhere before the French constitution of 1793. The Pennsylvania constitution established a unicameral system. Representatives were elected by nearly universal suffrage; all taxpayers over twenty-one years of age were both voters and eligible to all offices (but almost all citizens of Pennsylvania were taxpayers). The executive power was entrusted to a president elected by the house and assisted by a council. The president did not possess the right of veto and could exercise his powers only with consent of his council. Provision was made for a referendum. An embryonic court of constitutional review was set up in a Council of Censors, meeting once every seven years to investigate whether the constitution had been violated during that time. These institutions were imposed by the democrats, who had defeated the conservatives in the elections for the convention.

Events took a different course in Massachusetts. There one man, John Adams, played the leading role. He presented his ideas on a future constitution in his *Thoughts on Government,* published early in 1776. He held that the purpose of government should be the "happiness of the people" and that a republic could be founded only upon virtue. He came out as a partisan of the bicameral system, the annual election of officials including the governor, and a public educational system paid for by the state and not by the churches. On the other hand, he opposed election of a constitutional convention, holding that the existing assembly had the power to draft a constitution. Under his influence the Massachusetts assembly drafted a constitution in 1778 which in its broad lines reproduced the organization of the British government. The assembly decided, however, to submit this constitution to a referendum, in which it was rejected. Both the democrats and the Loyalists voted against it, though for different reasons. A convention was then elected, which adopted a constitution drafted by John Adams; he said that he drew his inspiration from the ideas of Locke, Sidney, Rousseau, and Mably. In fact the new constitution was not very different from its predecessor. It provided for a governor, a senate, and a house of commons. Suffrage was broad but in order to be eligible for higher offices one had to possess a large income. One article required citizens to attend church. This constitution was adopted in a referendum, but the number of voters was very small, less than a quarter of those registered.

Several of the new American state constitutions were prefaced by declarations of rights. The oldest, most generous, and the most important in its repercussions was the declaration of rights of Virginia of June 12, 1776. It affirmed notably that "all men are by nature equally free and independent," that they have the right to enjoy "life and liberty, with the means of acquiring and possessing property, and pursuing and obtaining happiness and safety." It recognized the sovereignty of the people, proclaimed the right of resistance to oppression, the separation of powers, guarantees for those indicted, on trial, or convicted of crimes, personal responsibility of officials, freedom of the press, and the free exercise of religion. Less than a month later, on July 4, 1776, the Continental Congress in Philadelphia proclaimed the abjuration of the sovereignty of King George III in a Declaration of Independence which repeated the essential rights of men who had been "created equal": "life, liberty, and the pursuit of happiness." However, the Declaration of Independence placed most emphasis upon the rights of citizens of the United States; it therefore has a less universal character than the declaration of rights of Virginia or the French declaration of 1789.

It took five years after the proclamation of independence before the first constitution of the United States, the Articles of Confederation, was adopted in 1781. It organized the new republic in the form of a federal union. In an excessive concern to preserve democracy, central authority was left with very little power. Although the federal government was able to bring the war to an end, it proved incapable of solving the problems which arose after return to peace: the maintenance or abolition of slavery, the financial crisis, the disorganization of trade and communications, and the offensive of the conservatives. A new constitution was adopted on September 17, 1787, by a convention meeting in Philadelphia and composed of the most illustrious men in the United States. After it was approved by the legislatures of almost all the states, the new constitution came into force on March 4, 1789. It organized the powers into three branches in accordance with the ideas of Locke and Montesquieu. The executive was entrusted to a president elected for four years and given very great authority; the legislative, to two chambers, the House of Representatives, whose numbers were proportional to the inhabitants of each state (slaves counting for three-fifths of a free man), and the Senate, composed of two senators from each state; the judiciary, to a Supreme Court and inferior courts. Despite an invocation to God, the constitution forbade the establishment of a state religion; the Anglican (Episcopalian) Church was disestablished in the states where it had been the official church before 1776. The new regime therefore introduced the separation of church and state along with a democratic system.

With the political organization of the former colonies of North America so profoundly transformed, it is undeniable that a political revolution had occurred. The question remains: Was it accompanied by a social revolution?

The American patriots abolished the feudal system just as the revolutionaries did later in France and the other countries of Europe. But only vestiges of the feudal system existed, and then only in some of the American states, so that abolition of feudalism attracted little attention. It remains true, nonetheless, that dues of a feudal kind were abolished in all states, particularly New York, and that laws establishing entails or primogeniture in inheritances were amended or repealed. Jefferson paid particular attention to the abolition of these last traces of feudalism.

Civil and political equality made great progress but was nowhere completely achieved. As later in Europe, no state gave women political rights, although there were some protests. The most serious violation of the principle of equality, however, was the maintenance of slavery in the southern states. To be sure, slavery was abolished and the slave trade forbidden in a number of northern states, and these laws were soon extended to most states north of the Potomac; but the southern states remained obstinately loyal to the preservation of slavery and considered that the "rights of man" applied only to whites. We may note that this notion was later held by a number of French revolutionaries, and that neither the Constituent Assembly in 1789 nor the Legislative Assembly in 1792 made any change in the status of slaves; not until the French democrats came to power in the Convention in 1793 was slavery abolished in the French colonies. It may be observed nonetheless that the American Revolution did raise the problem of the abolition of slavery. The problem became more and more painful in Europe and in the United States, where it led to civil war in 1861.

As for free men, most rapidly acquired all political rights. By 1800 suffrage was practically universal in seven of the sixteen states in the union. Nonetheless the practice of recruiting emigrants in Europe by contracts of indenture continued; those who signed such contracts remained subject to compulsory labor for periods of varying length after their arrival in America and were deprived of most civil rights as well as all political rights. The practice of contracts of indenture declined rapidly, however, and disappeared early in the nineteenth century.

The American revolution also bore a social character because it resulted in redistribution of landed property. The lands of the Loyalists were confiscated, just as later the estates of the émigrés were confiscated in France. The difference was that there were about 60,000 émigrés from the United States, or 24 per thousand inhabitants, while

France had only 129,000, or 5 per thousand. In proportion to the size of population, the lands of the American émigrés represented a value about equal to the expropriated wealth of the French émigrés. The Loyalist émigrés received an indemnity from the British government which can be estimated at 82 million francs, while the French émigrés received one billion francs from Charles X, or a little more than ten times as much, and France was ten times as heavily populated as the United States. The lands confiscated from the American Loyalists were redistributed, often in small parcels, and the number of small owners was thus multiplied. It must be observed, however, that in some states the governments did not follow this policy of systematically increasing the number of small owners. The lands confiscated from the great Loyalist families (Delancey, Bayard, Philipse) in southern New York State passed into the hands of other big landowners (Livingstone, Schuyler, Roosevelt). In Baltimore and Frederick counties in Maryland it was the big Whig proprietors who bought the lands confiscated from the Loyalists. In South Carolina an estate of 40,000 acres owned by the émigré MacCulloh was divided into lots of 200 acres, but there were only thirty-four purchasers for the last two hundred lots, so that although some buyers were satisfied with 200 acres, others put together estates of 5,000 acres. One Robert Raiford bought properties expropriated from a number of Loyalists and was able to create an estate of 1,000 acres. The estate of the Tory T. Hooper, 3,600 acres in extent, passed intact into the hands of J. MacKinsey. The greatest confiscated estate in America belonged to the Penn family in Pennsylvania. The Pennsylvania legislature took over its management by the Divesting Act of 1779, but it became state property and was not subdivided. The American revolution therefore caused a profound change in the distribution of property, as in France. In the absence of exhaustive studies, however, it is not possible to assert at this time that the number of small owners increased very much. The effect of the expropriation of the Loyalists in equalizing wealth was therefore relatively weak.

Like the other revolutions in the countries of the West, the American revolution endeavored to give all citizens a means of rising in the social hierarchy by making education more available. Numerous colleges and schools of medicine were founded; the first civil engineers were trained (until then almost the only engineers in North America had been Army engineers); the first law school was established by Judge Tapping Reeve at Litchfield, Connecticut, in 1784. The American Philosophical Society, which had been founded in 1734, increased the number of its publications and spread the new ideas in the fields of literature, philosophy, and science; the American Academy of Arts and Sciences was organized in 1780. The press experienced remarkable growth and contributed greatly to informing the rest of the world about the principal episodes and the new institutions of the American revolution.

The American revolution was also an economic revolution. Let us remember that the patriots rebelled so that they would not have to pay the taxes placed by England on certain raw materials and manufactured products, and also in order to escape the tea monopoly granted by the British government to the East India Company. American businessmen wished to create an American industry and to keep the whole United States market for themselves. A number of industrial and commercial businesses were organized after 1776, due to the dynamism of such men as Jeremiah Wordsworth, W. Duer, and Robert Morris. Many of these businesses were weak and vanished as soon as peace returned. Others were more durable. The Bank of North America, which opened in Philadelphia in 1789, played a role in the recovery of the United States similar to that of the Bank of England after the English Revolution of 1688 and the Bank of France in the reorganization of France under the Consulate. Where there had not been more than a half-dozen large industrial and commercial firms in the English colonies of America before 1776, eleven were established between 1781 and 1785, twenty-two from 1786 to 1790, and 140 between 1790 and 1795. The revolution in America contributed to the rise of capitalism perhaps even more than in Europe. Some American revolutionaries also wished to break the old commercial ties which linked North America to England; this was the purpose of the commercial clauses of the treaty of 1778 between the United States and France. During the war the interruption of communications between the United States and England (which in any case was partial, never complete) did result in significant expansion of Franco-American trade. With the return of peace, however, the previous economic relations between Great Britain and the United States were resumed on almost the same footing as before, to the great disappointment of the French government.

The revolution was not complete in the economic field, no more than it had been in the social. Nonetheless the revolution hastened the advent of modern capitalism in the United States, as it was to do in the other countries of the West.

The American revolution had immense repercussions in Europe. First of all it gave Europeans the feeling that they were living in an age which was about to experience stupendous upheavals. They drew lessons and encouragement from the American revolution. They realized that the doctrines of the philosophes were not mere utopias but could be applied in practice. Finally, the American revolution created what has been called the "American myth" in Europe. This was the image of a new, more democratic society, approximating what Rousseau had imagined in a golden age of the distant past. For a long time the Europeans believed that in America they had discovered the reflection of a primitive epoch when men were good, simple, and happy. It was only around 1850 that they began to see America as the image of the world of the future.

The various countries of Europe had different attitudes toward the American revolution, depending on the character of the news that reached them about American events. These reports came by the press (newspapers and books), by word of mouth (especially from veterans of the fighting in America), and by propaganda organized by official and unofficial representatives of the United States.

The European press was growing rapidly at the time of the American war. The press had been practically free in England since the end of the Wilkes affair in 1769; the number of newspapers in the United Provinces was increasing, and many had an international audience, like the famed *Gazette de Leyde*. Many new newspapers were established in the Austrian Netherlands and the principality of Liége; the most famous was the *Journal encyclopédique* founded in 1759 by Pierre Rousseau, who originally came from Toulouse in southern France. In Germany, where 260 newspapers had been published during the decade 1740–1750, 410 appeared between 1760 and 1770, and 718 in the following decade; twenty-nine of these new journals used the word "patriotic" in their titles. There was no country so small or distant that it did not possess its own newspaper, and all devoted a large place to news from America. In Russia the *Gazette de Saint Pétersbourg* and the *Gazette de Moscou* reported in great detail the military operations in America, the debates in the English Parliament upon the colonists' demands, the new constitutions of the American states, and the American Declaration of Independence. The writers Novikov and Radishchev greeted the birth of the new republic with joy. Numerous books about the United States were published in most countries of Europe. From 1760 to 1790 twenty-six such works were published in three languages and fifteen in four languages (French, English, German, Dutch).

Newspapers and books were received, read, and debated in the many discussion groups, some of which, like the Masonic lodge in Budapest, took the name of "American."

Veterans of the war in the United States, after returning to Europe, usually became agents of propaganda in favor of the American revolution, though sometimes quite unawares. The activities of the most celebrated—the Frenchman Lafayette, the Pole Kosciuszko, and the Italian Massei—are well known. But were not the Englishmen and Hessians of the British army and the veterans of Rochambeau's army also obscure propagandists? An American historian has located on the map of France the region from which each of Rochambeau's six thousand soldiers came. He obtained a series of dots which cover approximately the regions (Artois, Île de France, Flanders, and Poitou) where agrarian disturbances broke out in 1789 and 1790. Although the suggestion of a causal connection remains only a hypothesis, it warrants checking by precise studies.

The activities of the diplomatic representatives of the United States are also well known. Benjamin Franklin and after him Thomas Jefferson at Versailles, and Isaac de Pinto and after him John Adams at The Hague, did all they could to show the United States in the most favorable light. One way was to distribute the new legislative texts from America, particularly the state constitutions. The constitutions were read avidly and provoked much comment and vigorous debate, especially in France, the United Provinces, Belgium, and Switzerland. The American constitutions were published at least five times in France between 1776 and 1786, and once in Holland in 1787.

The reactions of the countries of Europe to the American revolution were varied. There was passionate controversy in England, Ireland, and the United Provinces; sometimes adversaries and partisans of the revolution even came to blows. Great Britain just missed having a revolution, while one actually broke out in the United Provinces. In Belgium, France, Germany, and Switzerland it was the educated public which first became interested in the American events, but they gradually became widely known among the people. The American revolution was not the cause of immediate disorders but had long-term effects. In Italy enthusiasm for Franklin and the democratic institutions of the United States developed only in 1796. Although Spain, like France and Holland, participated in the American war of independence, it seems to have remained rather indifferent to the American revolution. In Eastern Europe, Poland, and Russia, the *intelligentsia* kept informed of the events in America, but they were only a very small fraction of the population and were scarcely able to transmit the American ideals to illiterate masses.

Revolutionary Disorders in Great Britain

The American revolution led to a series of revolutionary disorders—sometimes of extremely grave character—in Great Britain, particularly in Ireland and in Yorkshire, as well as in London itself, between 1778 and 1781. If the various disturbances did not degenerate into a revolution, it was because they displayed different characteristics and had different origins. Yet these origins were all connected with the general causes of the revolutions in the West studied in Chapter One.

The disorders began in 1778 in Ireland. They were consequences of the American revolution and even more of the political and social organization of the island. As is known, the subjugation of Ireland by England was made tighter in the eighteenth century. The Irish Catholics, who formed a majority of the population, possessed few political rights and little land. The soil belonged almost completely to Protestants of English or Scottish extraction or to the Anglican "Church of Ireland." But the Irish Protestants themselves did not enjoy the same rights as Englishmen. Although they were represented by a majority of members in the Dublin Parliament, that assembly was subordinated to the Parliament in Westminster and was not its equal. The inhabitants of Ireland, Protestant as well as Catholic, accordingly had many reasons for discontent. When the English colonies of America revolted against the mother country, the Irish saw in the American insurrection both example and encouragement. The war in America had other repercussions in Ireland. It caused a reduction in Irish exports to the American continent and an economic crisis soon resulted. Furthermore, Ireland itself seemed threatened by attack from the American rebels. In 1778 the American privateer John Paul Jones made a raid on Belfast which aroused great anxiety. In addition, the French were preparing in Normandy a landing operation in Great Britain; Ireland seemed to be the target, as it had been during earlier Anglo-French wars.

The British government, which had sent most of its troops to America, decided to raise volunteers to defend Ireland. It called upon the Protestants in 1778, but their numbers were insufficient and Catholics had to be admitted into the ranks of the militia in 1779. The Irish Volunteers, who numbered 40,000 in 1779 and 80,000 in 1782, quickly became aware of their strength and began to demand reforms and increased liberty. They organized a boycott of English goods in imitation of the American rebels. Under the leadership of Grattan, a member of its lower house, the Dublin Parliament granted a subsidy to the King of England for only six months. In the House of Commons at Westminster the Irish were defended by the same men who had stood up for the rebels in America, notably Edmund Burke. The English government made some concessions. The Test Bill, which excluded Catholics from all public office, was repealed for Ireland; the Irish Parliament was declared autonomous; and the two kingdoms of Great Britain and Ireland were proclaimed equal. These concessions did not satisfy the Irish. In November 1783 they held a Grand National Convention in Dublin; it demanded that Irish Catholics be given the right to vote and that elections to the Dublin Parliament be held every three years. The Protestants of Ireland became frightened and the Irish Parliament rejected these demands. The war in America had just ended, and the British government was now able to send troops to Ireland. The Irish Catholics took refuge in clandestine activity, forming the secret society of the "United Irishmen," which adopted the demands formulated by the Dublin convention as the basis of its program.

While these events were occurring in Ireland, other events provoked by similar causes were taking place in England. Just as the revolt of the American colonists had incited the Irish to demand reforms, so it impelled some Englishmen to propose profound changes in British institutions. In 1780 John Jebb, a Whig, published a series of political demands which formed the basis of the program of the "Radicals" for almost a century. These demands included universal male suffrage, secrecy of the ballot, annual election of Parliaments, equal constituencies, with the number of members proportional to the population, salaries for members of Parliament, and eligibility of all voters to the House of Commons. "Associations" were formed to achieve these demands; they were especially numerous in London and Yorkshire, and the agitation became known as the "Yorkshire movement." It was essentially a movement of the bourgeoisie, but it developed an atmosphere of clamor and uncertainty which engendered extremely serious popular disturbances—the Gordon Riots in London in June 1780.

Although originally the goals of the London rioters were diametrically opposed to the objectives being sought by the Catholics in Ireland and the English Radicals, the London disorders were nonetheless part of the great revolutionary movement of the West. The Londoners rose at the call of Lord George Gordon, president of an association seeking repeal of the Catholic Relief Bill which Parliament had passed in 1778. This law, which was valid only for England and Wales, revoked a statute passed under William III which condemned Catholic schoolteachers to life imprisonment and the loss of the right to inherit land. In exchange for this minimal concession, the Catholics were to swear an oath of loyalty to the King and renounce recourse to any papal jurisdiction. This law had already caused disorders in Scotland; on February 2, 1779, two Catholic chapels were destroyed at Edinburgh and Catholic homes and shops were looted. The demand of the Irish Catholics for abolition of the Test Act, and the successes won by France and Spain—Catholic countries—in the American war increased the anxiety and discontent of the London people. The riots therefore seemed to be at first an attack upon the principle of religious toleration advocated by the philosophes. But, as we shall see, the riot soon degenerated into a revolt against the rich and the government which protected them. From this point of view the Gordon Riots closely resembled the great riots which marked the revolution in the West, particularly in France and Italy.

The riots began on June 2, 1780. Lord George Gordon had urged the Londoners to present to Parliament a petition demanding repeal of the Catholic Relief Act. He declared that if fewer than 20,000 persons were present, he would resign as president of the association organized to obtain the withdrawal of the law. A crowd estimated at no less than 30,000 demonstrators, perhaps as many as 60,000, crowded the streets to accompany the petition, which bore 44,000 signatures. The prime minister, Lord North, was jeered, along with Edmund Burke, the defender of the American rebels, who was considered to be favorable to the Catholics. When despite the demonstration the members of Commons decided to adjourn discussion of the petition, the crowd broke loose. It began to destroy Catholic chapels and to attack the homes of Catholics. The disorders did not cease with nightfall and were renewed on June 3, 4, and 5. On the sixth, the demonstrators were attacked by cavalry and forthwith turned their fury against the representatives of authority. The home of a judge and a police station were destroyed, the brand new prison of Old Bailey was burned down and its prisoners set free. On June 7 many other prisons were attacked and their gates opened. Numerous homes of nobles and rich businessmen were threatened. On the evening of Wednesday, June 7, thirty-six gigantic fires lit the sky of London; nothing comparable was to take place in Paris during the entire revolution. On June 8, when the venerable Bank of England was attacked, the burghers of London took up arms and formed a militia. On June 9 Lord George Gordon, along with numerous rioters, was arrested and imprisoned. Tried for high treason, Lord Gordon was defended by the Whig barrister, Thomas Erskine, and acquitted on February 5, 1781. In all, the riots caused 210 deaths and 248 wounded, including 75 who died in hospitals. The police made 450 arrests. One hundred and sixty persons were tried, 62 sentenced to death, and 25 hanged, including four women and a youth of 16. Thirty-two private homes were completely wrecked and 110 persons were reimbursed for losses amounting to a total of £30,000. Statistics on the occupations of the persons arrested show that 70 percent were wage-earners. It is apparent that this uprising was essentially provoked by economic difficulties caused by a rapid increase in population, a greater increase in prices than in wages, and the trade stagnation caused by the war in America. Characteristic was the reply given by an arrested rioter when it was pointed out that he had attacked the home of a Protestant: "Protestant or not, no one needs more than £10,000 a year—that's enough for anyone to live on." The attack upon the prisons must be interpreted as the expression of a vague aspiration for greater social justice. Hostility against the Catholics was only a pretext for the riots. If the demands of the bourgeois Radicals had had a social and not an exclusively political character, they perhaps might have been able to attract the discontented farmers and workers. Then a revolution would have occurred in England. But as a whole the British bourgeoisie were satisfied, for they had had a share in government since the revolutions of 1640 and 1688. They did not seek an alliance with the lower classes, as the French bourgeoisie did a few years later. In England the interests of the bourgeoisie and the lower classes were already extremely divergent by the end of the eighteenth century; they did not suffer, as in America, from the common oppression of a distant and almost foreign government, nor, as in France, from a still powerful feudal regime. Abolition of a few sinecures, some budgetary economies, the collective resignation of the North ministry, and above all the conclusion of peace with the United States were sufficient to satisfy them. Nonetheless the revolutionary movement was not dead. After the revolution developed in France, it reappeared in England.

The Revolutions in Geneva

At the same time that the revolution was developing in the United States and rumbling in Great Britain, it almost triumphed in Geneva. It may be asked: Can we compare the tiny republic of Geneva to the great states of the West? Can we draw a parallel between the disorders which took place there and those which occurred at London, and soon at Paris? We reply that we can, for although

Geneva had less than 30,000 inhabitants around 1780, its influence in the world greatly exceeded the number of its inhabitants, thanks to its writers, like Jean-Jacques Rousseau, its scientists, like Charles Bonnet and Horace de Saussure, and its bankers, like Necker. Geneva was a microcosm, and the events in Geneva were a reflection or prefiguration of those in America, Great Britain, the Low Countries, and France. Furthermore, the triumph of the revolution in Geneva signified its rapid extension to Switzerland, particularly the cantons of Bern and Zurich. The national struggles began to sharpen between the French-speaking Vaudois and the German-speaking Bernese, and the social struggles between the burghers of Zurich and the peasants of the rest of Zurich canton. In addition, there was an intellectual elite in all parts of Switzerland—at Bern, the physician Albert von Haller; at Basel, the Bernouillis, illustrious mathematicians; at Lausanne, César de Laharpe, tutor of Catherine II's sons; at Zurich, the illustrious pedagogue Pestalozzi, who endeavored to put into practice the doctrines of the philosophes.

Each canton in Switzerland had its own individual constitution at the end of the eighteenth century, but in all cantons the government, in spite of appearances, was in the hands of a few families, the "patricians" or "oligarchs." In Geneva the population was divided into four groups: the "aristocrats," who alone sat in the assemblies and governed the republic; the "bourgeois," who enjoyed the rights of citizens but did not sit in the councils; the "natives," or descendants of émigrés, who had come to Geneva during the course of the last two centuries; and the "inhabitants," or foreigners residing in Geneva. "Natives" and "inhabitants" enjoyed no political rights. The poorest artisans were recruited almost entirely among these last two groups. The publication of Jean-Jacques Rousseau's *Social Contract* in 1762 created a great impression in Geneva, where it sharpened the feeling of frustration on the part of the "natives." The book was condemned and burned by the executioner. Nonetheless a constitutional crisis broke out. It lasted six years and received only an imperfect solution in the compromise of March 9, 1768, which decreed that five families of natives would enter the ranks of the bourgeoisie each year. The conflict subsided for a while but recurred again around 1780. Why did it break out at that time? It is possible that the economic difficulties which were common to the whole of the West also affected Geneva and worsened the condition of the "natives." It is probable that the propaganda of the philosophes opened the eyes of the "bourgeois" of Geneva. It is certain that the example of the United States exercised a profound influence. In any case, after an armed demonstration or "insurrection," the General Council of Geneva adopted the "Charitable Edict" (*Édit bienfaisant*) on February 10, 1781; it granted the "natives" civil equality and made them members of the "bourgeoisie" after the third generation. But the Syndics, the executive power in Geneva, not only refused to apply the edict but exiled du Roveray, the state's attorney, who had defended the "natives." The crisis became more acute on April 7, 1782, when the Council of Two Hundred, the organ of the aristocracy, also declared that it would not apply the edict of February 10, 1781, which it said had been "imposed by violence." The following day, April 8, a Monday, the Genevan democrats, including du Roveray, Clavière (who was to become minister of finances in France in 1792), Marat (brother of Jean-Paul, the future "friend of the people"), and the lawyer Grenus, called the natives to arms. More than a dozen persons were wounded, one fatally, in the course of a scuffle. But the city hall was captured, and the members of the Council of Two Hundred were imprisoned or placed under house arrest. The "bourgeois" and the "natives," acting in alliance, decided the next day to renew the membership of the councils, and the aristocrats were expelled.

But not all aristocrats were arrested, and some were able to send messages abroad. They asked help from France, Prussia (whose king was the sovereign of the adjacent principality of Neuchâtel), the kingdom of Sardinia, and the cantons of Bern and Zurich. The governments of these states refused to recognize the new councils in Geneva. The little republic felt itself to be in danger. While republican clubs patterned on those in the United States multiplied, the citizenry worked on the fortifications and put the city in a state of defense.

Despite these measures, the powers which the aristocrats had called on for help decided to intervene. Although he had been favorable to the American revolution, French foreign minister Vergennes had come to the conclusion that the theories of Rousseau, from which the Genevans drew their inspiration, were indeed dangerous, since Rousseau "proclaimed that sovereignty resides in the people, who alone can grant it or take it back." France therefore sent six thousand men against Geneva, while the king of Sardinia sent four thousand and the Bernese two thousand. The Genevans, with a force of only one thousand, could scarcely offer resistance. Nonetheless the "committee of safety" replied to an ultimatum sent by the canton of Bern on May 13 that the "Genevans were determined to live as free men and to die as free men," a slogan which was later adopted in France. The siege of the city began on June 13, and food soon ran short. On July 1 the Genevan democrats recognized that further resistance was impossible and surrendered. The foreign troops occupied the city on July 2. For the first time since 1770 a revolutionary movement of democratic character was defeated by the counterrevolution.

The philosophes were indignant. In France Madame Roland exclaimed: "Virtue and liberty now find shelter only in the hearts of a few good men. Shame on all the rest, shame on all the thrones of the world!" The French philosophes were wrathful because the soldiers employed against the Genevan rebels had just returned from helping the American rebels to win their freedom. The Genevan democrats, especially Francis d'Ivernois, Clavière, and du Roveray, went into exile in France, England, and Neuchâtel.

They were given a warm greeting by the liberals. Mirabeau, in a *Mémoire* addressed to Vergennes, and Brissot, in his *A Philadelphian at Geneva,* took up the defense of the democrats. They lauded the moderation shown by the revolutionaries during the three months that they had held power.

An "edict of pacification" dated November 4, 1782, reestablished Geneva's former constitution. Circles and clubs were banned and the popular militia was disbanded. This edict was given the name of "Black Code" by the Genevan democrats. They began actively to prepare their revenge, whether they remained in the republic or went abroad, and they maintained contact with other democrats in the West. The revenge came in 1793, as we shall see; but then the Genevan revolution was bloodier than its predecessor and the leaders of the aristocracy perished. Meanwhile the events in Geneva had hardly ceased to hold the center of attention before revolution broke out again, in the Low Countries.

The Revolutions in the Low Countries

Like the American and Genevan revolutions and the disorders in Great Britain, the revolutions in the United Provinces (Holland) and the Austrian Netherlands (Belgium) derived from the general causes we have outlined above: the economic and social crisis due to the demographic pressure, the crop failures, and the perturbations caused by the American revolution. First came a revolt of the aristocratic corporations against the governing princes. In the United Provinces the revolution began with a struggle of the "regencies," or governing groups in the municipalities, and the provincial estates, against stadholder William V. In Belgium it began with the resistance of the municipalities and the provincial estates against the reforms which the sovereign of the country, Emperor Joseph II, desired to introduce. The popular classes then intervened in the struggle, as in most countries of the West.

In the United Provinces the stadholderate had been settled for more than a century in the Orange family. Around 1780 stadholder William V began to consider changing his title to king and strengthening his powers. Such a transformation could not happen except at the expense of the provincial states and the regencies. These corporations, encouraged by the victory of the United States, allies of the Dutch, reacted against the proposed innovations. The United Provinces soon were divided into three parties. The regents, composed of the upper bourgeoisie, especially in Holland, wished to maintain the traditional organization and were hostile to the creation of a centralized monarchy. The stadholder's party, or Orangists, were composed of a majority of the nobility (who were not very numerous in the Dutch republic), the patriciate of the provinces other than Holland, the Calvinist preachers, who were traditionalists hostile to the ideas of the philosophes, the Jews, who were numerous in Holland and the traditional protégés of the Orange family, and the poor fishermen of the maritime provinces. A third party, formed somewhat later, took the name of Patriots in imitation of the Americans. The Patriots counted in their ranks the intellectuals, the merchants, a number of whom had maintained their relations with the descendants of the Dutch settlers of New Amsterdam (now New York), an active minority of the nobility, and the workers of the towns. They were hostile to the establishment of a monarchy, of course, but did not wish to preserve the rigidified institutions of the United Provinces either. They desired to build a new, more democratic regime, with a more modern and efficient administration. Van der Capellen tot den Pol, one of the first Dutchmen to take the side of the American insurgents, was one of their outstanding leaders. As early as 1775 he had opposed the departure of a Scottish brigade in the service of the United Provinces which was scheduled to sail for America, and he sent £20,000 from his personal fortune to the insurgents. Van der Capellen translated the Englishman Price's *Observations on the Nature of Civil Liberty* into Dutch. Along with Van der Capellen we may mention Van der Kemp, de Luzac, Paulus, Vreede, and Schimmelpenninck, whom we will find again at the head of the Batavian republic in 1795. These Patriots, let it be noted, were burghers; they did not dream of sharing political power with the less favored classes of the nation, the fishermen and the poor peasants. Regents and Patriots alike were convinced that the defeat of England would result in a mortal blow to British commerce in the Atlantic, that French traders would gain all the resulting advantages, and that they could therefore count upon the support of France which the American rebels had received. The stadholder, on the contrary, sought the support of the kings of England and Prussia, to whom he was related.

After the war in America ended, the Patriots and the regents, who had been united during that conflict, demanded reforms from the stadholder. When he refused, Van der Capellen issued an anonymous *Appeal to the Dutch People.* An act of virtual rebellion, it proposed not only establishment of a more democratic regime but also overthrow of the stadholder. The regents became frightened and began to withdraw from the movement; the Patriots, on the contrary, organized civic banquets, formed leagues, and raised volunteer militia bands which were open to Catholics (as also happened in Ireland) and religious dissenters—a remarkable innovation in the United Provinces. A central committee was formed in Amsterdam, with committees of correspondence and clubs in every province. In July 1784 a delegation of Amsterdam burghers compelled the stadholder to dismiss the Duke of Brunswick, the commander of the army and his former tutor, and to conclude an alliance with France with the primary purpose of resisting the commercial competition of England and the possible revival of the port of Antwerp should the Scheldt river be reopened to international shipping, as Emperor Joseph II desired. Despite these concessions, riots broke out in the cities. Wearing of cockades of orange, the stadholder's color, was forbidden, while the black cockade of the Patriots was acclaimed. A kind of "mass levy" was decreed by the States (provincial assembly) of Holland. In September a riot at The Hague kept the stadholder in his palace in danger for three days. William V considered abandoning the United Provinces; the States of Holland withdrew William's titles of stadholder and captain general of the province; and the Patriots formed a committee of five members with the duty of reestablishing republican institutions and "saving our beloved fatherland." Using force, the Patriots seized power in 1787 in the provinces of Holland, Groningen, and Overijsel. They were not successful in the province of Utrecht, but the city of Utrecht itself was split in two, with the Patriots fortifying themselves in their districts. The Orangists were strong in Zeeland, thanks to the support of the fishermen; there was a sharp struggle between Orangists and Patriots, and several towns, of which Ter Goes was the most important, were pillaged. The stadholder, who had displayed extraordinary passivity, finally reacted. On May 27, 1787, he issued a manifesto protesting against the dismissal of the magistracies of Rotterdam and Amsterdam by the Patriots and demanding the return of his powers. On learning of the manifesto, the Patriots rose in Amsterdam on May 28. An Orangist was thrown into a canal. The next day homes of Orangists were looted, Orangist sailors and Patriot militiamen fought. On May 30 the district where the Orangist seamen lived was sacked by Patriots. At Utrecht the Patriot militiamen, commanded by Daverhoult (a future president of the Legislative Assembly in France), repulsed regular troops commanded by Orangist officers. It was obvious that if the situation continued much longer, the stadholder would be overthrown and a democratic republic established.

In imitation of the Genevan aristocrats, William V appealed to his brother-in-law, King Frederick William II of Prussia, and his father-in-law, King George III of England, to help him with armed force. While an English fleet cruised off the Dutch ports, a Prussian army entered the United Provinces. The Patriot militia was easily defeated and the Prussians occupied The Hague in September 1787, restoring the stadholder to his former powers.

As at Geneva, many Patriots went into exile. The consul of France at Rotterdam, on February 21, 1788, evaluated the number of Patriots who had left the United Provinces at 42,000. Most settled in Belgium or France. At the end of 1788 there were more than a thousand Patriot families receiving assistance at Saint-Omer and Gravelines, in the North of France. Among these Dutchmen were 619 workers, 383 masters of various trades, 230 merchants, 31 farm laborers and gardeners, and 15 former regents and gentlemen. The large number of masters and workers, as well as merchants, is striking. It was they who formed the majority of the Patriots. Had the Patriots won the support of the peasants and the fishermen, as happened in France three years later, they would unquestionably have been victorious. But the feudal regime had virtually ceased to exist in the United Provinces. Fishermen and peasants had more grievances against the burghers who exploited them than against the stadholder who protected them. They did not form part of the militia, which was limited to the artisans and burghers in the towns and was unable to resist the Prussian troops. Still, the Dutch Patriots did not give up the struggle, no more than the Genevan Patriots. After taking refuge in Belgium and France, they joined the Patriots of those countries and aided them in making their revolution, before returning to Holland in order to achieve the victory of the revolution in their own country.

At the precise moment when reaction was winning in the United Provinces, revolution began in Belgium. The reforms of Joseph II, an "enlightened" prince, had aroused the discontent of the provincial States and the municipalities, which were composed of members of the traditionalist aristocracy and the big bourgeoisie. Furthermore, the beginning of the Industrial Revolution had led to an increase in production and made more urgent the reopening of the port of Antwerp, which had been closed to shipping since the United Provinces had become independent in the sixteenth century. The revolution in Belgium originated in an alliance between the aristocracy, which was unhappy over Joseph II's innovations, and the big commercial bourgeoisie, which desired changes in the economic structure capable of increasing their business. But soon the petty bourgeois intellectuals, who were followers of the philosophes, joined the coalition. They desired a profound transformation of the organization of the state; their goal was a democratic form of government, in which they would be able to take part. As in the United Provinces, therefore, the coalition was quite disparate. It rapidly divided into "Statists," led by the lawyer Van der Noot, and "Patriots" or Vonckists, so called after their leader, Vonck.

In the first period of the Belgian rebellion, Joseph II faced a coalition of all who were angered by his clumsy reforms. Introduction of religious toleration and closing of the monasteries of the contemplative orders gave satisfaction to the Voltairean bourgeoisie, it is true, but aroused the discontent of the mass of the Belgian people, who were very attached to the traditional forms of religion (as was to be seen over the following twenty years). Suppression of guilds and introduction of free trade in grain, however pleasing to the big merchants, were badly received by the consumers, who feared another rise in prices. Finally, Joseph II gave no satisfaction to the democrats, who did not win increased participation in the administration.

In 1787 Joseph II took a step which drove the opposition into open revolt. Contrary to the terms of the "Joyous

Entry" of Brabant, the charter which he had subscribed at his accession, he revolutionized the entire administrative and judicial structure of the country. He abolished the old tribunals, which enjoyed great prestige, and replaced them with courts like those which he had just created in Austria. He also divided Belgium into new territorial districts, headed by intendants directly subordinate to the government at Vienna. Belgium, which until then had enjoyed virtual autonomy, was thus reduced to the status of an Austrian province. Indignation was rife. The former authorities refused to publish the reform edicts. There was talk of a tax strike. The revolutionaries adopted as a recognition mark a cockade with the black, yellow, and red colors of Brabant. The emperor replied by an act of force on January 7, 1789, rescinding the promises he had given in the "Joyous Entry."

It was a very unfavorable time for an act of force. The harvest of 1788 had been as bad in Belgium as in France; during the winter of 1788–1789 the price of food rose to its highest level of the eighteenth century. The agitation which marked the election of the deputies to the States General and the drafting of the cahiers in France spread to Belgium (and the Liége district, where the inhabitants protested the arbitrary rule of the prince-bishop). The revolution developed in Belgium at the same time as in France. But where the majority of the bourgeoisie and the peasantry in France remained united in a revolutionary bloc until 1792, as we shall see, the Belgian revolutionaries, having little support among the peasants (who were less burdened by manorial dues than in France), split apart. The Patriots or Vonckists desired to organize a regime like the government of the United States. They drew up a "Declaration of Independence of the Province of Flanders" and an "Act of Union of the Belgian Provinces," which reproduce passages of the American Articles of Confederation, sometimes word for word. The Statists, on the contrary, abhorred liberal reforms. They had in mind only restoring the institutions abolished by Joseph II. His death in February 1790 favored the Statists. The new Emperor, Leopold II, did not object to annulment of the reforms undertaken by his brother. In exchange, the Statists permitted Austrian troops to reestablish themselves in Belgium. The prince-bishop of Liége took advantage of these events to call in German soldiers, who occupied his little state. Like the Genevan and Dutch Patriots before them, the Belgian Patriots came to France as refugees. There they swelled the mass of revolutionary "Europeans" who urged France to go to war against Europe in the belief that only war could spread revolution on the continent and revive it in Switzerland, Holland, and Belgium. In 1789, therefore, the fate of the revolution in the West was bound up with what happened in the revolution in France.

chapter three

THE REVOLUTION IN FRANCE: SPECIFIC CAUSES; THE BEGINNING

If the revolutionaries of various European countries who took refuge in France expected so much from the revolution there, it was because France occupied a place of the first rank, perhaps even the very first place, in the Western world. In area France was the largest country in the West in 1789, except for the United States; the German (Holy Roman) Empire cannot be truly compared with it, because it was divided into so many states. With 26 million inhabitants France surpassed all other Western countries in population; Great Britain, which was second, had less than half as many inhabitants, although London was the biggest city in the Western world, with about one million inhabitants, Paris with 650,000 coming immediately afterward. The French state had larger revenues, almost 500 million livres, than any other state in Europe or America. This was more than the revenue of Great Britain, double that of the Hapsburgs, triple that of Prussia, Russia, Spain, or the United Provinces, twenty-five times greater than that of the United States. In the spiritual field, France's preeminence was conspicuous. French artists received orders from all Europe, while—even more important—the French language was considered a universal tongue, and the most celebrated philosophes wrote in French. Montesquieu, Voltaire, and Diderot were of course French. The *Encyclopédie* was essentially a French work. As for France's role in world politics, there might have been some doubt after 1763 and the defeats suffered by France on land, at sea, and in America during the Seven Years' War about what place France would hold. But her success during the War of American Independence restored her prestige. After 1783 France therefore shared with Great Britain the position of first power of the world. England surpassed France only in her industry, which had a lead of about twenty years, her system of credit, which was vastly more effective, and her international trade, which was very much more extensive. Success of the revolution in France would therefore have an infinitely greater significance than its triumph in any other country. However, not only did the revolution in France succeed from the very first, it also acquired very much greater intensity than elsewhere. Its achievements surpassed those of the American revolution; some of its economic and social innovations anticipated the great revolutions of the twentieth century. The French revolution derived these characteristics not only from the general causes which we have surveyed in the first chapter, but also from particular causes, the mutual relationship of the social classes, the fiscal crisis, and the crisis of institutions.

The Relations between the Social Classes in France around 1787

Although the social structure of France at the end of the eighteenth century corresponds in a general way to the pattern which we have drawn, its characteristics were more sharply accentuated than those of the other countries of the West. The most important of these characteristics, which gave the French revolution such an irresistible impetus from the very beginning, was the violent hostility, even hatred, of the common people for the privileged classes, especially the nobility. Why did such hatred exist? The nobility comprised only a small fraction of the population of France, about 350,000 persons or 1.5 percent of the population. To be sure, the nobility was not a caste. Entrance into the nobility had been relatively easy in earlier centuries and even during the first half of the eighteenth century. However, after 1750 the nobility tended to close in and to reserve for itself the principal positions in the state, to which the bourgeoisie previously could also aspire. The nobility not only possessed an important portion of the land, varying from about 15 percent in the South to 60 percent in some parts of the West, it also strove to keep for its members the majority of posts in the courts and the financial branch of government, the high administrative offices, all officer ranks of the army and the navy, and the bishoprics, archbishoprics, and great abbeys. The nobility strove to monopolize these places not in a vain quest for prestige but out of vital necessity. The fact was that part of the income of the nobility—a part that varied according to the individual but was always very substantial—came from the manorial dues, which had been permanently fixed many years before. The income from these dues became all the more inadequate as prices rose sharply. In order to maintain their "rank" and their resources, the nobility endeavored not only to keep all government offices, not only to increase the output of the lands which they farmed directly, but also to make their feudal rights more productive. They therefore organized a minute revision of their terriers, or registers of dues owed by their vassals. This endeavor has been correctly called the "feudal reaction." It greatly outraged the peasants, who were also unhappy over the burden of the tithes, a tax paid to the clergy and equal to a tenth of the crops.

As for the bourgeoisie, they were all the more exasperated to see the offices of state administration, the magistracy, the financial system, the high clergy, and the army escaping from them. Traditionally, as their wealth and power had increased, they had sent their sons into these posts. The French bourgeoisie, in fact, although they had been created and made wealthy by trade, unlike the English bourgeoisie did not continue to hold trade as their ideal. Engaging in trade did not prevent a man from taking part in government and administration in Great Britain, but in France, on the contrary, the bourgeoisie could not enter government except by buying offices. However, higher government posts carried with them a grant of nobility. After the end of the sixteenth century therefore the French bourgeoisie kept their savings for purchase of government offices for their children instead of investing them in trade or the new big industries. The increasing monopoly of these offices by the nobility reduced the number of posts at the disposal of the bourgeoisie. It is easy to understand why the bourgeoisie and the peasants formed a powerful if tacit alliance against the nobility. It was this coalition, which we do not find anywhere else in America or in the other countries of Europe, which gave the French revolution its distinctive coloration and impetus.

The Financial Crisis

Financial difficulties were common to all the states of the West in the eighteenth century, as we have noted. But they were greater in France than elsewhere. The deficit, which had been chronic since the reign of Louis XIV, had brought the state to the edge of bankruptcy in 1770. By Draconian measures which aroused sharp discontent among the privileged groups, Abbé Terray had been able to improve the situation while he was finance minister. Reestablishing France's financial situation was all the more difficult because the system of taxation was decrepit, incoherent, complicated, unequal, and unjust. There were four direct taxes: the taille, which in theory was imposed only on commoners but in practice was collected from persons in northern France and from landed property in southern France; the capitation, or poll tax, which all Frenchmen were supposed to pay but which the clergy and a part of the nobility had managed to escape; the *vingtièmes* ("twentieths"), an income tax, which was also supposed to fall on all taxpayers but likewise did not affect the clergy and was not paid by all the nobility; and the royal *corvée,* which was a tax in labor on the main highways imposed on peasants living nearby. The indirect taxes were collected not by the state but by a company of "farmers general" who paid the state a fixed amount in advance but kept the remainder of the receipts for themselves. Indirect taxes varied from place to place; in particular, the gabelle or salt tax was heavier or lighter in different regions. Tariff boundaries divided France into several regions. The ministers of finance at the end of the old regime felt that a system of such complexity and inefficiency could not be repaired but had to be abandoned; they wanted to replace it with another system of taxation in which every Frenchman would contribute to the needs of the state in proportion to his real income. Turgot, controller general of finances, under the influence of his friends, the physiocrats, proposed to Louis XVI in 1775 the introduction of a single proportional tax on land, the "territorial subvention." It would replace all other taxes, which would be abolished. His proposal aroused the discontent of all the privileged groups. Since establishment of free trade in grain had already led to a sharp rise in the price of bread and grave disorders (the Flour War), Louis XVI, under the pressure of a coalition of the discontented, dismissed Turgot in 1776. To replace him he called in the Genevan Jacques Necker, who had a reputation as a financial wizard.

Necker entered upon his duties just when France was becoming involved in the war in America. This conflict considerably increased the French deficit. Indeed, in order to finance French participation in the War of American Independence, Necker had to make loans at ruinous interest rates of eight and ten percent. In order to maintain confidence and to be able to continue borrowing, Necker made the budget public in 1781 under the title of "Report to the King" (*Compte rendu au roi*). In it, Necker reported that there was no deficit but a surplus of more than 10 million livres. Calonne, a successor of Necker, declared later that in 1781 the budget actually ran a deficit of more than 46 million livres. Necker actually had omitted from the budget the so-called exceptional expenditures, that is, the war costs. Nonetheless the *Compte rendu* had unprecedented success and gave Necker a lasting popularity among the mass of the people. He was praised for having listed the amount spent in pensions granted by the king to courtiers; the figure was considered to be enormous. On the other hand, the wrathful privileged groups did not forgive the minister and obtained his dismissal with the aid of Queen Marie-Antoinette (1781). The financial crisis remained unsolved, however. Now on top of it came a grave economic crisis. As we have seen, the economic difficulties were not limited to France but they probably were worse in France than anywhere else. Proof of this is to be found in the curves of prices of various food products and the graphs of births and deaths, which stop their regular rise and show sharp fluctuations. Births, which for some forty years had almost always shown a surplus in the countryside, now were exceeded frequently by deaths. Bad grain harvests due to unusually bad weather conditions were the essential causes of this crisis. In France a phenomenon peculiar to the country was added to the other difficulties. Despite governmental bans, the number of vineyards had been greatly increased during the eighteenth century. Wine grapes were much more profitable to the farmer than other crops; almost the entire harvest could be sold, and it brought quite sizable sums of hard cash into the hands of the vine grower, permitting him to improve his standard of living. But overextension of viticulture led to overproduction, which was in turn the cause of a fall in prices beginning in 1780. The farmers were all the more sensitive to this downturn in their income because during the preceding years they had believed that the sale of wine was enabling them to escape their age-old poverty.

Economic stagnation also affected industry and trade. Where in England the transformation of industry had reached the dimensions of a revolution, thanks to the invention of the steam engine and other machines, in France industry was modernized at a slow rate due to a lack of capital (the bourgeoisie, as we have seen, preferring to invest their savings in purchase of government offices rather than in acquisition of machinery). The formidable competition of England became felt as soon as peace was reestablished in 1783. English cloth began to dominate the markets of the Levant, where French cloth had been at a premium for more than a century. Difficulties resulted for the manufacturers in Languedoc who had been supplying these markets. The government expected that the development of trade between France and the United States would ease these difficulties, but its hopes were disappointed. The United States profited by the treaty of 1778 in order to export its raw materials to France and especially to the French Antilles, but it employed the income from these sales for the purchase of products manufactured in England. The French government nonetheless persisted in its liberal commercial policy. In 1786 it concluded a trade treaty with England which substantially lowered the tariffs in force in both countries. England, with its much more advanced industry, was the principal beneficiary of this agreement. On December 7, 1787, a new regulation extended the list of American goods admitted to the Antilles. The American merchants took advantage of the opportunity but did not increase their purchases in France. The economic and financial crisis in France reached its apogee around 1787. The internal deficit continued to get worse, rising to more than 130 million livres, or more than 20 percent of expenditures; and the balance of accounts with foreign countries, which had long shown a surplus, ran a deficit of almost 70 million livres in 1787, with imports of 611 million and exports of only 542 million. The difficulties of the industries were increased when the peasants, hit by bad harvests, reduced or halted their purchases of manufactured goods. Factories and handicraft workshops closed. Urban unemployment was now added to the rural unemployment caused by crop failures. Unemployment in both town and country was multiplied by the presence of large numbers of young people, a consequence of the demographic surplus of the previous twenty years. The unemployed, who received almost no assistance, wandered from town to town and through the countryside, living by begging and sometimes by banditry. At the end of the old regime the fear of brigands terrorized the inhabitants of the towns and countryside of France. The origin of these difficulties lay fundamentally in the economic and financial crisis. But by 1787 it was clearly apparent that, even if this crisis were solved, all other difficulties would remain. It was necessary to make profound changes in all institutions, and even to overthrow and replace them.

The Institutional Crisis

Although at the end of the old regime the French monarchy had the outward appearance of a powerful and centralized system with an absolute king by divine right at its head, aided by a chancellor, a controller general of finances and four secretaries of state, a governor, an intendant and a military commander at the head of each province, and a parlement to provide justice, this cohesion actually masked inconceivable disorder and confusion. The frontiers of the kingdom were not determined with precision; some villages did not know whether they were part of France or the German empire. The internal divisions of France were inconsistent and overlapping. The most ancient divisions were the ecclesiastical dioceses, which in the south sometimes served as the bases of civil administration. The bailiwicks and seneschalsies established in the thirteenth century had not been abolished, although their functions were much reduced. The provinces and the military governments were almost identical but did not have the same boundaries as the generalities, the districts under the authority of the intendants. A few provinces, it is true, had maintained their representative assemblies, the provincial estates. These estates were composed primarily of representatives of the clergy, the nobility, and the upper bourgeoisie. The peasants were not represented. The principal functions of these estates was assignment of taxes among communities for collection and sometimes financial administration of the province. Provinces without estates were called "election lands" because officials called *élus* (literally "elected," but actually named by the royal government) assigned the taxes. The justice rendered by a great number of royal, manorial, and even ecclesiastical courts with overlapping jurisdictions was costly and barbarous. It was legal to use torture on both accused and convicted prisoners. Magistrates were not appointed upon the basis of qualifications but purchased their "offices" (the system being known therefore as "venality of offices"); often, at the end of the old regime, judges inherited their posts. The magistracy had therefore become independent of the king during the eighteenth century. But the monarch could intervene in the course of justice at all times. He could imprison a subject by a secret warrant of arrest (*lettre de cachet,* or "sealed letter") in which no reasons were given, and he could release a prisoner by a "letter of grace." Many public services were not furnished by the state. Public education and support of the poor amounted only to 2 percent of the state budget; the church was entrusted with these services. In 1787, therefore, it seemed to be necessary not only to make a complete transformation of the fiscal system of the state but also a thoroughgoing reorganization of the other institutions of government.

However, the notion of social hierarchy remained deeply rooted in the upper classes. Although the bourgeoisie were jealous of the nobility, sometimes to the point of hatred, they considered themselves to be superior to the artisans and peasants. Within the third estate, a whole series of "bourgeois titles," the use of which was minutely established by custom, marked an unofficial but generally accepted hierarchy: One might not call "Madame" a woman who had the right only to "Mademoiselle," nor "Monsieur" an individual who should only be addressed as "Sieur." The bourgeoisie desired extensive and profound reforms; they were not yet thinking of a revolution in 1787.

The Aristocratic Revolution or Pre-Revolution (1787–1789)

The revolution in France did not in fact begin with a popular uprising or even with a riot instigated by the bourgeoisie, but with a revolt of the aristocracy. After Necker's departure in 1781, his place was taken by a number of men in turn; each remained in power a very short time and all proved incapable of balancing the finances of the state. In 1783 Calonne, the former intendant of Metz, who had a reputation for brains, was named controller-general of finances. For three years he attempted to meet the difficulties with Necker's method, that is, by borrowing. But by the end of 1786 the government's credit was exhausted and only one alternative remained: either bankruptcy or reform of the state's financial structure, that is, organization of a system of taxation truly proportional to individual income. Such a system could not help but meet the opposition of the privileged groups; in the first rank of the opponents were the parlements, which had the function of "registering" and "verifying" laws. In order to avoid the probable "remonstrances" by the parlements, Calonne thought it better to have his reforms accepted by an extraordinary Assembly of Notables summoned by the king—that is, by himself. Such an assembly was not an innovation, for kings had convened notables during the sixteenth and seventeenth centuries. All the same, assemblies of notables met rarely; they had been used primarily to avoid summoning the Estates General, which were composed of representatives of the three orders, the clergy, nobility, and Third Estate. The last Estates General had been held more than 170 years before, in 1614. In the face of the excited state of public opinion and the depression of the 1780s, it seemed prudent to avoid calling a meeting of the Estates General.

An Assembly of Notables was therefore summoned for early 1787. The plan of reforms prepared by Calonne comprised principally a new tax, the territorial subvention already proposed by Turgot and Necker, to be collected in kind from all income from land, without any exception; it would replace the "twentieths." Other taxes would not be abolished but would be reduced. Calonne also proposed amortization of the clergy's debts with the revenues received from allowing repurchase of the manorial duties collected by the church, a better utilization of the royal domain, which would be regranted as fiefs, a series of loans permitting extension over twenty years of the payments which the treasury was due to make during the next ten years, and establishment of a national bank capable of supporting the credit of the state. Several other administrative reforms were likewise proposed, in particular establishment of provincial assemblies.

The Assembly of Notables met on February 22, 1787. Contrary to Calonne's hopes, its members did not prove to be docile, although he had appointed them. Indeed, having been made the butt of satirical songs and caricatures, they insisted on showing independence. Although they accepted Calonne's principles, they rejected all his proposals.

Louis XVI then dismissed Calonne and called upon the man who seemed to be the leader of the opposition in the Assembly of Notables, Loménie de Brienne, archbishop of Toulouse. Brienne soon realized that only Calonne's plan would permit meeting the deficit and balancing the budget. He therefore retained its essential elements, notably the territorial subvention.

The notables remained intransigent, declaring that "only the authentic representatives of the nation had the right to grant a new tax." In effect, they were demanding that the Estates General be summoned. Several notables made specific reference to the Estates General, notably Lafayette in a speech on May 21 which drew much comment. At Brienne's request, Louis XVI dismissed the assembly on May 25.

Brienne had got rid of the notables but he had not renounced his reforms and now had to get them accepted by the parlements. But the hostility of the "sovereign courts" was almost certain after the opposition of the notables, who included the presiding justices of all the parlements. Nonetheless, Brienne went forward and attempted to introduce a whole series of reforms. In order to avoid increasing the deficit, he opposed France's armed intervention on behalf of the Dutch Patriots when they were threatened by Prussia and England. Such an intervention, if successful, would unquestionably have consolidated the revolution in the United Provinces, but, contrary to the calculation of some French leaders like Marshal de Castries it would have precipitated revolution in France. Brienne introduced economies, notably in the king's household and in the pensions given to courtiers. Some ceremonial army units were abolished and the number of marshals and generals reduced. But Brienne maintained the nobility's monopoly of officer commissions and the practice of punishment with the flat of the saber that had been introduced into the army by Count de Saint-Germain, so that the Third Estate felt no gratitude to Brienne for his reforms in army administration. The army itself was discontented; the soldiers and noncommissioned officers were unhappy because all prospect of promotion to higher ranks was closed, the noble officers because some of the privileged units had been abolished and a new regulation required that they give up their traditional abuses.

A more important reform was establishment of provincial assemblies, as Turgot, Necker, and Calonne had already proposed. Each community would have at its head a municipal assembly, presided over by the (manorial) lord and composed of the richest inhabitants elected by property suffrage. The lord, the syndic, the parish priest, and two deputies of each municipality would meet to form a "departmental assembly." Each of these departmental assemblies would name a part of a provincial assembly, in which the Third Estate would have a number of deputies equal to that of nobility and the clergy combined. This reform did not apply, however, to the "estate lands," which retained their former organization. Still, this reform, such as it was, constituted a true revolution, for it introduced the principle of election into all local government. The election of these assemblies, whose members at first were chosen half by the king and half by co-optation, caused continually increasing agitation throughout

France. Brienne's intention, like Turgot's, was to crown this system by a "national assembly," which would replace the Estates General and have a better-chosen membership. This purpose was thwarted by events.

Other reforms in the area of justice were made by a collaborator of Brienne's, the keeper of the seals, Lamoignon. Legal procedure in criminal cases was made more humane; arrests on criminal charges could be made only on the basis of open warrants; and torture was abolished. Furthermore, the jurisdiction of manorial courts was reduced. Finally, although the government did not reenact the Edict of Nantes which Louis XIV had revoked in 1685, it considerably lessened the effect of the revocation by granting civil status to Protestants in the edict of November 19, 1787. This was not yet equality, or hardly even tolerance, but it was nonetheless real progress in this direction, made over the protests of some parlements and the assembly of the clergy of France.

All of these reforms constituted an important achievement. If they had been continued, especially if satisfaction had also been given to the basic wishes of the bourgeoisie and the peasantry, revolution might have been averted. But the key element of this achievement—financial reform—was missing. Although the parlements accepted Brienne's administrative reforms with more or less good grace, their hostility to any system of taxation tending to destroy the privileges of the higher orders was a certainty. As early as July 2, 1787, the parlement of Paris, expanded into a court of peers by attendance of the dukes of the peerage, rejected a proposal to bring stamped paper into general use, as the British government had attempted to do in North America. It demanded the production of the state accounts before pronouncing on any kind of new tax. On July 26 the court of peers repeated the demand of the assembly of notables that the Estates General be summoned. It is probable that at this time a majority of members of the court had in mind an assembly of estates composed in the same manner they had been at their last meeting in 1614, when the clergy, the nobility, and the Third Estate each had the same number of deputies.

This resistance did not prevent Brienne from presenting to the parlement on July 30 an edict which replaced the tax of twentieths by a territorial subvention to be paid by all landowners. Again the parlement refused to register the edict. Malesherbes realized clearly that this was an act of rebellion. He told the king: "I say that the parlement of Paris at this moment is only the echo of the entire nation. It is the parlement which speaks because it is the only body which has the right to speak; but we must not conceal from ourselves that if any assembly of citizens had this right, it would make the same use of it. It is therefore with the entire nation that we have to deal."

On August 6, the king commanded the parlement, which was summoned to Versailles to meet in a *lit de justice* (a session in the presence of the king sitting on a "throne [*lit*] of justice"), to register the financial edicts. This the parlement did, but the next day, meeting in Paris, it declared "null and illegal the entries made yesterday in its registers." The revolt of the privileged corporations, which was similar to that which we have already observed in other countries, was reaffirmed. The people of Paris, believing that the parlement was defending the "rights of the nation," in Malesherbes' words, acclaimed the magistrates. Encouraged, they multiplied their attacks and accused Calonne of having ruined the finances of the state. The government reacted by exiling the parlement to Troyes on August 14. The departure of the parlement led to outright rioting in Paris, which encouraged the magistrates to be firm. On their arrival in Troyes, they declared that "only the Estates General can probe and cure the wounds of the state." The other sovereign courts of France and a host of pamphleteers supported the revolt of the aristocratic parlement. The government gave in, withdrawing the edict on stamped paper and the plan for a territorial subvention, recalling the parlement to Paris, and promising to summon the Estates General in 1792. The ministry pledged to remedy the financial situation by rigorous measures during the five years before the Estates General met. The basic reason for these measures of capitulation was that the government needed loans, and it was indispensable that they be registered by the parlement.

In order to obtain this registration more easily, the government called a surprise meeting of the parlement in a royal session on November 19, 1787. The palace where it met was surrounded by troops. After having heard speech after speech for eight hours, Louis XVI promised to call the Estates General "before 1792" and ordered registration of the edicts on the loans. The Duke of Orléans rose and with unheard-of audacity declared that "this is illegal." "No, it is legal, because I wish it," replied the king. This was an imprudent affirmation of royal absolutism at a time when the government no longer had the means to make itself obeyed. The exile of the Duke of Orléans and the arrest of two councilors of parlement only increased revolutionary agitation in Paris and throughout the kingdom. During the winter of 1787–1788 the parlement and the dukes of the peerage increased their efforts on behalf of those whom the government had punished on November 20; at the same time, in an act of broader significance, they also protested the use of sealed warrants of arrest. On April 17 the king declared quite correctly that if he bowed before the demands of the parlement, "the monarchy would be nothing more than an aristocracy of magistrates, as contrary to the rights and interests of the nation as to those of the sovereign." An aristocracy of magistrates, in accordance with the ideas of Montesquieu—this was precisely what numerous members of the privileged classes throughout the West wanted. But to achieve it they needed the support of the Third Estate, or at least of the bourgeoisie. It was in order to obtain this support that the parlement of Paris appealed on May 3, 1788, to the "fundamental laws of the kingdom," notably "the right of the nation to grant tax revenues freely through the organization of Estates General summoned in the regular manner with its regular membership . . . the irremovability of magistrates . . . the right of each citizen never to be sent to trial before anyone other than his natural judges . . . the right not to be arrested at the command of anyone whatsoever except in order to be placed in the hands of his competent judges without delay." Although the parlement proclaimed in the same declaration that "the privileges consecrated by law and tradition are inviolable," public opinion went into raptures over the parlement, "not in order that the parlement might become powerful or the most popular of corporations," as Tocqueville wrote, "but because it was the only body in France which remained sufficiently big, strong, and organized to struggle against the royal power." The fourteen provincial parlements and sovereign councils adopted an attitude identical to that of the parlement of Paris. They led the opposition to the monarch but remained all the while irrevocably committed to the traditional organization of society, inequality of the orders and preservation of privileges. Among the most vehement may be numbered the parlements of Grenoble, Besançon,

Rennes, Dijon, Pau, and Bordeaux. At the same time that the parlement of Paris had been sent to Troyes the parlement of Bordeaux refused to register the edict creating provincial assemblies and was exiled to Libourne. All the parlements showed themselves irrevocably hostile to the creation of a system of taxation equal for all.

What was at stake for the French monarchy in May 1788 was whether it would permit itself to be dominated by a body of aristocrats who held their power only because of their wealth (since they had purchased their offices), or would impose its own will. The monarchy attempted to have its way by the coup d'état of May 4, 1788. Brienne and his keeper of the seals, Lamoignon, decided to employ the same methods that Maupeou had used in 1771; a "plenary court" would henceforth register laws common to all of France (while the sanction of the Estates General was being awaited). The parlements were left only with the right to register regional decisions. On the other hand, their judicial functions were reduced by the creation of forty-seven "great bailiwicks." The plenary court was composed of the magistrates of the Grand Chamber of the parlement of Paris, the princes of the blood, the peers of the realm, and a certain number of high dignitaries. In Brienne's mind this plenary court could become the future upper chamber of a constitutional regime; a lower chamber would be added, as in England.

These reforms seemed to challenge the declaration of May 3. When the court of peers protested, two of its most influential councilors, D'Emprémesnil and Montsabert, were arrested and imprisoned. The edict had to be registered by means of a *lit de justice* on May 8, and in the provinces during the days that followed. This forced registration was the signal for a revolt of the aristocracy, led by the members of the parlements.

In all the parlements, the chief justices protested indignantly. At Rennes, when the session ended, the intendant was threatened with stoning; the parlementarians were thereupon exiled by sealed letters (*lettres de cachet*), which caused another riot so fierce that the intendant had to flee. Even worse happened at Grenoble. On June 7, the day when the members of parlement who had been ordered by sealed letters to go into exile were due to leave the city, a crowd sacked the military headquarters and then climbed to the rooftops in order to pelt the police with tiles. This "Day of Tiles" resulted in four deaths and some thirty injured but prevented the departure of the members of the parlement. At Pau the people rose up on June 19 and reestablished the parlement in its functions by their own authority. Everywhere the police were overwhelmed. The army repressed the riots in unwontedly mild fashion. It was discontented over the recent reforms and its officers were in general bound by family ties to members of the parlements. The police, who had been punished on several occasions for having brought charges against individuals cheering the parlements, were extremely indecisive. The revolution was making progress. If the royal government had been able to base itself upon the bourgeoisie or the peasantry, it would unquestionably have triumphed, as Gustavus III did in Sweden. But in the spring of 1788 the Third Estate still thought that the members of parlement were the "fathers of the people" and their best defenders. In some regions, particularly Dauphiné, the commoners supported the parlementarians with great vigor. In Dauphiné, in fact, the Third Estate even seized leadership of the movement; a lawyer named Mounier took the initiative of convening a meeting of about a hundred notables in the city hall of Grenoble on June 14, 1788. They decided in turn to hold a meeting on July 21 of all 491 representatives of the three orders at the château of Vizille, without asking the government for permission; there were 276 representatives of the Third Estate, as against 165 nobles and 50 churchmen. The assembly at Vizille called for restoration of the parlements, but this demand was eclipsed by others for a meeting of the Estates General in the near future, with as many deputies from the Third Estate as from both privileged classes, and for reestablishment of the provincial estates of Dauphiné. The assembly at Vizille had immense repercussions. It also proved that the program formulated by the parlementary aristocracy was already out of date. The demand for summoning of the Estates General, with double membership for the Third Estate, became the order of the day.

Loménie de Brienne saw all the advantage which he could gain from this movement of public opinion. He decided to support those who were beginning to be called "Patriots" or the "National Party," after the example of the American and Dutch revolutionaries. It was at this time that he declared: "Since the nobility and the clergy are abandoning the king, who is their natural protector, he must place himself in the hands of the commons, in order to crush them both with its help." The decree of the council of July 5, 1788, authorizing all Frenchmen to publish their views on the meetings of the estates, in fact established freedom of the press. In reality Brienne was seeking above all to win time, but the decree of July 5 cemented the party of the Patriots. The clubs formed in 1787 were reopened and new ones were founded. A "Committee of Thirty," whose principal members were Adrien Duport, Mirabeau, Condorcet, Target, Lacretelle, Du

Pont de Nemours, Roederer, Lafayette, Talleyrand, Mounier, and Barnave, seems to have furnished leadership to the clubs. The clubs wrote, published, and distributed pamphlets replying to the appeal issued by Brienne on July 5. Sieyès was the author of one of the most famous, *What is the Third Estate?* All demanded the summoning of the Estates General, not "in the old forms," as the members of parlement demanded, but with double membership for the Third Estate and a vote by head. They assigned to the Estates General the task not just of introducing a few fiscal reforms but also of drafting a constitution in the image of those adopted by the American states.

Brienne unquestionably could have put off the summoning of the Estates General had not a sudden financial crisis developed early in August when the treasury found itself unexpectedly empty. In order to assure the success of a new loan, Brienne suspended the plenary court on August 8 and announced that the Estates General would meet on May 1, 1789. This measure proved insufficient and Brienne had to resign on August 24. He was replaced by Necker, who had the confidence of the Patriots.

Repeating Calonne's tactics, Necker hoped that the privileged classes would voluntarily consent to a double membership of the Third Estate and a vote by head. He recalled the parlement; the demonstrations which followed in Paris degenerated into riots. He also recalled the Assembly of Notables on November 6, 1788; to his great disappointment, it advocated holding the Estates General "in the form of 1614," as the parlement of Paris had already done on September 21, and denounced "the revolution which is being prepared." Supported by public opinion, Necker overrode this opposition. On December 27 he obtained from the royal council a decision that the king would accept the double membership of the Third

Estate, but he could not persuade them to decide whether voting would be by head or by order; that important decision would be taken by the Estates General itself. The vote of the notables definitely broke the old alliance between the parlementarians and the Third Estate, just as the ministerial decision of December 27 broke the new alliance between the government and the bourgeoisie. The Patriots prepared to oppose the coalition between the royal government and the privileged groups which they now foresaw. In January 1789 Mallet du Pan, a Swiss observer, reported what was happening: "The public debate has changed character. . . . It has become a war between the Third Estate and the other two orders."

The French Revolution of 1789

In 1789 the revolution in France changed character. During the two previous years the aristocracy supported by the people had opposed the government; now the aristocratic resistance split up and weakened. It was replaced by a revolt of the bourgeoisie, which was soon supported by a gigantic uprising of the peasantry. The momentary conjunction of these three movements at the beginning of August led to the collapse of the old regime and the proclamation of the "immortal principles" upon which it was intended that the new regime would be built not only in France but in all modern Europe. It was therefore the breadth of the revolutionary movement as well as the will of its leaders which made the revolution of 1789 in France infinitely more radical and in certain of its aspects more permanent than those which occurred in the other countries of the West.

The year 1789 began with elections to the Estates General. The conditions of the balloting were established by a decree of January 24. The suffrage was very wide, for an elector had only to be twenty-five years of age and a registered taxpayer. No property requirement was required to be eligible. However, voting for the deputies to the Third Estate included several stages while the nobility and most of the clergy voted in direct elections. The electors were instructed to give their delegates lists of their grievances.

The meetings at which deputies were elected and the grievance lists (*cahiers de doléances*) drawn up were held in almost complete freedom; the government decided to observe full neutrality. The influence of the bourgeoisie enabled them to win inclusion of their essential demands in the cahiers of the Third Estate and especially in the general cahiers, which were prepared in the capitals of the bailiwicks. These demands—adoption of a constitution, abolition of privileges, sometimes abolition of guilds (although ideas about this were divergent), and freedom of trade—had already been put forward in numerous pamphlets since July 5, 1788. The monarchical form of the state was never called into question. In the 60,000 cahiers drawn up by the peasants and the artisans, we find principally complaints against the feudal system as well as the special demands of individual communities.

The cahiers of the privileged orders demonstrated the general attachment of the members of these two orders to the person of the king but recognized that profound reforms had to be made. They denounced the arbitrary character of the government and sketched plans for a more efficient administration. Few of these cahiers indicated any intention of renouncing either privileges or the feudal system.

Between February and May 1789 the elections of deputies to the Estates General and the preparation of the cahiers maintained the agitation which had continued almost uninterrupted for two years. The worst economic crisis in half a century caused a rise in the price of food, a slump in the sale of manufactured products, unemployment, and misery. Everywhere in France hungry crowds prevented transport of grain over the highways. In some localities bourgeois militia were formed by early May to maintain order. In Paris bad rioting broke out on April 27 and 28 in the faubourg Saint-Antoine, where two industrialists were accused of trying to cut wages. The wallpaper factory of Réveillon, one of the purported wage-cutters, was destroyed. Enforcement of order was lax; the police and the army, who had their own complaints against the government, were not eager to put down disorders, especially since some of those who had shown such zeal had themselves been punished. Nonetheless these disorders do not appear to have had great influence either on the election of deputies or the preparation of the cahiers. The deputies were chosen only from the ranks of the clergy, nobility, and bourgeoisie; not a single peasant or worker was elected to the Estates General. Among the bourgeois named, one half were members of the legal professions, principally lawyers. The others included merchants, industrialists, rich landowners, intellectuals, scholars and scientists, and a few Protestant ministers.

The Estates General were solemnly opened by the king on May 5, 1789, at Versailles. A long debate began at once over what was apparently only a procedural question; actually the very existence of the Estates General, as well as their ability to act effectively, was at stake. The question was whether the powers of the deputies would be verified in separate meetings of each order, as had been done in 1614, or in plenary session. Separate verification meant that the deputies would certainly continue to vote by order, that is, the demands of the Third Estate would run the risk of being rejected by the other two orders. Verification in plenary session would almost certainly give a majority to the Third Estate, which had the support of a strong contingent of parish priests. On May 6, under the influence of deputies from Brittany, the Third Estate refused to constitute itself as a separate house and its representatives took the title of "deputies of the commons," in imitation of the lower house of the English parliament. The nobility, on the contrary, rejected a vote by head by 141 to 47; the clergy did likewise, but only by 133 to 114. The two privileged orders then began to verify the powers of their own members, while the deputies of the Third Estate remained "immobile," as Mirabeau urged, "in order to be strong in the face of the enemy."

Finally, on June 10, the Third Estate solemnly invited the two other orders to join it in order to proceed to "verification of powers in common." Parish priests among the deputies of the clergy began to join the Third Estate on June 13. On June 17, at the proposal of Abbé Sieyès, a deputy of the Third Estate from Paris, the assembly of the Third Estate, with a number of parish priests in attendance, "considering that it represented 98 percent of the nation," declared itself the "National Assembly." It also took upon itself the right to consent to taxation and provisionally confirmed existing taxes; this hinted at the possibility that, if the king and the privileged orders rejected their proposals, they might proclaim a tax strike, after the example of the Belgian Patriots. This declaration was an extremely grave threat for the royal government, for it was already short of funds.

These decisions overcame the last hesitations of the

clergy. On June 19 they accepted verification of powers in common. On the other hand, Louis XVI, under the pressure of the nobility, decided in favor of resistance on the same day. On June 20 the meeting hall of the Third Estate was closed on his order. The deputies thereupon moved to a nearby indoor tennis court; there, amid general enthusiasm, they took an oath proposed by Mounier "never to disband and to meet wherever circumstances might require until the constitution was adopted and set on a firm foundation."

Despite this impressive demonstration, the king, at the urging of his brothers and the queen, decided to quash the decisions of the Third Estate. A "royal session" modeled after the *lits de justice* held in the parlement took place on June 23. The king began by announcing a complete program of reforms but spoke neither of voting by head, nor of tax equality, nor of the abolition of the feudal system. After the royal speech was read the Third Estate remained in the hall and reaffirmed the decisions which it had taken "in the name of the nation." Mirabeau epitomized its resistance when he declared to the king's emissary: "Go tell those who send you that we are here by the will of the people and that we shall leave our places only by the force of bayonets."

Louis XVI seemed to accept the situation. Agitation had spread to the streets, and, although the king had enough bayonets at his command to drive out the deputies, he did not have enough troops to check the riots which were brewing in Paris. He therefore allowed the majority of the clergy to join the Third Estate on June 24; forty-seven deputies of the nobility followed on June 25. On June 27 the king went so far as to invite all recalcitrant deputies to join the "National Assembly."

The "juridical" revolution had apparently been completed and there had been no resort to violence.

But the king and the aristocracy accepted the accomplished fact only in order to win time and to mass troops around the capital; when that had been done, the assembly would be dissolved. The troop movements increased the anxiety which gripped every one's mind at the spectacle of the assembly's impotence. After its first meeting on May 5, it took until July 7 to elect a "constitutional committee," and it did not declare itself a "National Constituent Assembly" until July 9. During these two months the peasants and the bourgeois became convinced that the privileged classes were in agreement to resist the popular demands, that they were about to obtain the dismissal of the Estates General, that they wished to "starve the people," and in general that there existed an "aristocratic plot" to defeat the "will of the people." Townsmen and country-dwellers became frightened and began to take up arms. Once armed, the people frightened each other. Everywhere it was believed that "brigands" in the service of the "aristocrats" were approaching. The large number of unemployed men—"with neither hearth nor home"—who wandered through the countryside explains this fear of brigands to some extent.

At the beginning of July a collective "fear" gripped the entire countryside of Normandy. At the same time, excitement was at a peak in the cities, particularly in Paris. The fear and suspicion were explained by Marat in a pamphlet published on July 1—the people thought that the government was going to dissolve the assembly. On July 12, in a prelude to the act of force contemplated by the king, Necker's dismissal was announced. This was the real cause of the popular uprising that followed in Paris. On July 14, during a series of attacks on armories, the

Parisians seized the Bastille, which was not only an arsenal but also a royal prison and the symbol of the king's arbitrary power. The rebels seized power in Paris. The permanent committee of Parisian electors established on July 12 transformed itself on July 15 into a "commune" or insurrectionary city government; the bourgeois militia also established on the 12th became the National Guard of Paris. The Parisians adopted as a sign of recognition a cockade in which the white of the Bourbons was added to the blue and red of the colors of the city of Paris. After some uncertainty on what attitude to take, Louis XVI, at the strong urging of several high-ranking noblemen of liberal tendencies, decided to move the troops away from Paris and to recall Necker. On July 17 he went to Paris; his presence ratified, as it were, the success of the Parisian revolution.

The revolution spread to the provinces like a powder train. In the cities the armed people seized municipal powers more or less completely and formed national guards recruited principally from the bourgeoisie. Often these actions were accompanied by measures to regulate the price of bread and to maintain a check upon the grain traffic. In the countryside the peasants, impatient for the abolition of the feudal system which they had demanded in most of their cahiers, stormed the châteaux; they demanded and burned the old charters which fixed their obligations towards the lords. Where there was resistance, they sometimes went so far as to burn down the manor houses. The rebels also frightened each other; everywhere "brigands" and "aristocratic plotters" were accused of starting the disorders. This mentality explains the outbreak of this "Great Fear" during the second half of July; this strange phenomenon distinguished the French revolution from the revolutions which occurred in other countries of the West. The Great Fear had a decisive effect upon the course of the revolution in France. The rural world, which for centuries had been so submissive and so passive, was now in arms; it demanded the abolition of the feudal system with far greater violence and unanimity than it had shown in the cahiers.

After the aristocratic revolution, which began in 1787 and was directed against royal absolutism to the extent that it imperiled aristocratic privileges, after the revolution of the jurists and lawyers, which began on May 5, 1789, and was intended to win a victory for the principles of freedom and equality of rights by the sole strength of reason and procedure, there now suddenly erupted the most violent peasant war that France had known for centuries.

It had been the intention of the bourgeois, who were the only representatives of the Third Estate in the National Assembly, systematically to prepare a constitution proclaiming respect for property along with individual freedom and equality before the law. But they now saw with fright that property itself was being threatened. The feudal dues and the tithes which the peasants demanded be immediately abolished were forms of property owned not only by the nobility but often also by bourgeois. In some regions of France, as for example Dauphiné, the bourgeois national guards and armed peasants clashed violently. But the Great Fear and the peasant uprisings which accompanied it were an inescapable death sentence for the feudal system.

The entire program of activity which the National Assembly had worked out at the beginning of July was disturbed. It was urgent to bring the peasant uprising to a halt, lest bourgeois property itself come under attack. A tacit alliance was sealed between the peasants and the bourgeoisie. The deputies of the Third Estate defended the most essential peasant demands in order to limit the revolutionary movement. This was another of the very original aspects of the revolution in France. The alliance between the peasants and the bourgeoisie permitted the revolution to attain immediately its most radical and definitive results. During the night of August 4 the liberal deputies of the nobility, under the influence of deputies of the Third Estate, declared to the National Assembly that feudal rights constituted property of a special kind, which had often been usurped or imposed by violence, and that it was legitimate to verify these rights and to suppress those which appeared to be unjustified. In a great wave of enthusiasm the mass of the representatives of the clergy and the nobility consented to the "sacrifices" awaited by France with such impatience. The Assembly decreed the abolition of the feudal system and the privileges of persons, towns, and provinces; it also proclaimed equality before the law and the suppression of tithes. These spectacular decisions were at once broadcast by thousands of newspapers, pamphlets, and illustrated broadsides. The repercussions were profound. The rural disorders abated and the assembly was able to resume its labors in calm.

The Declaration of the Rights of Man and the Citizen

The Constituents (as the deputies to the National Constituent Assembly were henceforth called) had decided early in July to begin their work with a "declaration of rights," as the members of the constitutional conventions in the American states had done. Such a declaration was in conformity with the theories of the philosophes and it was a demand in many of the cahiers. The objections of the moderates, who held it to be dangerous, were brushed aside. Debate began on August 4 and it was adopted on August 26.

The French "Declaration of the Rights of Man and the Citizen" offers some significant differences from the American declarations. The American declarations remained very specific, very "American"; this was true even of Virginia's, the broadest. The French deputies, on the contrary, desired to prepare, in Mirabeau's words, "a declaration applicable to all ages, all peoples, all moral and geographical latitudes." In it are to be found neither the name of a nation nor the description of a system of government; it is as valid for a monarchy as for a republic. It is truly universal. This assured its prestige and constitutes its greatness.

The French declaration was a compromise among drafts presented by various deputies, Sieyès and Lafayette in particular, and its articles are not arranged in a rigorously logical order. The primary stress is upon freedom. Men are born free and remain free. Freedom is "the right to do anything which does not harm others." The judicial basis of freedom of opinion and freedom of the press is defined; but the declaration also explicitly provides that the expression of opinion may not disturb the public order established by law. It makes no mention of freedom of religion (being satisfied with religious toleration), nor of freedom of residence, industry and trade, meetings, associations, and teaching.

Equality holds a lesser place than freedom in the declaration. Although the first article affirms that men are born equal, equality does not figure among the "imprescriptible" rights. Article 6 specifies that the law is equal for all, establishes equality in the courts, and opens all government positions to every citizen. Fiscal equality—

the absence of any tax privilege—is established by Article 13.

The right of property does figure among the "natural imprescriptible rights," and the final Article of the declaration repeats that "property is inviolable and sacred." After the peasant risings of July, property owners needed reassurance.

According to Article 3, sovereignty resides in the nation. Since the national sovereignty is indivisible, the three orders (estates) are abolished. Law is the expression of the general will; consequently all attacks upon the public order must be put down. Respect for the public order is assured by the separation of powers, to which the declaration devotes an entire article.

In addition to these fundamental principles, other articles of the declaration take up the armed forces, finances, which are assured by "a public contribution, freely consented," and the responsibility of government officials. Finally, the right of resistance to oppression is proclaimed; thereby the July uprisings were made lawful.

The declaration of rights was the work of the bourgeoisie directed against the old regime; it was also, in Mirabeau's phrase, furnished with "restrictions, precautions, and conditions" designed to prevent the peasants and workers from using it as a weapon against the bourgeoisie. It was at the same time a condemnation of the abuses of the absolute monarchy and the foundation on which to build the new order. Placing itself under the aegis of the "Supreme Being," it preserved the primacy of Catholicism. It passed over freedom of industry and trade in silence despite the influence of the physiocrats, because there were deep divisions among the deputies of the Third Estate on this question. Freedom of association was not mentioned because the Constituents desired to reduce the number of religious congregations; some even wanted to suppress them entirely.

The French Declaration of the Rights of Man is therefore neither a servile copy of the American models nor a hasty transcription of the ideas of the philosophes. It was the work of men who took into the closest consideration the historical circumstances in which it was written. Although composed by French bourgeois of the eighteenth century in their own interest, the significance of the declaration far exceeds the interests of the bourgeoisie. The "immortal principles of 1789" which it proclaims continue to be invoked, by some with enthusiasm, by others ironically. It became the dogma of the Revolution, the catechism of freedom and equality, "the credo of the new age," in Michelet's phrase.

Louis XVI was first to be disturbed by the "explosive character" of the declaration. He refused to give his approval either to the Declaration of Rights or to the decrees enacted in order to put into practice the principles adopted on the night of August 4. As for the National Assembly, when it began to discuss the constitution, its divisions came out into the open. The "Monarchians" (*monarchiens*) led by Mounier, desired a monarchy "in the English style," with two houses and the king having a right of absolute veto. They were opposed by the Patriots, who were hostile to the royal veto and desired a single legislative chamber. This conflict led Louis XVI into believing that a second act of force against the deputies might succeed. Again he moved troops into the Paris region. Again the people of Paris replied by a riot to the concentration of armed force, which was accompanied as in June by renewed food shortages and rising prices. The fact was that only a popular insurrection could compel the king to give his sanction to the abolition of the feudal system and the Declaration of Rights, that is, to the creation of a new regime. On October 5 a parade of women, followed by "conquerors of the Bastille" and the national guard of Paris, marched to Versailles. The king's gesture in approving the decrees did not succeed in calming the demonstrators. After massacring a number of guardsmen and breaking their way into the queen's apartment, they took the royal family to Paris on October 6. The king, henceforth virtually a prisoner in the palace of the Tuileries, became a hostage of the Patriots. On October 12 the National Assembly followed the king to Paris, which became the capital. The assembly, accepting Sieyès' theory of its constituent power, then decided that as a national constitutional assembly it was superior to the king, and that he could not reject any articles in the new constitution. This was not the view of the Monarchians. Several Monarchians left the assembly, some even went abroad to join those great lords who had fled Paris and become émigrés immediately after July 14.

For two years the National Constituent Assembly governed France in sovereign manner; indeed, its rule was virtually a dictatorship. It renewed France's political, administrative, economic, social, and even religious structure, always with the twofold concern of avoiding a return of the former privileged classes to power and at the same time preventing the mass of the people from exercising to the full the rights which it had proclaimed. The assembly's ability to carry out this policy was limited, however, by popular pressure. In Paris the assembly debated before galleries which were constantly filled with listeners who did not hesitate to demonstrate noisily their approval or opposition. After October the people were organized into revolutionary bodies throughout France. There were the municipalities, the national guards (which began to form local federations as early as August, and regional federations beginning with November, and celebrated a "national federation" or meeting on July 14, 1790), and, not the least, the clubs. These clubs usually originated in the debating societies which had been created after 1750, or were inspired by the English, American, Genevan, and Dutch political clubs. During the first years of the revolution there were clubs of every political shading, but the most numerous were the clubs of "Friends of the Constitution." It became usual to call them the "Jacobin" clubs, because the Friends of the Constitution in Paris met in a former convent of Jacobins (Dominican friars). The Jacobin clubs were linked by a network of correspondence.

All these revolutionary organs exercised their influence upon the National Assembly by means of petitions and the press, which publicized their discussions and their slogans. The freedom which the press had enjoyed since May 1789 permitted a great increase in the number of newspapers. They represented all shades of opinion, from *The King's Friend* to Marat's *Friend of the People*. The most revolutionary and violent journals were read with greatest avidity. The press kept the citizenry on the alert, and the citizens, through their organizations, attempted to make the National Assembly follow their lead. It was amid such conditions that the assembly attempted to construct a new regime during the two years from October 1789, to September 1791.

chapter four

THE WORK OF THE FRENCH REVOLUTION FROM 1789 TO 1792

The essential goal of the National Constituent Assembly was to construct a new regime which would guarantee to the bourgeoisie the peaceful exercise of power and eliminate the possibility of either a return to absolute monarchy, or rule of the aristocracy, or rule of the mass of the people. They envisioned this regime as a constitutional monarchy established upon the rational basis proclaimed in the Declaration of the Rights of Man and the Citizen.

The assembly proceeded to destroy the institutions of the old regime as soon as new institutions had been created to take their place. But not all of the old institutions were destroyed; some were continued either in their old forms or somewhat modified. The Constituent Assembly therefore did not build the new France from scratch; yet the Constituents never felt the least compunction about preserving the past and never hesitated to destroy inherited institutions.

The achievement of the Constituent Assembly has many aspects. Its political work, which its members unquestionably considered to be their most important accomplishment, was the least enduring, for it collapsed after two years. Its social, economic, and administrative achievements, on the other hand, left much deeper traces, which still persist in the structure of present-day France. We shall begin our analysis by examining these essential aspects of the work of the Constituent Assembly.

Social Achievements

The society of the old regime was built upon hierarchy and privilege, which is to say upon inequality. Contrariwise, in its first article the Declaration of the Rights of Man proclaimed equality before law. The Constituent Assembly attempted to create institutions to put this principle of equality into practice. Because it attempted to reserve the reality of power for the bourgeoisie, the assembly met major difficulties in this endeavor and was not wholly successful.

Although on August 4, 1789, the Constituent Assembly abolished personal servitude (there were still 1.5 million serfs in France) and the three orders into which Frenchmen had been divided, although it granted civil rights to foreigners and actors, a proposal to give equality to Jews aroused very sharp debate and was only enacted by the assembly on September 27, 1791, three days before its final adjournment. Equality also presupposed the removal of all discrimination between Negroes and whites as well as the abolition of slavery. This was the logical consequence of the first article of the Declaration of Rights. But the French colonists, represented in the assembly by such influential deputies as the Lameths and Barnave, did not even accept civil equality between whites and free "colored men." After some hesitation the assembly finally accepted the position of the colonists. They did so in order to avoid the revolt which was forecast, it was explained. In fact the assembly thereby prepared a later explosion in the colonies which brought far greater harm to the planters than honest application of the principles of 1789 would have done.

The most important immediate consequence of the principle of equal rights was the opportunity for all Frenchmen to be appointed to any position in the state. The nobility thereby lost their monopoly of the higher offices. Actually only the bourgeoisie benefited from this change, for only they possessed the education necessary to hold these posts or the wealth necessary to acquire such education. In the army, however, where courage could still take the place of learning and sons of peasants and artisans could rise to the summit of the revolutionary hierarchy as a result of circumstances (the emigration of noble officers and the long wars of the revolutionary period), it could now be truly said that "every soldier carried a marshal's baton in his knapsack." All in all, upward social mobility became more rapid and more frequent than before the revolution.

Even more important in its consequences, however, was the abolition of the feudal system, adopted amid enthusiasm by the National Assembly during the night of August 4, although under the pressure of the peasant uprising. During the days that followed, the owners of manors strove to limit their concessions as much as possible. The decrees applying the decisions of principle taken on August 4 were only adopted on March 15, 1790, and the peasants found them unsatisfactory. The new decrees drew a distinction between the rights of feudal (manorial) overlordship, which the assembly presumed to have been usurped, and rights of "feudal contract," which it assumed derived from contracts made between the landlords and the peasant tenants. The rights of overlordship included honorific and personal obligations, which were abolished without payment. The tithe, which had been a very heavy burden for the peasants, was also abolished without compensation; but the landowners were the principal beneficiaries of this measure, for they ceased to transmit the tithes to the church although they continued to collect them from their tenants and sharecroppers.

On the other hand, most of the manorial dues, or "real rights," were not actually abolished outright but had to be bought back by the peasants at prices they found difficult to pay. Repurchases were to be made by individuals, not the state or communities, and no system of credit was provided to make the repayments easier to meet. Until the dues were completely repurchased, they still had to be paid, together with the arrears for thirty years. It was obvious that if this law were enforced the feudal system would last for many long years. The discontented peasants rose in rebellion again in many regions. It was only later, in 1792 and 1793, after the fall of the monarchy, that the Legislative Assembly and the Convention which followed it gave satisfaction to the peasants by abolishing all dues of "feudal character" without any compensation. Thereafter no servitudes on either person or land existed within the continental territory of France. The right of property became absolute, in the Roman sense of the term, and the transfer of land was vastly facilitated.

Economic Achievements

Circumstances rather than theories led the Constituent Assembly to make important reforms in the field of economics and finances. The Estates General had been summoned essentially in order to solve the financial crisis. Even before May 1789 many financiers considered that the best way of meeting the governmental deficit would be to sell the property of the clergy for the benefit of the state, which in return would be responsible for payment of the salaries of churchmen and the costs of religious activity.

Abolition of the tithes on August 4 proved that the assembly would not hesitate to follow this path. On August 6 the first proposal to put the property of the clergy at the disposal of the nation was presented from the rostrum. Discussion was long and sharp. Mirabeau and Talleyrand clearly posed the terms of the problem: The wealth of the clergy would be placed at the disposal of the nation in order to pay off the debt of the state; in return the government would provide for the costs of religious worship and pay the salaries of clergymen, although without maintaining the scandalous gap between the incomes of parish priests and bishops. Some deputies argued that it was necessary to take the clergy's wealth in order to remove its status as an estate. At last the wealth of the clergy was nationalized on November 2. The properties appropriated from the churchmen were to be employed to back the assignats, a form of paper money, with which the state would pay its indebtedness. Assignats could be used for the purchase of "national property," as the former ecclesiastical holdings were designated. Assignats so used were to be returned to the treasury and burned.

This decision had a considerable influence upon the history of the French revolution. It resulted in inflation and the devaluation of the assignat, and hence in a rise in prices and a higher cost of living; another consequence was a massive transfer of property, which passed from the hands of the clergy to the ownership of the bourgeoisie and prosperous peasantry.

The sale of "national properties" began in May 1790. Credit facilities were granted to purchasers; they had to pay only 12 to 30 percent of the purchase price in cash, depending on the kind of property; the balance could be paid over twelve years at 5 percent interest. The assembly hoped to assist the peasants by these arrangements. Only a small sum was necessary as a down payment for purchase of "national property," but the landless day laborers had used what little money they had to buy bread at very high prices during the spring of 1789, and many small landowners reserved their savings for the repurchase of feudal dues. Furthermore, although some lots were small and inexpensive, many were vast and the minimum acceptable price was very high. Sales were held at auction and bids on part lots were permitted only if their combined figure was higher than the highest bid offered for the same land as a single lot. The sales were very successful at first, but as we have said, it was especially the bourgeois and the prosperous peasants who profited. Nobles and parish priests were also among the buyers. Poor peasants could make purchases only by forming groups. The distribution of landed property in France was profoundly changed, but to the profit of the prosperous classes. The number of landless day laborers did not decline significantly.

The assignats were put to use at once to pay the government's debt. But the obligations inherited from the old regime were soon swollen by new indebtedness when the Constituent Assembly decided to abolish the former "venal" offices with compensation to the owners. New issues of assignats appeared in rapid succession. But Frenchmen did not accept them without suspicion; they had unhappy memories of the collapse of the paper money issued by Law's bank between 1716 and 1720. By 1791 devaluation of the assignats began. Devaluation would probably have been limited, and to some extent even beneficial (for it was at first a stimulant to the economy), if the financial situation had not forced the treasury to have recourse to new and bigger issues. The fact was that taxes were no longer being collected and the treasury was empty. Instead of being used for reimbursement of the state debt—the purpose for which they had been established—assignats began to be used for payment of current expenses. Inflation and devaluation continued at an accelerating rate. In 1792 the assignat dropped a third in value; when the decline became even more rapid, a grave monetary crisis resulted which did not terminate until 1797, with withdrawal of the assignats and a partial bankruptcy.

The Constituent Assembly did not foresee these difficulties and methodically pursued its economic activities. However, its members were divided on economic policy, and their divisions reflected the actual economic life of the nation. In one camp were the big merchants, the big industrialists, and all who advocated complete freedom of industry and trade, which assured the omnipotence of the employer over his workers and staff; in the other camp were those who were attached to the traditional forms of handicraft production and desired to preserve guild organizations and production regulations, most of which were not in accordance with the principle of economic freedom.

Abolition of feudalism contributed greatly to the emancipation of the land, as we have seen. But there also existed servitudes on the soil—rights of usage, the stubble right, collective communal property—which were not of feudal origin and were not immediately abolished. After long debate the supporters of economic freedom won a partial victory. The freedom for any man to enclose his lands and to till them as he pleased was proclaimed, but the stubble right was abolished only in artificial meadows; a law introducing division of communal lands, to which the assembly was favorable, was drawn up but no decision was taken on it. In practice, landowning farmers found these reforms to their advantage, but day laborers were very strongly opposed to abolition of the common lands and the stubble right, which enabled them to keep a few goats or sheep. Furthermore, the right of enclosure could be exercised only with great difficulty, for in many parts of France the multiplicity of small holdings in the "open fields" made enclosure a practical impossibility. Despite these difficulties, the agrarian reforms of the Constituent Assembly were continued by the Legislative Assembly and the Convention. These reforms resulted in reduction of the average size of holdings and an increase in the number of landowners, and greatly strengthened the individualism of the peasantry.

In the areas of trade and industrial production, the Constituent Assembly was even more deeply divided. It did not even begin discussion of these matters until February 1791. Opponents endeavored to prove that the guilds enjoyed exclusive privileges and therefore should be abolished on the basis of the decisions of August 4. Abolition of the guilds was finally voted, but the Constituent Assembly also adopted the proposal of deputy Le Chapelier to maintain in force the old police ordinances which forbade workers to associate in journeymen's leagues (*compagnonnages*), to form "coalitions" (unions), or to strike. The Le Chapelier law was voted under the pretext of maintaining freedom of labor, but it was in accordance with the ideas of the economists and the interests of the capitalist bourgeoisie. It passed almost without debate; not only was there no representative of the workers in the

Constituent Assembly, but it must be added that the problem of labor did not arise in 1791 in the same terms as it did fifty years later, for the Industrial Revolution had hardly begun in France. Still it is true that in the Le Chapelier law the interests of employers won out under the pretext of economic liberalism. It was only repealed in the second half of the nineteenth century, by the law of 1864 which permitted strikes and the law of 1884 which legalized trade unions.

It was also on the basis of the principles of freedom and freehold property that the Constituent Assembly repealed the law on mines of 1744, which had required prior authorization from the government to use the subsoil for mining and thus limited the rights of the owner of the land. The Constituent Assembly returned full ownership of the subsoil to the owner of the land, but thereby disorganized operation of the mines and generated interminable lawsuits.

As for trade, the Constituent Assembly applied the principle of the economists, *laissez faire, laissez passer*,[1] at least as far as trade within the territory of continental France was concerned. All tolls and customs dues on imports and exports collected at the frontiers, within the country, and at city gates—and in general the majority of indirect taxes—were abolished. Government revenues were to come essentially from three direct "contributions" —the land contribution, the personal property tax, and licenses on businesses and trades. Jurisdiction over fairs and markets was reduced to the most elementary police regulations; all price-fixing was abolished. This measure encouraged an increase in prices and caused discontent among the poor, who feared famine. New disorders caused

1. Loosely, "do not interfere or penalize" or "hands off."—*Trans.*

by the free movement of grain occurred in different parts of France.

Complete freedom of trade was to be favored by a system of uniform weights and measures, which was approved in principle. Freedom of trade led to development of banks, financial companies, and in general all forms of credit. Trade in securities was made nearly free. The profession of bond and mercantile brokerage was opened to all without restriction.

The Constituent Assembly showed itself to be less liberal with regard to foreign trade. In this area the interests of the big merchants no longer coincided with the principle of free trade. To be sure, the assembly abolished the privileges and exemptions which some ports such as Lorient and Marseilles enjoyed, and it suppressed the monopolist trading companies like the India Company. But it maintained a protectionist tariff and indicated its opposition to the trade treaties with the United States (1778) and England (1786), which had lowered tariff rates.

Colonial trade remained strictly regulated. Despite the violent protests of the deputies from the colonies, who desired freedom to trade as they pleased, the system of "Exclusion," permitting the colonies to trade only with the mother country, was maintained. On the other hand, perhaps in compensation, the Constituent Assembly established colonial assemblies with sole authority to legislate regarding persons and property in the colonies; these assemblies maintained the inequality between whites and "colored people," the slave trade, and slavery.

Most of the economic reforms of the Constituent Assembly endured. They continued to be in force long into the nineteenth century, some surviving even to our own day.

Administrative Achievements

The administrative achievements of the Constituent Assembly were also very enduring. They were indispensable reforms demanded by a majority of Frenchmen, for the complexity and incoherence of the monarchical administration scandalized eighteenth-century men infatuated with rationalism. A large number of the cahiers demanded a thorough administrative reform, such as had been in preparation for some years. The monarchical administration itself had desired to substitute a sensible organization of the national territory for the hodgepodge of "provinces," "bailiwicks" and "seneschalsies," civil and ecclesiastical "dioceses," "estate lands" and "election lands," "military governments" and "commanderships-in-chief," and unequal and illogical judicial districts.

In 1787, in connection with the establishment of provincial assemblies, the royal government had also conceived a plan for special districts for the allocation (in old French, *département*) of taxes. In 1789 the geographer Letrosne proposed an administrative division of France suggested by the federal system of the new United States of America; his plan called for 25 generalities, 250 districts, 4,500 wards, all approximately equal in shape. In approving the design of the project as a whole, Condorcet felt that it would be necessary to "reconcile changes with local convenience." Mirabeau declared: "I should want a division based upon geography and facts and adapted to the localities and circumstances, not at all a mathematical division, which is almost perfect in theory but in my opinion, would be almost impossible to put into practice. I should want a division intended not only to establish proportional representation but also to bring the administration of men and things closer together and to permit greater participation of the citizenry in the work of government. Last, I propose a division which will not seem—shall we say?—too novel; a division which will permit—if I may be so bold as to use the terms—a compromise with prejudices and even with errors, and will be desired equally by all provinces and be founded upon familiar relationships." The Constituent Assembly accepted Mirabeau's ideas.

Reorganization was facilitated by the abolition of provincial and communal privileges during the night of August 4. The Constituent Assembly divided France into eighty-three "departments," but decided that the "former boundaries of provinces should be respected whenever there is neither real advantage nor absolute necessity for discarding them." Brittany was given five departments, Provence three, but the two small provinces of Aunis and Saintonge were combined to form a single department. The departments were given the names of their most characteristic geographical features, which they still retain. An effort was made to set the boundaries so that the capital of each department would be no more than a day's travel from its most distant point.

The departments were divided into up to nine districts. It was intended that residents would be able to make the round trip from their homes to the capital of the district in a single day. Each district comprised a number of cantons. The primary unit remained the parish, which dated from the early Middle Ages; it was now called the "commune."

Each of these divisions was to be administered by representatives of taxpayers, chosen directly in the commune and by two-stage elections in the district and the department. Councils at the head of the commune, the district, and the department were divided into two sections; one—a directory in the department and the district, a mayor and municipal officers in the commune—was given the executive power, and the other—a general council in the department, the district, and the commune—was deliberative. The king was represented by a procurator syndic, who was elected, not appointed. This was the most complete administrative decentralization which France has ever known. Each department was like a little autonomous republic. If the departments fell into the hands of opponents, the revolution would be in jeopardy. Not surprisingly, centralization had to be reestablished in 1793.

These new divisions had to be provided with courts, all alike and with perfectly defined jurisdictions. The capital of the canton received a "justice of the peace," in imitation of Holland and England. He was more an arbitrator than a judge; his task was to avoid trials rather than to suggest them. Assisted by two other citizens, he presided over the police court of the canton, which had the duty of punishing minor crimes. In each district capital there was a civil court, and in the departmental capital a criminal court. All judges were elected from the ranks of graduate lawyers and were paid by the state. In criminal cases it was the citizens themselves who decided upon indictments and guilt. A jury for accusations was composed of eight citizens drawn by lot from one list, and a trial jury of twelve citizens was likewise chosen by lot but from a different list. The judges, brought in from the district tribunals, merely fixed sentences. All courts were to judge according to uniform codes. The Constituent Assembly began drafting these codes but was able to complete only the penal code. Inspired by the humane ideas of Beccaria, it abolished torture and barbarous punishments and increased safeguards for the accused. Nonetheless, despite a speech by Robespierre, the death penalty was maintained. Appeals in civil cases went from one district tribunal to another; the Constituent Assembly, not wishing to revive the former parlements, did not create appellate courts. It did establish national tribunals: the Court of Invalidation (*tribunal de cassation*), composed of one elected judge from each department, which had the duty of examining not the substance of cases but only their form; and a High Court which would meet in exceptional cases to try crimes by ministers and high officials as well as crimes against the security of the state. This judicial system was logical, coherent, and humane. It made justice totally independent of the king but, as a consequence of the system of property qualifications for the ballot, it placed justice in the hands of the bourgeoisie. Incontestably one of the most successful reforms, it was the work of an assembly more than half of whose members were lawyers.

In military matters the Constituent Assembly was much more hesitant. The assembly legalized the militia bands which had been formed spontaneously in July and August 1789 by making them a "National Guard." In the minds of the members of the Constituent Assembly as well as of the guardsmen themselves, they were not an army but a force whose sole function was to maintain order within the country and to safeguard the "conquests of the revolution." Despite the appeal of Deputy Dubois-Crancé in favor of universal military service, obligatory and equal for all, the Constituent Assembly retained the professional army, although promotion to even the highest ranks was opened to all soldiers. Nonetheless the royal army soon began to disintegrate when its aristocratic officers went abroad in emigration. Often the soldiers rebelled against commanders who were hostile to the revolution. The Constituent Assembly became more and more inclined to call upon the National Guard to defend the country and the revolution. After June 1791 it ordered the formation of battalions of volunteers selected from the National Guard; an army of citizen-soldiers wearing blue uniforms, with white jackets and red braid, took shape at the side of the old royal army, which wore white uniforms. The navy was also reorganized, and all naval ranks were opened to every citizen, especially merchant marine officers.

Political Achievements

The fundamental objective of the members of the Constituent Assembly, as we have seen, was to establish a constitutional monarchy, which they hoped would last as long as the ten-centuries-old absolute monarchy. In this endeavor they met almost total failure. The constitutional monarchy organized by the National Constituent Assembly lasted less than a year. Its fragility was a result of the fears of a majority of the deputies, who dreaded both giving the king too much power and entrusting the people with too much authority. The regime which they created therefore lacked strength and soon collapsed.

The Constituent Assembly began by transgressing one of the fundamental principles which it had proclaimed in the Declaration of Rights—equality. At Sieyès's suggestion, it introduced a subtle distinction among French citizens. Only the more prosperous, the "active citizens" (about two-thirds of the total), participated in political life. The remainder, called "passive citizens," enjoyed only civil rights. To be an active citizen one had to pay direct taxes equal to three days' wages. Because of the unequal distribution of taxes, the percentage of active citizens varied very widely; and they were proportionally much more numerous in the countryside than in the towns. The large majority of peasants who owned at least their cottages was included among the active citizens, while artisan journeymen who lived in rented rooms remained passive citizens. It must be noted, however, that the active citizens directly elected only the municipal councils. The Legislative Assembly, the general councils of the departments and the districts, and the judges were named at the second stage by electors who had to be chosen from among the 50,000 wealthiest Frenchmen, who owned or enjoyed the income from property worth from 150 to 400 days' work, depending on the locality.

The Legislative Assembly was elected for two years. It received important powers: the initiative and the passage of laws, the voting of a budget which was not subject to the royal veto, the decision on war and peace, the right to address the people by proclamations. Still the king retained many elements of strength. Although he was no longer "king of France by the grace of God" but merely "king of the French," his person remained "inviolable and sacred." The succession to the throne was still governed by the Salic Law, that is, it was hereditary in the male line by order of primogeniture. The king named and dismissed the six ministers who were responsible only to him and had to be selected outside the membership of the assembly. The king continued to lead the army and the navy, since he named the majority of their officers. He was the director of France's diplomacy and proposed the declaration of war or conclusion of peace to the assembly, which had the power of decision. His principal prerogative was the right of suspensive veto. If he refused to approve a law it could become effective only if two successive legislative assemblies confirmed the vote of the first assembly. Thus the king could delay enforcement of a law for a period varying from two to six years. On the other hand, the king could not dissolve the assembly.

This constitution, which presents many analogies to the Constitution of the United States, required profound agreement between the executive and the legislature in order to function successfully. It was not possible to create such agreement because the two branches were deeply distrustful of each other and each desired to utilize to the full, and more, the prerogatives granted it by the constitution. Furthermore, the religious problem, rising unexpectedly, caused significant worsening in the relations between the king on the one hand and the assembly and new authorities of the nation on the other. The religious question deepened the crisis in France. Some historians see in it one of the essential causes of the partial failure of the French revolution.

The Religious Achievement

The Constituent Assembly included in the Constitution of 1791 a whole series of dispositions relating to the Catholic church. It may be wondered why it took up so delicate a matter. It should be noted, first of all, that during the old regime the church and the state were so closely intertwined in France that the reform of one inevitably caused an upheaval in the other, even though not a single cahier demanded that the Estates General make any deep changes in the organization of the church. Furthermore, it was financial necessity which first compelled the assembly to take up the question of the church. We have seen that the abolition of tithes during the night of August 4 and then especially the nationalization of the wealth of the clergy led the assembly to promise that the state would provide for the costs of religious worship, in particular the salaries of priests. But the payment of salaries required that the number of clergymen be determined; it seemed logical too to modify the ecclesiastical districts so that they would coincide with the new administrative divisions. The Constituent Assembly thus moved inexorably toward giving the clergy a "civil constitution." Debate on this problem revealed from the beginning the variety of attitudes among the deputies on the question of religion. None was an advocate of "separation of church and state," none demanded it or even conceived of it. The majority of the deputies were imbued with Gallican and Jansenist ideas and favored a return to the church of the early days of Christianity—that is, a simple, austere church in which priests and bishops were elected by the faithful. A few anticlerical deputies, disciples of Voltaire, Helvétius, and Holbach, took advantage of the opportunity to reduce the power of the church.

The civil constitution of the clergy abolished the regular clergy, declaring that the state no longer recognized their vows and forbidding such vows in the future. Ecclesiastical districts were patterned on the administrative divisions. There was one bishop for each department, which meant extinction of fifty-two dioceses. The eighty-three remaining bishoprics were distributed among ten ecclesiastical metropolitan districts (archbishoprics). Priests would be paid by the state. A decision of utmost gravity provided that bishops would be elected by the electoral assemblies of the departments, and parish priests by the district electoral assemblies. Parish priests could choose their assistant priests. Canonical institution was to be given to priests by the bishops and to bishops by the metropolitans. Bishops were forbidden to ask the pope for confirmation; they might write him only "in witness of the unity of faith and communion." "Ecclesiastical functionaries," like all other officeholders, were to take an oath "to be loyal to the nation, the law and the king, and to maintain the constitution with all their strength." The Church of France thus became a national church, practically independent of the pope.

The civil constitution of the clergy, adopted in July 1790, was greeted quite favorably by the lower clergy but a number of bishops were very hostile to it. Most awaited a decision by the pope before committing themselves. Louis XVI wanted to know the pope's decision before ratifying the civil constitution, but, under the pressure of the Constituent Assembly, he had to give his sanction on August 24, 1790. Pope Pius VI could hardly accept innovations of such fundamental character in the organization of religious life. He was indignant that he had not been consulted before these changes were decided. Furthermore he felt deep hostility to the principles of 1789. He was not without justification in accusing the French revolutionaries of encouraging disorders in his possessions of Avignon and Comtat-Venaissin. He was encouraged in his opposition by the French ambassador, Cardinal Bernis, whose duty it was to urge him to accept the civil constitution. Nonetheless Pius VI hesitated for a long time, thinking that the various questions in dispute with France could be made the subject of an inclusive negotiation. Finally the Constituent Assembly tired of waiting and decided on November 27, 1790, to put the civil constitution into force and to require the oath of loyalty from priests and bishops. The pope replied with the briefs of March 10 and April 13, 1791, which formally condemned the civil constitution.

This decision caused a schism in the Church of France, an event of the highest importance in the history of the revolution. There were now two churches, the "constitutional church" recognized and paid by the state, whose members had taken the prescribed oath, and the "Roman church" loyal to the pope, whose priests were "refractory" and refused to acknowledge the civil constitution. Almost all bishops and about half of the priests were "refractory." As a natural consequence, the refractory church gave significant support to the counterrevolution; yet, if we take into consideration the attitude of the parish priests during the Estates General in 1789, this gain of strength by the counterrevolution could not have been anticipated. In addition, the religious question profoundly disturbed all Frenchmen, from Louis XVI down. The king bitterly repented having given his sanction to the civil constitution. He would only accept a "refractory" priest as his chaplain, and it was largely because the people of Paris wished to prevent him from hearing mass celebrated by a refractory that he decided to flee the capital. The flight of the royal family took place on June 20, 1791, but they were captured at Varennes, en route to the French-German frontier, where the king had concentrated troops and the émigrés had gathered. The collusion of Louis XVI with the counterrevolution was more obvious than ever.

The flight to Varennes had important consequences for the course of the revolution. On the one hand it developed patriotic and national sentiment by revealing the most profound beliefs of Louis XVI; on the other hand, the first "republican" demonstrations were held, reinforcing the fear of evolution toward a more democratic regime felt by a majority in the Constituent Assembly.

As soon as the Constituent Assembly learned of the king's flight, it suspended Louis XVI from his duties and took over the full powers of government in France, exercising both executive and legislative duties. A republic now existed *de facto*. But at the same time the Constituent Assembly, in order to be able to reestablish the monarchy, pretended to give credence to the idea that the king had been kidnapped. Many Patriots did not believe this tale. After June 21 they began to demand the establishment of a true republic in France. The assembly was frightened by this campaign. On July 17 a republican petition was to be signed by Parisians on the Champ de Mars, a parade ground. The assembly ordered the mayor of Paris to disperse the demonstrators by force. Martial law was proclaimed. The National Guard under Lafayette fired on the crowd; there were some fifty dead. During the days that followed, republicans were arrested and their newspapers suspended.

The Constituent Assembly then attempted to backtrack. Between July and September 1791 it amended the constitution, restricting the number of "electors," reducing the freedom of the clubs, and making the civil constitution of the clergy an ordinary law which could be easily abrogated. After solemnly restoring Louis XVI to his powers, the National Constituent Assembly ended its sessions on September 30, 1791. It believed that it had reestablished the union and the concord of the nation. Actually the religious schism, the flight to Varennes, and the fusillade on the Champ de Mars had intensified the divisions, not only among Frenchmen, but also between the revolutionaries and the counterrevolutionaries throughout Europe. The success of the revolution in France revived the hopes of the revolutionaries who had been defeated or disappointed in Great Britain, the United Provinces, Belgium, and Geneva. Throughout western and central Europe, even as far as Poland, men gave themselves to the cause of the revolution. Henceforth not only France but Europe and the United States as well were divided into two camps.

chapter five

REVOLUTION AND COUNTER-REVOLUTION IN THE ATLANTIC WORLD (1789–1794)

The revolution in France was not an isolated phenomenon. Although more violent in France than elsewhere, its causes and its goals were the same. The French revolution was only an episode of the revolution of the West. A number of contemporaries realized this. For example, Camille Desmoulins gave his newspaper the title *The Revolutions of France and Brabant.* Barnave explained in his *Introduction to the French Revolution,* written in 1793, that this revolution was only the summit of a movement common to all Europe. Other contemporaries less sensitive to the relationship of great international forces believed that the movements observed in the different countries of Europe were the result of a vast effort of propaganda undertaken by the French revolutionaries. They denounced the activity of a "propaganda club," whose headquarters they located sometimes in Paris and sometimes in the provinces, which was supposed to be sending emissaries, pamphlets, and journals to all Europe. Still others held that the origin of all the revolutionary movements consisted in a plot of freemasonry. Among them was Abbé Barruel, who published a *History of Jacobinism* in Hamburg in 1798. Historical research has never been able to prove the existence of the "propaganda club," and it has shown how silly was the theory of a Masonic plot. What propaganda there was, was spontaneous and due to the contagion of the French example; it was known throughout the Western world by means of newspapers, books, plays, letters, and prints, which were in great demand everywhere. The letters of foreigners traveling in France and the accounts of Frenchmen living abroad played an essential role in this propaganda, although there cannot be detected in these documents any intention to incite revolution outside of France. Naturally it was in the countries where revolutionary movements had failed some years earlier that the example of France worked with greatest effect. The reawakening of the revolutionary forces occurred first in Great Britain, the United Provinces, the Low Countries, and Switzerland.

Revolution and Counterrevolution in Great Britain

The conclusion of peace with the United States in 1782–1783 and with France, Spain, and the United Provinces in 1783, enabled the British government to resist the pressure of the Irish revolutionaries and the English radicals. Concessions appeased the politicians and a return to normal economic conditions pacified the masses. But they were aroused again by news of the revolution in France, which was greeted with enthusiasm by a large part of the British people. Protestant Dissenters applauded the emancipation of religious minorities in France, the nationalization of the wealth of the clergy, and the reduction of papal power over the church in France. Radicals like Fox and Erskine, intellectuals like Thomas Paine and Godwin, poets like Robert Burns, Wordsworth, Coleridge, and Southey, men of the people like the shoemaker Thomas Hardy and in Ireland the members of the secret league of the United Irishmen—all were notable among those who cheered the events in France.

Some were not satisfied just to cheer. They wished to organize a revolution which would establish more equality among the social classes in England and give political rights to Catholics in Ireland. Were these revolutionaries, as some have said, exclusively rich bourgeois, cultivated and liberal men, "aliens in their own land," isolated from the people who hated them as extremely harsh employers, men who lacked the means of political pressure upon the ruling classes? Where do we find authentic representatives of the common people among them? Historians are still debating these questions and it is too early to come to a final conclusion. In any case, it is true that numerous clubs and societies were formed to develop the revolutionary movement in Great Britain. A Society of the Revolution, founded to commemorate the English revolution of 1688, already existed; during its meetings it voted declarations in favor of the French revolution, and one of its members, a Unitarian minister named Richard Price, expressed opinions favorable to a new British revolution. Among the recently established associations, the most important was the Corresponding Society of London, founded on January 25, 1792, on the model of the Jacobin clubs of France. It created a true revolutionary network throughout the country. The Society of Constitutional Information had branches especially in Scotland and Ireland. The British Revolutionary Club, founded on November 18, 1792, celebrated the victories won by the French armies at

Valmy and Jemmapes as successes of the entire revolutionary cause. These societies and clubs returned to the program of reforms which had already been presented to Parliament during the eighties: recognition of the "rights of man," extension of the suffrage, and parliamentary reform. There was, it is clear, no more question of social equality here than there was in France at the same period. Burke calculated that this program had the approval of more than 80,000 British Jacobins. In any case, their demonstrations remained peaceful and did not go beyond speeches and petitions. The fact was that many of the problems which were very acute on the continent scarcely existed in England. There were no fiscal privileges in Great Britain. The nobility engaged in trade and the bourgeoisie shared in power. If manorialism still existed, it was much less burdensome than in France and, most important, included neither dues on the transfer of land nor obligatory labor service. The tithe was a burden only in Ireland. Social inequality was certainly very great; since the beginning of the Industrial Revolution—that is, about 1770—a proletariat of working men was coming into being. But the bourgeoisie and the aristocracy were not divided by any profound antagonism and they tended to combine against the poor classes, whereas in France the bourgeoisie and the aristocracy remained enemies, despite the efforts of Lafayette and Mirabeau. Therefore the union of the bourgeoisie and the peasantry, which as we have seen gave the French revolution its special character and impetus, did not occur in Great Britain. This explains the enormous success which greeted Edmund Burke's book, *Reflections on the Revolution in France,* when it appeared in November 1790. Burke endeavored to show that the diabolical character of the revolution in France was due to its break with the traditions inherited from the past and its efforts to create an artificial new order without deep roots in the history of the country. The bourgeoisie easily accepted Burke's point of view and deserted the revolutionary clubs and societies, which were closed by the government. Soon the war against France ranged England in the camp of the counterrevolution and permitted the government to prosecute those who persisted in admiring the revolution.

The Revolution in the Low Countries

Reaction had been triumphant in the Low Countries, since 1787 in Holland and 1790 in the Austrian Netherlands. The Patriots, who had taken refuge in France in large numbers, prepared to renew the revolutionary movement in their countries with the aid of the French patriots.

Of the 40,000 revolutionaries who had fled the United Provinces in 1787, more than five thousand still remained in France in 1789. They had settled in Paris and the northern region, where some plied the professions of merchants and bankers. Others, without steady jobs, impatiently waited until the revolution would permit them to return home. They formed "Batavian" clubs and corresponded secretly with their fellow Patriots who had remained at home and reorganized their ranks despite police surveillance. The dissolved Dutch clubs secretly reappeared in the form of "reading societies." In December 1791, a Dutch refugee, Brahain-Ducange, declared in the Jacobin Club of Paris: "Societies which share our principles have already been formed in many cities including Amsterdam, Leiden, Dordrecht, Haarlem, and Utrecht. There are thousands of Jacobins in our populous and flourishing cities." This report was confirmed some months later by Caillard, a secret agent sent by the French government to the United Provinces. He estimated the number of Jacobins in the country at many thousands. At Amsterdam, he reported, the secret clubs had more than five thousand members. Dutch patriots who had emigrated to France and the Jacobins who had remained in the United Provinces were preparing a new revolutionary explosion, to be set off when French troops entered Holland.

The Patriots of Belgium and Liége were in the same state of mind. The leaders of the two parties which had attempted to establish an independent Belgium had taken refuge in France when the Austrian troops returned in 1790. They also settled in Paris and the frontier district. Some participated in the French revolution; among them were Walckiers, a rich and influential banker, and Lebrun-Tondu, who became the French minister of foreign affairs in 1792. They published a "Manifesto of the United Belgians and Liégeois," drawn up by Lebrun, although one of their Patriot leaders, Vonck, refused to sign it as too democratic. (Vonck died shortly afterwards on December 1, 1792.) The Statists were even more moderate. They hoped to establish a Belgium as a kingdom under the scepter of the young duke of Béthune-Charost. In any event, neither Patriots nor Statists could hope to succeed except with the assistance of French armies. Therefore Belgian refugees of both parties urged France to go to war, and they associated by preference with the Girondins, who had proposed a warlike program since December 1791.

The Revolution in Switzerland

Many Genevans had taken refuge in France after the failure of the revolution in 1782. Among them was Clavière, who became the French minister of finances in 1792. There were also revolutionary exiles in France from other

Swiss cantons, especially Freiburg, Neuchâtel, and Vaud. The Swiss exiles in Paris formed a Helvetic Club, whose bylaws declared that they desired to "spread freedom to those Swiss cantons where the aristocracy have perverted the original institutions of the country." The members of the club not only corresponded with their friends who had stayed in Switzerland, but also flooded the country with revolutionary newspapers and pamphlets. Laharpe, a Vaudois who was the tutor of the young children of Catherine II at St. Petersburg, kept carefully informed of the progress of the revolution; he encouraged his compatriots to make the Vaud country, then a vassal province of the canton of Bern, an equal and independent canton. Faced by the storm which threatened to shake Switzerland, members of the patriciate like Karl Müller von Friedberg at Saint-Gall and Peter Ochs at Basel proposed reforms; but no heed was paid to them. Agitation continued. In 1790 the peasants of the Schaffhausen and Valais districts demanded changes in the feudal (manorial) system. In the Valais the peasants rose in arms in 1790 and presented demands in 1791. The government of the canton arrested numerous peasant rebels; five were sentenced to death and executed, and two others were exiled. In the Porrentruy district, which was under the overlordship of the bishop of Basel, the peasants presented similar demands. The bishop called in Austrian troops, who restored order. This action gave the commander of the French troops, General Custine, a pretext to occupy the bishopric of Basel as soon as the war began in April, 1792, and to proclaim a "Rauracian Republic." In the canton of Zurich, it was such intellectuals as pastor Lavater, the writers Escher and Usteri, the painter Füssli, and the pedagogue Pestalozzi, who were favorable to the revolution. The closing of the Austrian and French frontiers to Swiss textiles on the eve of the

Revolution had created a grave economic crisis in the canton of Zurich, which had an extensive textile industry. The peasants near Zurich, who lived in virtual subjection to the adjacent city, formed a revolutionary club in the village of Stäfa. When the club published a grievance list, the *Mémorial,* in 1794 it was considered to be guilty of conspiracy and was harshly repressed.

In Geneva the "natives," after their defeat in 1782, reorganized and prepared to resume the struggle. On December 5, 1792, they seized power in alliance with the "bourgeois." Now the Genevan aristocracy could no longer count on their former allies, and the democrats were able to grant the right of citizenship not only to the "natives" but also to the "inhabitants." Clubs with a Jacobin flavor were established in increased numbers. Soon a revolutionary committee was in control of the affairs of the canton; a revolutionary tribunal condemned eleven aristocrats to death. Geneva thus was able to carry out a revolution by its own efforts, although it paralleled the revolution in France.

The Revolutionary Movements in Central Europe

In central Europe the Enlightenment had profoundly penetrated the circles of the educated. In a number of states rulers made important reforms in the organization of the administration and the judiciary. In these states the bourgeoisie benefited by the changes and considered that they were ahead of the rest of Europe; they believed that France was only catching up with them in 1789. Nonetheless some revolutionary spirit persisted among members of the Masonic societies, in particular the "Illuminated" of Bavaria, among the peasants of the German Rhineland, whose conditions closely resembled those of the French peasantry, and among the lesser nobility of Hungary, who had been eliminated from power by the reforms of Joseph II. In these circles the French revolution was greeted with enthusiasm. Information about the revolution came by means of books, newspapers, and travelers' accounts. *The German Chronicle,* a newspaper edited by the Swabian Christian Schubart, devoted its columns principally to the events in France. When German news almost completely vanished from its pages, Schubart changed its name to *The Chronicle*. Sieveking, a wealthy Hamburg merchant, organized a meeting on July 14, 1790, to celebrate the anniversary of the fall of the Bastille. The participants wore the tricolor cockade. The poet Klopstock sang an ode which he had composed for the occasion:

> Had I a hundred voices, they would not suffice to sing
> The freedom of Gaul, they would be too pale
> for so divine a subject.
> What have the enfranchised Gauls not done! They have
> Enchained even war, most horrid of all the monsters! . . .
> Alas, my Fatherland, it was not thou who scaled
> The peaks of Freedom and gave to all the peoples round
> The shining example! It was France.
> (*Sie, und nicht Wir.*)

Two years later, Sieveking and his friends organized a society which quickly took on the aspect of a Jacobin club. It was not long before the authorities in Hamburg decided that the club's activities were subversive and ordered it closed.

At Königsberg in Prussia, the famous philosopher Kant expressed admiration for the French revolution, at least in private. Tradition has it that he only once changed his route as he walked from his home to the university, when he learned the news of the capture of the Bastille. In any case, everything Kant wrote after 1789 was profoundly influenced by the revolution in France. His friends and his disciples were considered to be Jacobins by the Prussian police and were put on a blacklist. Another Prussian philosopher, Fichte, who taught at Jena, took sides more openly with the revolution. His *Appeal to the Prince on Behalf of the Demand for Freedom of Thought,* published anonymously in 1793, was wholly imbued with the new ideas. He explained the revolution to his contemporaries in another book, *Contributions for the Purpose of Correcting Public Judgments on the French Revolution.* Like Sieveking, Fichte founded a society which soon turned into a quasi-Jacobin club and came under suspicion. Fichte apparently was already thinking of inspiring an insurrection in Germany. Other writers and philosophers, such as Herder, Schiller, and Goethe, without taking sides so openly, also expressed their sympathy for the revolution. All these demonstrations however, remained quite platonic.

It was otherwise in Austria and the Rhineland, where true conspiracies were organized to change rapidly the old order of things. In the Austrian states, notably Lower Austria, Styria, and Carniola, the reforms of the enlightened despots Joseph II and Leopold II had resulted in vigorous agitation. The privileged corporations resisted these reforms, which were intended to augment the power of the sovereign. In their struggle against the privileged corporations the monarchs had sought the support of the bourgeoisie and even the prosperous peasantry. They subsidized pamphleteers, who wrote tracts to prove that the bourgeois and the peasants were not playing the role in the provincial diets to which they had a right. But the revolution in France frightened Joseph II—and his successor Leopold II even more. They abandoned some of their reforms and restored some of the privileges which they had taken from the nobility and the clergy, thereby arousing the discontent of bourgeois and peasants. The news from France sharpened both their discontent and their desire to improve their situation. Peasants assembled threateningly before manor houses. At the request of the peasants, bourgeois—usually the authors of pamphlets hostile to the privileged corporations—prepared petitions expressing the grievances of the peasantry. Josef von Sonnenfels, Andreas Riegel, and F. Haas, an inkeeper at Graz, called for organization of a constitutional government with a chamber representative of the four estates (clergy, nobility, bourgeoisie, and peasantry). Leopold II did not systematically resist these demands, but he died on March 1, 1792. His son and successor, Francis II, aged only twenty-four years, was a determined adversary of the revolution and refused all concessions. The malcontents then formed clandestine clubs, called Jacobin by the authorities. These clubs attempted to make contact with the French revolutionaries. They propagandized in favor of the revolution and organized a conspiracy against the emperor's government. The members of the conspiracy were finally discovered; the leaders were condemned to death in 1794 and their confederates received prison terms.

In the Rhineland it was intellectuals, notably Forster, the librarian of the university of Mainz, and Johan von Müller, secretary of the archbishop of Mainz, who spread the revolutionary ideas. By 1790 the bourgeoisie were presenting demands and the peasants were in agitation. The authorities reacted with particular violence because France was so close; they were encouraged in their counterrevolutionary measures by the presence of increasing numbers of French émigrés. The worst compromised revolutionaries left for France; among them was a priest, Euloge Schneider, who took up residence in Alsace in June 1791. Most of the others remained at home and organized a revolution when the French troops entered the Rhineland in the autumn of 1792.

In Hungary, as in Austria, the agitation originated in the policies of the enlightened despots. During his reign Joseph II had endeavored to reduce the powers of the Hungarian diet, which was composed almost solely of noblemen, and to Germanize the administration of the country. The Hungarian nobles were naturally hostile to this policy. Joseph II sought the alliance of the peasants against the nobles, and abolished compulsory labor service, which was very burdensome in Hungary. However, with the start of the revolution, Joseph II, and even more Leopold II after him, attempted to regain the support of the nobility; they therefore put off abolition of compulsory service. This measure aroused the anger of the peasants without rallying the entire nobility to the emperor. Some minor noblemen who dreamed of a more liberal regime wrote a "Hungarian Declaration of the Rights of Man and the Citizen" as well as a "Constitutional Act." In 1793 Emperor Francis II banned these two documents. As in Austria, the opposition retreated into clandestine clubs. Two secret societies, the Reform Society and the Society of Jacobins, were organized by Professor Martinovicz, who had written reformist pamphlets in 1790 at the behest of Leopold II. The membership of each society was drawn from a different social class. The Reform Society appealed to the lower nobility; a "catechism" prepared for its use demanded the abolition of the privileges of the clergy and the magnates and the creation of an independent Hungarian national state. The members of the Society of Jacobins were democrats and mainly bourgeois. Its catechism demanded proclamation of a republic and emancipation of the peasants but did not specify how land would be distributed to them.

The principal members of these two societies were put in contact with the Austrian Jacobins by Martinovicz. When arrested by the Vienna police on July 24, 1794, he informed against the Hungarian Jacobins. Their leaders were arrested in August and brought to trial. Eighteen were sentenced to death and executed.

It is doubtful that the conspiracy of the Hungarian Jacobins could have succeeded. The social structure of Hungary was very different from that of France, west Germany, and Austria. The peasants were almost all illiterate serfs. The conspiracy included mainly intellectuals, only a small number of bourgeois, and some liberal noblemen. They would have been supported by neither the magnates nor the peasants, so that their defeat was a certainty.

In Poland a revolution better prepared than Hungary's and led by the king himself had precisely the same result—a major defeat. One fundamental reason was that the two countries had similar social systems. The population of Poland in the late eighteenth century comprised a mass of 8 to 9 million peasant serfs, a little more than a hundred thousand nobles, and probably a slightly smaller number of bourgeois employed in various public offices and the liberal professions. Commerce was left in the hands of Jews, who were treated as foreigners. The government was weak. The king did not inherit the crown but was elected by the diet, which itself was paralyzed by the *liberum veto* (the requirement of unanimity for all decisions).

King Stanislas Poniatowski, a former lover of Catherine II, wished to change these conditions and to strengthen the powers of the government. He could count upon a portion of the nobility and the bourgeoisie, for during the preceding years the education of these classes, reorganized by the celebrated Commission of National Education, had advanced greatly. The new ideas had penetrated into Poland; foreign newspapers were read eagerly and Polish newspapers increased in number, numbering about ten in 1791. Father Switkowski's *Political and Historical Memorial* described in detail the capture of the Bastille and enthusiastically reported the events of August 4, 1789. "France is like a stormy sea . . ." the *Memorial* declared. In February 1790, Switkowski wrote that "the year 1789 has been the most extraordinary of the contemporary era. Since the crusades, there has been no period like ours." Father Switkowski even approved the civil constitution of the clergy. In 1791 three Polish Patriots founded the *National and Foreign Gazette* which devoted most of its news reports to the French revolution and tried to develop a reform movement in Poland.

It was in this atmosphere that Stanislas and the leaders of the Patriots—Jan Potocki, Malachowski, Kollontai, Czartoryski, and several bourgeois and professors—decided to impose a new constitution on the diet by a coup d'état. The Polish constitution of May 3, 1791, was the first European constitution written under the influence of the French revolution; it actually predates the French constitution of 1791, which was promulgated only in September. The terms which it employed bore a striking resemblance to those of the French constitution. Chapter V of the Polish charter proclaimed that "all power essentially emanates from the nation." It specified that the executive, legislative, and judicial powers in the government of Poland were to be separate. The house of nuncios (deputies) was to be "the image and the repository of the supreme power of the nation . . . the true sanctuary of the law"; it would pass general laws, decrees, the budget, and declare war and peace. The nuncios represented not their province but the "entire nation," as in France. Innovations of the first importance were the abolition of the *liberum veto* and the establishment of hereditary monarchy. Election of the king would occur only in the event of the extinction of the reigning dynasty. The king was to be assisted by a council of six ministers. Judges were to be elected; civil and criminal codes would be prepared. "The national army" would take an oath of fidelity "to the nation and to the king."

It appeared therefore that Poland was going to take a lead among countries equipped with modern institutions, along with the United States and France. But actually the Polish constitution of May 3, 1791, covered realities very different from those to which the American constitution of 1789 and the French constitution of 1791 applied. In the minds of the drafters of the constitution, the "Polish nation" were the nobility and the bourgeoisie. Although the Polish nobility was very numerous, including in their ranks many very poor gentry, they still represented only a small fraction of the population. The condition of the peasant serfs and the Jews was not improved. The privileges of the nobility remained very broad. One of the two houses, the Senate, was composed solely of members of the upper nobility and clergy. The nobles elected deputies by direct suffrage to the house of nuncios, where they formed a majority; the deputies of the bourgeoisie and the towns were elected by indirect suffrage. The regular courts tried only members of the nobility. There were special tribunals for the bourgeoisie; the peasantry were only placed "under the protection of the law" and in fact remained subject to the arbitrary decisions of their landlords. The social structure of Poland, which was like that of the rest of eastern Europe, therefore falsified the meaning of the words and phrases of the constitution of May 3.

Nonetheless this charter might have hastened the indispensable transformation of Poland. But this was not to be. It aroused the wrath of the magnates and, even more important, it worried Poland's neighbors, Russia, Austria, and Prussia, who were already considering a second partition of Polish territory. On the other side, some liberal noblemen and educated bourgeois held the constitution of May 3 to be inadequate. Because they called for the emancipation of the peasants, they were called Polish Jacobins.

Russian and Prussian troops entered Poland in 1792. The invasion had two consequences. The May 3 constitution was abrogated and a new, more radical and more democratic insurrection developed under the leadership of Kosciuszko in 1794. Kosciuszko and his friends wrote a new constitution. Its provision for abolition of serfdom might have roused the mass of the peasantry to defend against invaders a state in which social equality became a reality, but the majority of the nobility opposed Kosciuszko's project, and the rebels split into "royalists" and "friends of liberty." These divisions weakened the resistance of Poland's defenders. Russians and Austrians crushed the insurrection before any measure on behalf of the peasantry was actually taken. The social structure of Poland and Hungary did not make them favorable terrain for the development of the revolution.

The Revolutionary Movements in Italy

In 1789 Italy was still only a "geographic expression." It was divided into a large number of states, with the kingdoms of Piedmont-Sardinia and Naples and the Papal State the most important. Austria was master of Lombardy, and it had great influence in Tuscany through the intermediary of the Hapsburg ruler in Florence. The economic and social structure of Italy differed in the various regions. North of Rome it was similar to that of France. The feudal system had almost completely disappeared; the bourgeoisie were powerful; many peasants either owned their land, or were tenants or sharecroppers, although there were many farm laborers as well. South of Rome the feudal system, which had been introduced by the Normans in the tenth century, was harsher than in France. The nobility owned estates usually of immense size, known as latifundia. The bourgeoisie were important only in towns; but Naples was undeniably the most populous city of Europe after London and Paris. Throughout Italy the Catholic clergy enjoyed great influence, but they were divided. Jansenism, reduced mainly to criticism of the power of pope and bishops, had many disciples. The Enlightenment had penetrated everywhere; numerous discussion societies had been formed; Masonic lodges made their appearance even in Rome.

It is not surprising therefore that revolutionary clubs were formed by 1789 in the principal cities of North Italy and Naples. The police began to track down partisans of the new ideas. Buonarroti at Pisa and Ranza at Vercelli were persecuted for their opinions and had to take refuge in Corsica. Nevertheless an increasing number of clubs continued to meet in cafés and backrooms of pharmacies, where liberal bourgeois and noblemen discussed the French declaration of rights. Sometimes peasants suffering from the economic crisis demonstrated and invoked the example of the French revolution. At Rueglio and Dronero in northern Piedmont, peasants attacked bakers and the municipal authorities, shouting, "Long live Paris! Long live France!" At Bologna, in papal territory, Luigi Zamboni, a student, organized a conspiracy with some comrades. Betrayed to the police, Zamboni and his friend de Rolandis were arrested, sentenced to death, and executed on April 23, 1796, several days before French troops entered the city. Revolutionary clubs were formed in Naples as early as 1790. When the French naval squadron of Latouche-Tréville anchored in the port of Naples in December 1792, the members of the clubs made contact with the revolutionary officers and sailors and established a vast clandestine organization in the city, divided into "conversations," or cells, and "commissions," which included several "conversations." In 1794 this organization split. The more democratic members founded the "Reomo" club (*Repubblica o morte,* "the republic or death"), led by Andrea Vitaliani, a clockmaker known for his enthusiasms and his tendency to violence. The moderates named their club "Liomo" (*Libertà o morte*). The two clubs were finally discovered by the police. Fifty-six Neapolitan Jacobins were arrested; Andrea Vitaliani and two others were sentenced to death and executed. Many of the Patriots fled Naples and took refuge in France or Italian territories occupied by the French. Like the Batavian, Belgian, and Swiss Patriots, the Italian refugees had but one idea—to prepare a revolution in Italy with the aid of the French army.

The Countries of Europe Least Affected by the Revolution

Certain countries of Europe were less affected by the revolution because their political evolution and their social structure were unfavorable to development of the revolutionary movement.

In Spain, for example, the government took a clear

position against the French revolution as early as 1789. The Spanish Inquisition, which was still powerful, aided the government in tracking down revolutionary books and pamphlets which were smuggled across the Pyrenees or through ports. A few Spaniards working from Bayonne and Perpignan who nonetheless attempted to spread the revolutionary ideas in Spain met a solid barrier. Several attempts to form revolutionary groups inside Spain were discovered quickly. Among these were the associates of Picornell y Gomila, who were arrested in Madrid during late 1794 and early 1795. They were tried, sentenced to death, then pardoned. The power of the Catholic church, its influence over the nobility and the bourgeoisie, and the illiteracy of the mass of the peasantry, explain the attitude of Spain.

Contrariwise, it was the reforms accomplished by Gustavus III in Sweden which explain the revolution's lack of influence there. As we have seen, in order to strengthen his own power and break the power of the nobility, Gustavus III had made the coup d'état of 1772 and then governed with the aid of the bourgeoisie. By the act of Union and Security of 1789, he granted all Swedes equality of rights. The anger of the nobility mounted steadily; finally, on March 16, 1792, several noble conspirators assassinated the king as he was leaving a masked ball. Equality of rights had entered so deeply into the customs of Sweden, however, that the nobility did not dare to touch the essential provisions of the Act of Union and Security. Equality before the law was soon followed by a degree of economic equality; the government began a massive division and redistribution of the land, each peasant receiving a plot of about equal value. In Sweden, the royal revolution prevented a popular revolution.

The situation was totally different in Russia, where

there were an immense mass of illiterate peasant serfs, an aristocracy of educated officials, and a very small bourgeoisie. The intellectuals closely followed the events in France, which the few newspapers that did exist reported with accuracy. Novikov, Radishchev, Krylov, and many others hailed the revolution. The government of Catherine II was most deeply disturbed by Radishchev's book, *A Journey from Petersburg to Moscow,* which advocated the abolition of serfdom. The author was arrested, tried by the criminal court, and given a death sentence which was commuted to exile to Siberia. Novikov was sentenced to fifteen years in prison. After the trial of Radishchev, the empress examined "all membership lists of secret meetings and free scientific societies." Although the echoes of the revolution continued to reach Russia, they remained virtually without influence because of the very structure of Russian society.

The situation was the same in the Balkans, which was under the rule of the Ottoman Empire. Only Greek merchants who had business contacts with France and a few intellectuals had much knowledge of the revolution. Rhigas, who lived in Vienna, translated the "Marseillaise" into Greek and wrote a "Hymn to Liberty." In 1797 he and his friends were arrested by the Austrian police and turned over to the Turks. Rhigas' works, although they had little effect when they were written, still became precursors of the reawakening of the Balkan peoples.

The Revolutionary Movement Outside Europe

The revolutionary ideas spread through the world. Their most important bearers were groups or colonies of Frenchmen. In western Asia, where Frenchmen were fairly numerous in the ports of the Levant, revolutionary clubs appeared in Smyrna and Aleppo. At Constantinople, Frenchmen even planted a liberty tree and donned tricolor cockades; several Moslems imitated them. In the French colonies of the Indian Ocean (the French settlements in India and the Mascarene Islands), the colonists also formed clubs, but the burning question debated in the Constituent Assembly—the equality of colored people and the problem of suppression of slavery which was concealed beneath it—found almost no echo among them. Slaves and freedmen remained in ignorance of the debates in France until 1793, and calm continued to reign. The situation was different in the French colonies of the Atlantic. From 1789 on, the French colonists of Santo Domingo, Martinique, Guadeloupe, Tobago, and Saint Lucia followed with passionate interest the debates in the National Assembly on the fate of "free men of color," that is, freedmen and their descendants. A majority of the colonists were implacably opposed to any concessions to such "free men of color," believing that any concession to them would be a forerunner of the abolition of slavery. But the colored freedmen, some of whom were large landowners and had delegates in France, rose in rebellion late in 1789 against the intransigence of the colonists. The disorders worsened until the slaves themselves revolted.

The echo of these disorders reached the neighboring Spanish colonies, which had already been strongly affected by the proclamation of independence by the British colonies of North America. Despite the Inquisition and the police, the Enlightenment continued to penetrate into Central and South America. The Creole bourgeoisie and nobility read Voltaire, Rousseau, and Abbé Raynal. As early as 1781, the father of Simón Bolívar was complaining that the Creoles were even more harshly treated by the Spaniards than black slaves. Insurrections broke out sporadically; there was one in New Granada in 1781 and another in Guiana in 1788. (In the Portuguese colony of Brazil, a dentist named Tiradentes after his trade was arrested in 1789, charged with plotting against the government, and received the death penalty in 1792.) It must be noted that the Creole bourgeoisie of continental America, like the Creoles of the French islands, aimed primarily at their own accession to power; they had no intention whatever of granting equality of rights to the Indians or freeing the slaves.

This reservation did not keep the Creoles from enthusiastically greeting the news of the French revolution. A Spanish translation of the Declaration of the Rights of Man was written by a high Spanish official, Nariño, and published in several hundred copies at Bogotá in 1793. Distributed through the neighboring regions of New Granada, Peru, Venezuela, and Mexico, it aroused the curiosity of the Creoles, who were almost the only literate colonists. It also provoked an immediate reaction by the authorities. On November 1, 1794, the captain general of Caracas ordered the seizure of the "seditious lampoon" and the arrest of Nariño and his friends, who included two French doctors. They were charged with having sought to establish in New Granada "an independent republic after the fashion of that at Philadelphia." Found guilty and transported to Spain, Nariño was eventually released and devoted himself to the emancipation of his country.

At Quito, Santa Cruz Espejo, one of the rare Indians who had received a higher education and become a doctor and writer, was arrested in 1792 and imprisoned at Bogotá, where he made the acquaintance of Nariño. After his release he returned to Quito, where he founded a newspaper and a club, "The School of Concord," which made preparations for liberation of the country. Espejo's agitation caused his rearrest and imprisonment, and he died in jail. In Mexico, the priest Hidalgo followed the news from France with attention and dreamed of an independent Mexico.

A number of Creoles from Latin America were in Europe when the French revolution began. They took it as an example and an encouragement for their own countries. The Argentine Belgrano, who was in Spain in 1789, spread the revolutionary ideas at Buenos Aires after his return in 1794. More important was the Venezuelan Miranda, who was traveling through Europe when he heard the news of the revolution; he hastened to France, enlisted in the French army, fought at Valmy and Jemmapes, and became a French general. When he later returned to his own country, Miranda became the "Precursor" of independence. The Brazilian Manuel Arruda de Camara was a student at the university of Montpellier at the time of the revolution; on his return to Brazil he founded a secret society, the "Areopago de Itambé," with the independence of Brazil as its aim.

Between 1789 and 1794 the entire Atlantic world was shaken by the French revolution, even more than it had been by the American revolution.

The Beginning of Counterrevolution

In the face of this gigantic revolutionary movement, the counterrevolution began to organize. First of all, it needed a doctrine. It had to explain its reasons for preferring the old regime to the new, or even for proposing an organization of society different from that advocated by the philosophes. The French theorists Cazalès, Abbé Maury, Mirabeau-Tonneau (brother of the revolutionary),

Sénac de Meilhan, Count Ferrand, Abbé Barruel, and Abbé Duvoisin were unable to galvanize the masses between 1789 and 1792 either by their writings or their speeches. On the other hand, the Englishman Burke, whose influence we have already discussed, the Swiss Mallet du Pan, and Joseph de Maistre, a subject of the king of Sardinia, all published important works hostile to the revolution. They emphasized the "providential" character which they found in the revolution, asserting that it had been sent by God to punish men for their irreligion; they asserted the inadequacy of revolutionary institutions without links to the past. Burke, Joseph de Maistre, and later the Frenchman Bonald did propose reconstruction of society, each in his own manner—Burke by praising tradition, and de Maistre and Bonald by prescribing theocratic organization.

In England, as we have seen, Burke's *Reflections* aided powerfully in halting the revolutionary movement by turning the bourgeoisie against it. The police took advantage of this change of attitude to strengthen their action against English and even more against Irish revolutionaries. Translated into German, the *Reflections* won great influence throughout central Europe, where it aroused a section of the intellectuals against the revolution; among them was the German Gentz who became the most notable of Burke's disciples. The German princes, led by Emperor Francis II, abandoned their programs of reforms and began to hunt down the liberals.

In France the counterrevolutionary groups were quite heterogeneous. They usually included noblemen and some bourgeois. Some groups desired to restore the old regime, and others favored more or less extensive reforms, from as little as the program presented by Louis XVI to the Estates General on June 23, 1789, to the English-style monarchy proposed by Mounier and his friends in September 1789. These groups were soon strengthened by entry of refractory priests, who refused the oath required by the civil constitution of the clergy. But the kernel of the counterrevolution was formed by the émigrés.

The emigration movement had a precedent in Calonne's departure abroad in 1787, but it really began when the count of Artois, the king's brother, quit Versailles after July 14, 1789. The emigration grew continually from 1789 to 1793. The nobles and refractory priests went to Savoy, Switzerland, Piedmont, England, and especially the principalities of the Rhineland. The officers who left the army after the military mutinies of 1790 and 1791 assembled particularly in the Rhineland. The émigrés, remembering the recent history of Geneva, Holland, and Belgium, hoped that a foreign intervention would quickly bring the revolutionaries to their senses and restore the old order. Louis XVI and Marie-Antoinette addressed an appeal to their cousin, King Charles IV of Spain, as early as 1789. After they became virtual prisoners in the Tuileries in October, they continued to seek the aid of Austrian troops; Emperor Joseph II, it should not be forgotten, was Marie-Antoinette's brother. He died on February 20, 1790, but his successor, Leopold II, met the king of Prussia at Pillnitz after the failure of the attempted flight of the French royal family and together they issued the first warning to France on August 27, 1791. This declaration was unquestionably a response to the repeated demands of Marie-Antoinette and Louis XVI. The sovereigns of Prussia and Austria were not really greatly worried about the troubles which disturbed France and gravely weakened its position in Europe. What they did fear was that principles proclaimed by the French revolutionaries might seriously perturb the established public international law of Europe.

The principles which to them seemed most dangerous were the sovereignty of the people and especially the right of self-determination of the peoples which followed from it. Frenchmen claimed this right of self-determination from the very beginning of the revolution. At the federal meeting of the national guard held near Valence on November 29, 1789, Languedocians, Provençaux, and Dauphinois—inhabitants of provinces incorporated into France in the late middle ages—announced their intention of being French equally and identically with all other Frenchmen. Even more significant was the federal meeting at Strasbourg on June 13, 1790, where more than three thousand delegates of the national guards of Alsace, Lorraine, and Franche-Comté proclaimed that they were Frenchmen not because treaties made by their sovereigns in the past had joined their provinces to France but because they themselves wished to be French.

When applied to Alsace, this doctrine of self-determination became pregnant with international complications. If Alsace was considered French by the same title of ownership as any other province, there was no reason to grant the German princes who possessed seignorial rights in Alsace special indemnities as compensation for the abolition of their rights. So ran the argument presented from the rostrum of the Constituent Assembly by deputy Merlin of Douai on October 28, 1790: "Today . . . when the sovereignty of the peoples has finally been consecrated in such noteworthy fashion . . . what does it matter to the people of Alsace or to the French people that the Alsatians were joined to France by a treaty concluded in the era of despotism? The Alsatian people join the French people because that is their wish. . . . Treaties made by princes do not determine the rights of nations."

The new theories profoundly transformed international law. In a Europe where most states had been shaped by the accidents of wars and dynastic successions and included peoples of different languages, traditions, and customs, at the same time that the same aspirations and culture were separated from them by artificial frontiers, these ideas were immensely subversive. Avignon and Comtat Venaissin, papal possessions which formed an enclave in French territory, Savoy, which was a province belonging to the king of Sardinia, and parts of the Austrian Netherlands asked to join France by virtue of this right of self-determination of the peoples. On June 12, 1790, the Avignonese presented a request to the Constituent Assembly for union with France. Debate on their petition ran to great length because members feared that granting it would lead to war and because the assembly had solemnly declared that France renounced all wars of conquest. Nevertheless the assembly finally voted for annexation on September 13, 1791.

This decision, by reaffirming the new international law, spread alarm through the courts of Europe. Beyond doubt it contributed more to the declaration of Pillnitz than the pressure of the émigrés. Still, the emperor and the king of Prussia did not expect that they would need to resort to war; they thought that their declaration would scare the revolutionaries into backing down.

What happened in practice was the contrary of what they expected. The declaration of Pillnitz, coming immediately after the French king's flight, and added to the blustering of the émigrés, caused a stiffening of national pride in France. A great number of patriots, with Brissot and the Girondins at their head, came to believe that only war would make it possible to defeat the counterrevolution, by compelling its supporters in France, in particular the royal family, to unmask. The Dutch and Belgian Patriots and the Swiss, Savoyard, Italian, and German refugees in France also pressed for war in the hope of liberating their countries. A minority of Jacobins led by Robespierre were lavish with warnings that war would either ruin the revolution or establish the military dictatorship of a victorious general in France. The warnings were to no avail, for they were disregarded. The royal court also secretly pressed for war, expecting that it would bring deliverance. Leopold II, the peaceable emperor, would unquestionably not have precipitated hostilities, but he died suddenly on March 1, 1792. Francis II, his son and successor, did not share his moderation. The new emperor sent France a virtual challenge to battle. On April 20, 1792, Louis XVI proposed to the Legislative Assembly that war be declared against the king of Bohemia and Hungary (i.e., against the emperor rather than the Holy Roman Empire as such). This proposal was passed amid enthusiasm, with only seven votes opposing. The war which began here lasted almost without interruption until 1815. It contributed greatly to the expansion of the revolution and changed the face of the world.

chapter six

WAR, TERROR, AND THE DEMOCRATIC REPUBLIC IN FRANCE

The war that began on April 20, 1792, did not work out as its promoters intended. It did not bring the deliverance of the royal court or the restoration of absolute monarchy; neither did it give power to the Girondins, who themselves perished during the struggle. It did bring the military dictatorship foreseen by Robespierre, but not until it had led to numerous unforeseen vicissitudes—the Reign of Terror, revolutionary government, and audacious innovations in economic and social policy which were precursors of the future.

The start of the war and the defeats which soon followed aroused both the fear and the national exaltation of the mass of the French people. The large majority of the bourgeoisie, the artisans, and the peasants united to meet the danger; but the bourgeoisie had to make temporary concessions to popular demands. In addition, the revolutionaries felt that they could not meet the domestic danger except by terrorizing their adversaries. War therefore led to terror. Until 1792 the revolution had spilled blood only rarely and accidentally; now it became sanguinary. Violence and murder, instigated by war, were erected into a system of government.

Violence and terror were advocated by the "sans-culottes."[1] The sans-culottes did not form a social class in the modern sense of the word. They were a very heterogeneous group, composed of agricultural workers, small artisans, and shopkeepers; possessing little education and strong patriotism, they were quick to the most primitive reactions. Violence and terror frightened the bourgeoisie, but the danger was such that they permitted these means to be used in order to save France and the revolution. The bourgeoisie, who had been in power since the autumn of 1789, therefore temporarily revised their attitudes and ideas. They accepted the notion that it was necessary to sacrifice the freedom of the individual and the economy for a time in order to preserve the freedom and independence of the nation. They consented to suspension of individual freedoms in order to increase economic and social equality. Thus the war generated a new regime. Although it proved to be ephemeral, the revolutionary regime served as an example and a guide to the increasing number of theorists of social equality in Europe.

The war also gave renewed hope to the Patriots of all countries. Those who had settled in France and the fugitives who later joined them organized foreign legions as part of the French armies; their purpose was to deliver the peoples still subjugated by the old regime. The revolu-

1. Literally, "no breeches"—that is, those who did not wear the knee-breeches of the aristocracy but the trousers of ordinary folk.—*Trans.*

tion became a liberator. But also it became a conqueror. Many Patriots, believing their fatherlands too weak to exist in independence, were tempted into asking France to annex their countries despite the deep feelings of their fellow citizens. These requests to the young republic for its aid and protection also awakened in many French hearts the old instincts of conquest and domination. Some saw France, the "Great Nation," as the liberator; others, as the conqueror.

The war thus changed the course of the revolution. Without war there would unquestionably have never been a reign of terror; but without the terror the victory of France in the war would not have been possible. And without military victory the revolution would probably have triumphed neither in France nor beyond its frontiers.

The Fall of the French Monarchy

If the war were to prove of advantage to either the Girondins or the aristocrats, it had to be swift and decisive. But it began with French defeats and soon threatened to drag out. Other political forces won the time to act.

The Girondins believed that the Austrian troops, worn out by five years of fighting the Turks and infected by revolutionary propaganda, would offer no great resistance to the French armies. They did not believe that Prussia, the "enlightened" state par excellence, would join Austria, although Prussia had intervened in the Dutch revolution in 1787. But Prussia did support Austria as provided by the Pillnitz declaration. France therefore had to fight the famed Prussian army, which still lived on the reputation of its great victories at Rossbach and Leuthen during the Seven Years War.

The first engagements between French and Austrian

troops at the frontier of the Austrian Netherlands ended in a French retreat. The French soldiers shouted "Treason!" and massacred two of their generals, and a number of officers went over to the enemy. Fear spread throughout France, but was strongest in the capital. The Legislative Assembly, suspicious that the royal family was sending information to the enemy, passed decrees designed to strengthen the national defense and to prevent the king from attempting a coup d'état in conjunction with the advance of the enemy forces. The royal bodyguard was disbanded; refractory priests were ordered deported; an encampment of 20,000 "Federals"—volunteers recruited from the national guard and brought to the capital to defend it and to celebrate the anniversary of "Federation Day" of 1790—was organized under the walls of Paris. Encouraged by the enemy successes, Louis XVI vetoed the decrees. The sans-culottes of the Paris quarters rose in rebellion at the instigation of the Girondins, invaded the Tuileries, and paraded for eight hours before the king. Believing that he had already won the game, he firmly refused to withdraw his vote and dismissed the Girondin ministers whom he had called to office in April. The king's resistance encouraged counterrevolutionaries of every stripe. Lafayette, who had an army under his command, went secretly to Paris and attempted to organize a coup d'état. Numerous groups sent congratulations to the king. Meanwhile the Austrians, the Prussians, and the émigré army intensified their pressure on the frontiers of France.

In the Legislative Assembly the Patriots—both Girondins and Robespierrists—reunited in the face of danger. Disregarding the royal veto, the assembly on July 11 proclaimed that the "fatherland was in danger" and authorized the Federals to come to Paris for the celebration of July 14, despite a royal ban. In any case, many were already on their way, notably the Marseilles Federals. They marched toward the capital to the inspiring strains of the "War Song of the Army of the Rhine." Composed on April 16 at Strasbourg by Rouget de l'Isle, a captain of engineers, the "War Song" was soon given the name of "La Marseillaise." It was a call to fight the aristocrats inside and outside France who hoped to return France "to its ancient slavery," and it became the anthem of the revolution in its struggle with the forces of counterrevolution. Meanwhile the Girondins, fearing that they would lose control of the people, secretly negotiated with the king in the hope of returning to the government. Thus it happened that the fall of the throne—the logical conclusion of the Girondin's theories—was prepared without them and even over their opposition. It was the Paris "sections," led by Robespierre and the most democratic elements of the Jacobins, which took the initiative in proclaiming the king's dethronement.

All the while Louis XVI had remained passive. Calmly and confidently he awaited the entry of the Austrians and Prussians into Paris. He even asked the invaders to intimidate the revolutionaries in advance of their entry by a proclamation. A violent and maladroit manifesto was drawn up by an émigré and signed by Brunswick, the commanding general of the Prussian army. It threatened Paris with "military execution and total destruction" if the royal family were subjected to the slightest offense. Like all the means of intimidation to which the king had had recourse since the start of the revolution, Brunswick's manifesto produced a result contrary to his expectation. The manifesto, which became known in the French capital on August 1, roused most Parisians to anger. A secret directory of Federals prepared an insurrection for August 10, while the section of the "Quinze-Vingts" (a hospital for the blind) in the Saint Antoine quarter, demanded that the Legislative Assembly depose the king even earlier.

When the assembly adjourned on August 9 without coming to a decision, the uprising was begun during the night. An insurrectionary commune was established in the city hall in the place of the legal commune (municipal government). During the morning of August 10, the Tuileries was stormed by the Federals; the Swiss Guards offered weak resistance but ceased fire on the command of the king. The royal family took refuge in the meeting hall of the Legislative Assembly but that body itself was at a loss in the face of the new forces, which were certainly under the leadership of Robespierre and perhaps also of Danton, one of the leaders of the Cordelier club.

The Legislative Assembly could only bow before the victors of August 10. It suspended the king and permitted the commune to imprison him in the tower of the temple. It entrusted the executive power to a Provisional Executive Council under Danton's domination. On Robespierre's proposal it decreed election of a new constitutional assembly to be elected by universal suffrage. Called a "Convention," like the body which had written the new constitution in the United States, the new assembly had the task of providing a new regime for France. On July 30 passive citizens were accepted as members of the national guard. The revolution of August 10 marked not only the dethronement of a king who was strongly suspected of treating with the enemy, with the establishment of universal suffrage and the entry of the passive citizens into the national guard, but also it constituted a new stage in the rise of democracy. But democratic government was being born amid difficult conditions. In order to resist the powerful opposing forces, it had to have recourse to terror from its very inception.

The First Terror

The Prussian army, with the émigré army in its train, penetrated French territory on August 10. They seized the frontier fortifications without difficulty. On September 2 Verdun, the last fortress covering Paris, fell. The peril continued to mount. In the eyes of the Patriots, the capitulation of the fortresses could be the result only of treason; as far as Verdun was concerned, they were not wholly wrong. Fear increased rapidly and incited the masses to acts of violence intended to terrorize both domestic and foreign enemies. A whole series of revolutionary measures was ordered by the three authorities—the Legislative Assembly, the insurrectionary commune of Paris, and the Provisional Executive Committee—which shared power in mutual rivalry. Commissioners sent by these authorities to the provinces and the armies were instructed to use emergency measures, especially raids on homes, arrests of suspects, aristocrats, and refractory priests, and arming of volunteers.

The news of the capture of Verdun by the Prussians prompted the new authorities in Paris to call the citizens to take arms and fly to the borders to defend the fatherland and the revolution. But there were also fears that the aristocrats in the jails of Paris would take advantage of the departure of the Patriots in order to break out and massacre the volunteers' families. Fear of aristocratic conspiracy reappeared. Ringing of the tocsin and firing of alarm cannon increased the excitement of the crowd. Groups of exasperated revolutionaries seized the prisons on September 2; during four days they massacred prisoners, sometimes after a summary trial. There were about 1,300 victims, or about half of all those in prison. A circular of the committee of surveillance of the commune of

Paris called upon the people in the provinces to imitate the Parisians, and a number of executions resulted. Danton, who was minister of justice, apparently gave his approval.

The Legislative Assembly, in an attempt to rally quickly the support of the petty bourgeoisie and the peasant masses, promulgated a whole series of social measures to satisfy the most urgent demands of the people, and thereby completed the revolution of 1789. These measures were abolition without compensation of all feudal dues for which the manorial lord could not present the original warrant; sale of the lands of the émigrés in small lots; division of the communal lands; inventorying and requisitioning of cereal grains; establishment of a civil register of births, marriages, and deaths; dissolution of those religious congregations which still existed; deportation within two weeks of all refractory priests; and the introduction of divorce. However, the assembly refused to make price-fixing, which had been introduced by some local authorities, a general rule for the entire country.

It was especially the army which received impetus from the popular uprising. General Dumouriez, who had been in command since the beginning of the war, combined all his forces in the Argonne, to the rear of the Prussians. Forced to about face, the Prussians prepared to attack the French army encamped on the heights of Valmy on September 20. An overwhelming majority of the French troops were professional soldiers, but several battalions of volunteers were present. Dumouriez also had excellent new artillery at his disposal; manufactured shortly before the revolution from the designs of the engineer Gribeauval, these cannon were being used in combat for the first time. The fury and precision of the French cannonade and the boldness of the French troops, who calmly awaited the attack with cries of "Long live the nation!", discouraged the Prussians, who were already suffering severely from dysentery, torrential rains, and a very poor supply service. The great German poet Goethe, who was present, at once understood the significance of the Prussian withdrawal. "From this day and this place," he said, "dates a new era in the history of the world."

The armed nation and the will of the people had apparently taken the measure of the schemes of the sovereigns and the counterrevolutionaries. In fact, the Prussians withdrew not only because they had been impressed by the firmness of the French troops and because of their own difficulties, but also because the Prussian king was concerned by events in eastern Europe. Catherine II of Russia, having strongly pressed Austria and Prussia to intervene in France, was now taking advantage of their absence in order to attempt seizure of another portion of Poland. The king of Prussia wished to maintain the balance of power with Russia by also annexing a part of Poland. Along with the battle of Valmy, the events in Poland, by distracting the attention of Prussia, saved France and the revolution.

The Convention and the Beginning of the French Republic

At the very moment on September 20 when the battle at Valmy was coming to a close, the National Convention—the new constitutional assembly instituted in August—was opening in Paris. The elections had been held under the rule of universal suffrage, but the mass of the moderates, frightened by the first wave of terror, abstained; scarcely one-tenth of the electors took part in the ballot, but they were the most revolutionary tenth. The Convention therefore included only a minority of royalists and was composed principally of lawyers, bourgeois, and small merchants. There were only two workers among the 750 deputies.

The Convention abolished the monarchy as soon as it met and decreed that its acts would be dated from Year I of the Republic. While awaiting adoption of a new constitution, it maintained the institutions established by the Constituent Assembly. Some revolutionary organizations which had been formed spontaneously after August 10 and which were responsible for the reign of terror continued to function, thereby demonstrating again the close dependence of domestic politics upon the course of battle. The insurrectionary commune of Paris was dissolved, however.

The Convention, composed almost totally of members of the bourgeoisie, did not possess the faintest tinge of socialist ideology. Its members had not the slightest intention in engaging in a vast redistribution of wealth, and even less of reviving the economic controls abolished in 1789. Some of them believed, however, that it was necessary to make concessions to the sans-culottes, at least for the time being, in order to retain the popular support which had made victory possible in September 1792. They were ready to accept some price-fixing, recognition of the revolutionary initiative of the Parisian sections, and subordination of private interests to the interests of the nation. The proponents of these concessions were members of the "Mountain."[1] The Girondins distrusted the sans-culottes and were absolutely opposed to price-fixing, which they considered to be an unacceptable attack

1. The more extreme democrats in the Convention, so-called because they sat on the higher benches in the hall.—*Trans.*

upon property. They had connections with the big businessmen of Paris, the major ports, and other big cities. The majority of the deputies formed a middle "Plain" or "Marsh" of the indecisive. It should be noted that there were no parties in the modern sense of the word in the Convention, and even less in the country. Furthermore, all members of the convention were sincere and ardent patriots. Their purpose was to drive the foreign troops out of France and to obtain conditions of peace that would safeguard the new institutions from foreign intervention.

At first everything went splendidly for the Convention. The retreating Prussians and the Austrians soon left French soil and the French revolutionary troops occupied the Austrian Netherlands and most of the Rhineland after the victory of Jemmapes. The kingdom of Sardinia, which had joined the coalition, was invaded by the French; in the two Sardinian provinces which they occupied, Savoy and the county of Nice, they were acclaimed by the population.

The Dutch, Belgian, and Swiss revolutionaries were in raptures. They saw the day approaching when freedom would be established in their lands too. The Girondins, who originally had a majority in the Convention, had connections with the foreign Patriots who had taken refuge in France and were very responsive to their pressure. In addition, the ministry of foreign affairs had been confided to Lebrun-Tondu, who before 1789 had been the managing editor of one of the most important Patriotic journals in the Austrian Netherlands. The Girondins, who had already pressed for war the year before, now thought that victory was certain and decided that it was time to transform the war into a struggle for spreading the revolution. On their proposal the Convention adopted a decree on November 19, 1792, which proclaimed: "The

National Convention declares in the name of the French nation that it will grant brotherly assistance to all peoples which may desire to recover their freedom, and instructs the executive power to give the necessary orders to bring aid to all peoples and to defend citizens who have been or may be molested in the cause of freedom." The decree had immense reverberations.

But together with this tendency to make the revolution a movement of liberation, another tendency took shape which transformed the revolution into a conqueror. Some occupied regions, notably Savoy, had asked with undeniable spontaneity and unanimity that they be joined to France. Many revolutionaries believed that all "liberated" peoples would react in the same way, and that in any case France should be extended to its natural frontiers—the Rhine, the Alps, and the Pyrenees—so that it could protect and defend the revolution. They therefore favored French annexation of Belgium and the Rhineland. Referendums on annexation proposals were organized in the cities and provinces of Belgium, but despite the pressure of the French army only a small number of voters cast ballots. At Mainz, a "Rhenish Convention" approved annexation by France, although only a minority of the population was favorable. The former bishopric of Basel, after having formed an ephemeral Rauracian Republic, was also annexed and became the department of Mont-Terrible.

The sovereigns of Europe, already disquieted by this policy of annexations, were no less troubled by the trial and execution of Louis XVI. The Convention had been very divided over this issue. The moderates and many of the Girondins thought that keeping the king in prison until peace was made would be sufficient. But the Mountain, supported by the Parisian sans-culottes, demanded that an example be made by punishing the royal traitor. This would make any restoration impossible, for the king's execution would destroy the very principle of monarchy. When papers incontestably establishing that the king had had intelligence with the enemy were discovered in an iron chest in the Tuileries, the arguments of the Mountain were reinforced. Louis XVI was sentenced to death, although by a majority of a single vote, and he was guillotined on January 21, 1793. His execution stunned Europe. In the Convention it sharpened the divisions between the Girondins and the Mountain, and even more between the regicides and those who had not voted for the death of the king.

The execution of Louis XVI, the Girondins' policy of conquests and annexations, the opening of the Scheldt river, which had been closed to seagoing trade by the Dutch since 1583, the revolutionary agitation in numerous European countries—all these gave a new impetus to the war. An immense coalition—known to history as the "First Coalition"—was formed against France. England, which had been struggling against revolutions since 1773, and then Spain joined with Austria, Prussia and Sardinia, while Empress Catherine II gave her lofty approval. Portugal and most of the German and Italian states also entered the arena. In all Europe only Turkey, the Scandinavian states, and Switzerland remained at peace with France.

Government of Revolution and National Defense

The considerable forces put into the line by the coalition compelled the French army to give way. Many volunteers who had enlisted for only a single campaign had returned home. Dumouriez was beaten at Neerwinden in Belgium on March 18. He put the responsibility for his defeat upon the government, treated with the Austrian general Coburg, and attempted to march upon Paris with his army. But when his troops refused to obey he went over to the enemy, taking with him as prisoners Beurnonville, the minister of war, and four commissioners from the Convention who had come to arrest him. Dumouriez's betrayal disorganized the national defense and created a political crisis in France. The deterioration of the economic situation during the winter made the political situation even worse. As a result of massive issues of the assignats, the paper currency lost more than 50 percent of its value; the price of grain was not controlled and rose constantly; the cost of living increased. The Girondins, who had desired the declaration of war in 1792 and the war of conquest of 1793, seemed all the more responsible for the crisis because they had been closely linked to Dumouriez, the traitorous general.

The crisis resulted in the formation of many revolutionary institutions, as in August 1792. Committees of surveillance and revolutionary battalions reappeared. The Jacobin clubs, in which the sans-culottes more and more took the place of bourgeois, increased their activity, and intervened with increasing frequency and effectiveness in political and administrative life. The number of arrests without government orders increased. Lists of suspects were prepared. In Paris the sections which were dominated by the sans-culottes and directed by the commune accused the Girondins of paralyzing the Convention and the government and bringing the revolution to ruin. The struggle in the Convention between the Mountain and the Girondins was exacerbated. It ended with a victory of the Mountain, on June 2, 1793, when an insurrection of Parisian sans-culottes imposed on the assembly the arrest of 29 Girondin deputies and two Girondin ministers. The decision of March 10 to raise 300,000 recruits for the army served as the pretext for an insurrection in the Vendée and neighboring departments. News of the June 2 insurrection in Paris resulted in counterrevolutionary risings in Normandy, the Bordeaux region and most of the southeastern France. Soon more than sixty departments were in opposition or open revolt against the Convention, where the party of the Mountain was in control. It was a struggle not between two political theories but between two social groups: the upper bourgeoisie, who were frightened by the progress of the revolution which they had unloosed, and who now had the support of the monarchists; and the middle and small bourgeoisie, who were ready to use the most exceptional measures in order to assure the "public safety" and had the support of the mass of sans-culottes.

Immediately after June 2 the Mountain adopted a new constitution in the hope of reassuring ordinary Frenchmen and inducing the rebels to lay down their arms. The new fundamental law, it was felt, should allay their fears. The Convention had begun debate on a new constitution when it first met, but had delayed adopting specific provisions during the conflict between the Girondins and the Mountain. After the fall of the Girondins the constitution was rapidly completed. The constitution of Year I (1793) was vastly more democratic than the constitution of 1791. It established universal direct male suffrage and the referendum; proclaimed the right of self-determination of peoples and the brotherhood of free nations; declared in its first article that the purpose of society was the "common happiness"; affirmed the right to work, assistance, and education, but maintained the definition of property given in the Declaration of Rights of 1789, rejecting the changes proposed by Robespierre. Economic freedom was also clearly reaffirmed, but so was the right of insurrection. The constitution gave the legislative power to an assembly elected for a single year, and the executive power to a council of ministers chosen from outside the membership of the assembly and subordinate to it. This constitution was approved in a referendum by 1,800,000 affirmative votes, but it was obvious that circumstances did not permit it to be put into immediate effect. The text of the constitution was therefore deposited in a cedarwood ark which remained, unmoved and unopened, at the foot of the presiding officer of the Convention. Although never put into force, the constitution of 1793 played an important role in history. It officially placed the problems of social democracy before the world for the first time. It became a source of ideas and encouragement to later democrats, from Babeuf and Buonarroti to Louis Blanc, Barbès, and Jaurès.

With the constitution thus put away for the future, the Convention organized emergency government for the present. On October 10 it proclaimed that the government of France would be "revolutionary"—that is, not subject to the constitution—until peace. The revolutionary government was brought into being by a number of separate measures; most of these were not part of any general plan but were taken under the pressure from the sans-culottes during the crisis of the summer of 1793. A decree of 14 Frimaire Year II (December 4, 1793) to some extent codified the revolutionary government.

The executive power was actually entrusted to two committees of the Convention. The first, the Committee of Public Safety, had been set up under the name of the Committee of General Defense on January 1, 1793, at a time when relations between France and England were becoming strained. Reorganized and reduced to nine members after Dumouriez's treason, on April 6, 1793, it was given the task of running the government, with the exception of financial and police matters. The committee underwent another reorganization after the elimination of the Girondins. What has been called the Great Committee, consisting of twelve members, was formed in July and August 1793, when the danger on the frontiers and in the rebellious departments was growing worse and a cruel famine was being felt.

The Great Committee governed France by dictatorship for a year and saved her from invasion. Its members did not all share the same views by any means. We can distinguish between the moderates, Robert Lindet, Lazare Carnot, and Prieur of La Côte-d'Or, who were specialists in military and economic problems; a Left, composed of Robespierre, Saint-Just, and Couthon, who had the political leadership of the country, and to whom may be added Jean Bon Saint-André and Prieur of La Marne, who were concerned with maritime affairs; the extremists, Billaud-Varenne and Collot d'Herbois, who were linked with the sans-culottes; in the center, Barère, the eloquent eternal conciliator; and finally, on the Right, Hérault de Séchelles, a former member of the Parlement of Paris.

The Committee of General Security, established as soon as the Convention met, was the successor to the Committee of Surveillance of the Legislative Assembly. It was also composed of twelve members after September 1793; it remained on duty for nine months and had supreme control over the political police.

These two committees were responsible to the Convention, which could overturn them during the monthly reelection of their membership. Together they formed what was in fact, though not in name, the government of France. The local revolutionary committees of surveillance were legalized and given charge of watching suspects; but they often considerably expanded their functions. The role of the popular societies or Jacobin clubs was officially recognized; they were given the task of supervising the work of the authorities. The elections were suspended and the power to change the membership of the administrative councils was given to representatives on mission, aided by the popular societies. On the other hand, the "revolutionary armies" which had been formed in numerous departments for the purpose of arresting suspects, requisitioning food in the countryside, and supplying the markets, were suppressed as too intractable. The most powerful centralization that France had ever known succeeded the extreme decentralization established by the Constituent Assembly.

These measures brought immediate results. The civil war, in which as many as two-thirds of the departments were engaged against Paris at one time or another, receded. The Federalist insurgents in Normandy were defeated at Pacy-sur-Eure on July 13. Most of the departments rallied to the Convention and the revolt was concentrated in three distinct centers—the Vendée; Lyons; and Provence, with the rebellious cities of Marseilles and Toulon. Regular army forces were dispatched against the rebels.

The sans-culottes of Paris, by means of the insurrections of September 4 and 5, 1793, compelled the Convention to adopt measures of the greatest severity for the purpose of suppressing the counterrevolutionary uprisings and preventing new outbreaks. Taken all together, these measures constitute the Reign of Terror. As early as the month of March 1793, as we have noted, imprisonment of suspects had begun. After the popular demonstration of September 5, a decree of September 17 established different categories of suspects and ordered their arrest. It is still difficult for historians to determine how many Frenchmen were imprisoned under this decree; estimates vary from 300,000 to 500,000 persons.

Revolutionary tribunals were established to try the suspects. The first extraordinary tribunal had been established in Paris on August 17, 1792, but the slowness of its proceedings had provoked the September massacres and it was suppressed on November 29. After Dumouriez's betrayal, a revolutionary tribunal was reestablished in Paris. Under the pressure of the demonstrations of September 5, 1793, it was divided into four sections, of which two functioned simultaneously. Tribunals and military commissions were organized in the provinces, especially at Nantes, Bordeaux, Lyons, Orange, Marseilles, Toulon, and Cambrai.

At least 17,000 suspects were sentenced to death. However, if summary executions and deaths in prison are taken into account, the total number of victims of the Terror must be evaluated at 35,000 to 40,000. This was about the same number that died during the great civil wars of the sixteenth century, but it was very much lower than those lost in the Russian, Spanish, and German hecatombs of the twentieth century.

The different regions of France were unequally affected by the Terror; 89 percent of the death sentences were handed out in districts which were in rebellion—in the western departments, the valley of the Rhône, and the frontier zones in the north and east. There were no death sentences in six departments and less than ten in thirty-one departments.

Workers contributed the largest contingent (31 percent) to those tried by revolutionary jurisdictions; second in number were peasants (28 percent). Aristocrats and priests were not a large part of the total number of victims in absolute numbers, but were a very large number in proportion to their class.

The Terror raged from October 1793 to July 1794. Its aim was fundamentally political and repressive; it did not at all seek the extinction of a social class, as has sometimes been claimed. It was essentially an instrument of national and revolutionary defense. The committees of government (the committees of Public Safety and General Security) not only had to defeat the enemy within France; they also had to repel the invaders on all France's frontiers. The war against the European coalition had to be waged on the land and at sea. In this struggle France could overcome the obvious inferiority of her forces provided that she was able to utilize her demographic resources to the full. With about 26 million inhabitants, France was the most populous state of the European continent; indeed, when her area and her resources are taken into account, she was overpopulated. The mass of the unemployed which resulted from France's overrapid demographic growth provided a pool from which recruits for the army could easily be drawn.

The formation of the national guard led to the establishment of the principle of obligatory universal military service. In February 1793 the Convention decreed a call-up of 300,000 men (it will be recalled that this levy served as a pretext for the revolt in the Vendée), but it proved inadequate. Under the pressure of the sans-culottes of Paris, the Convention decreed a levy *en masse;* unmarried men eighteen to twenty-five years old were required to join the army, but everyone else in the nation had to work towards a single goal—war and victory.

Massive production of arms, equipment, and foodstuffs was necessary in order to equip and feed so many troops. France was the only country in continental Europe whose industry was sufficiently developed to be able to meet these needs rapidly. Additional arms factories were established; all textile mills had to work for the army, and everywhere shops were set up to make uniforms and shoes. Shortages were filled by requisitions. Scientists were mobilized to improve existing equipment and to design new means of warfare. The French army put to use for the first time the semaphore telegraph invented by Chappe and the balloon developed by Conté. By the spring of 1794, one year after the invasion began, the Committee of Public Safety was able to bring numerically superior forces into action against the enemy on every frontier.

Economic and Social Precursors

Financing such massive war production would have been an almost insoluble problem under the old regime. Now, however, the assignat provided the government with almost unlimited means of payment. All it had to do was print paper money. Unprecedented and immense inflation resulted, and in turn at once caused increased prices and a rising cost of living.

The high cost of living was a consequence not only of the increase in the means of payment placed at the disposal of the nation; it was also a result first of the mobilization, which took large numbers of able-bodied men from the land and reduced production, and second of the continuing bad harvests. After the famine of 1788–1789, the years 1791, 1792, and 1793 were also years of shortage. Worst of all, the markets were badly supplied, because the harvests were too small and the peasants would not accept payment in assignats, which dropped steadily in value.

The price of food rose constantly higher; all commodities were affected.

Not surprisingly, those who suffered from hunger and the high cost of living came to believe that the revolution had not achieved its goal. This was the attitude of the sans-culottes in the cities, especially Paris. As we have already observed, the sans-culottes did not constitute a social class in the modern sense of the word. They included petty bourgeois, shopkeepers, artisans, clerks, and independent workers; proletarians in the present sense of factory workers were only a minority. The sans-culottes' feeling about property rights was very different from that of the bourgeoisie. Like the peasants, who stubbornly defended communal usages, they favored basing the right of property upon personal labor and the needs of all. On September 2, 1793, the "sans-culottes" section in Paris demanded that the Convention set a rigidly fixed price on articles of prime necessity, the wages of labor, and the profits of industry and commerce. Their petition added: "'Aha!' the aristocrats, the royalists, the moderates, the intriguers will tell you, 'this is an attack upon property, which is supposed to be sacred and inviolable.' That's true. But aren't these scoundrels . . . aware that the only foundation of the right of property is the extent of physical need?" The sans-culottes, we see, wished to preserve the right of property and at the same time to limit its consequences. These views were therefore opposed to the ideas of the revolutionary bourgeoisie and even more of almost the entire membership of the Convention. In short, the sans-culottes aspired to an equality which would be not only "an equality of rights" but also an economic equality expressed in wages and the distribution of food. Their ideal was a society composed of small and equal landowners and independent small producers. The sans-culottes had a quite anarchical conception of government. They favored direct government by the people deliberating in primary assemblies and voting aloud. Their principal spokesmen, Hébert, Jacques Roux, and a group who were called the *Enragés* ("Mad Dogs") were not original thinkers who persuaded the people to follow them; on the contrary, their newspapers and their speeches were merely the sounding boards of the sans-culottes.

Take the speech of Jacques Roux to the Commune of Paris on June 21, 1793: "What is liberty when one class of men can starve another? What is equality when the rich man by his monopoly exercises the right of life and death over his fellow men? Liberty, Equality, Republic, they're all just a phantom. . . . Isn't the most effective, the most certain and the most deadly way to bring about the counterrevolution this exorbitant price of goods which rises so much every day that three out of every four citizens can hardly pay for their food?"

Under the pressure of the sans-culottes to resist the rising cost of living, the Convention, despite its repugnance for such measures, had to introduce price-fixing on a scale vastly more inclusive and strict than any ever decreed under the old regime. A law establishing a "general maximum" of prices and wages which the sans-culottes vehemently demanded during the insurrection of September 5 was enacted on September 29, 1793. The committees and the "revolutionary armies" found it necessary to employ the system of terror in order to compel the peasants to supply the markets at the maximum prices. A law of July 26, 1793, decreed the death penalty for hoarders. In fact it was almost never applied, but the threat it held and the activities of the revolutionary institutions were sufficient to improve the supply of markets and stores. Ration cards were distributed in Paris and some other cities.

Improvement of the food supply constituted only a part of the sans-culottes' program. They also demanded equalization of wealth by additional taxes upon the rich and redistribution of land. At the same time, some sans-culottes made an attack upon the Christian religion itself, accusing the "constitutional" clergy of the crime of moderation equally with the refractory clergy. In 1790 a "revolutionary" religion had been organized, with civil festivals and commemorative holidays like July 14, "Bastille Day." The sans-culottes often added a cult of "martyrs of freedom" and sought to de-Christianize France. The majority of the Committee of Public Safety, and Robespierre personally, were hostile to these tendencies, which risked arousing the mass of Frenchmen against the revolution and paralyzing the national defense. Although the committee got the Convention to adopt the revolutionary calendar, which was certainly the most anti-Christian measure of the revolution, it also permitted Danton and his friends, who were called the "Indulgents," to initiate a struggle against both the sans-culottes' program and the Terror. At the same time the committee gave a modicum of satisfaction to the sans-culottes by the "Ventôse decrees," which ordered that the property of recognized "enemies of the revolution" be distributed among the poor. This measure could bring results only over a long period of time and in any case was difficult to carry out; it was really designed to calm the sans-culottes when their leaders and spokesmen, Hébert and the Enragés, had just been arrested for making increasingly violent attacks upon the policies of the Committee of Public Safety and for preparing a new insurrection. But Danton and his friends were also arrested in order to prevent the revolution from taking the path proposed by the Indulgents, which would soon lead to a compromise peace and restoration of the king. Hébertists, Enragés, and Indulgents were all brought before the revolutionary tribunal, sentenced to death, and executed on March 24 and April 5 and 13, 1794.

The Committee of Public Safety under the leadership of Robespierre was all-powerful for a period of four months. It exercised a virtual dictatorship. But the execution of the sans-culottes' leaders had alienated the people of Paris from the committee. "The revolution is frozen hard," wrote Saint-Just. The Committee of Public Safety governed by means of the Terror and in the name of virtue in order to achieve the victory of the revolution. In the hope of rallying the masses to its side it repudiated the de-Christianization movement, but it attempted to implant a deist religion, "the cult of the Supreme Being," instead. The committee also adopted a program of social security, by establishing the "Great Book of National Charity," which provided grants for the able-bodied poor, assistance at home for the ill, and support for the aged. At the same time the principle of free compulsory elementary education was proclaimed and slavery was abolished in the colonies. But there was no chance at the time that these innovations would endure, especially since their application had to be delayed for lack of money.

The Downfall of the Revolutionary Government

The Terror, the titanic effort of national defense, and the measures of economic and social compulsion achieved the anticipated results. The counterrevolutionary risings within France were defeated. Marseilles was recaptured on August 24, Lyons on October 9, and Toulon on December

18, 1793. The Vendée rebellion was crushed on December 23; although the insurrection in western France was continued in a guerrilla war—the *chouannerie*—it was more troublesome than truly dangerous. By the spring of 1794 almost all the French armies had been reorganized and were facing the foreign enemy. They went over to the offensive, won numerous partial victories, and on June 26 gained the brilliant victory of Fleurus, which reopened the gates of Belgium to the French.

With the civil war terminated and the invasion repulsed, the Terror and the measures of economic and social compulsion which accompanied it became intolerable. At the very time that the battle of Fleurus was being won, there had been a new upsurge of the Terror. As a measure of centralization, most of the revolutionary tribunals and the military commissions in the provinces were abolished and the trial of suspects was concentrated in Paris. On 22 Prairial (June 10), Robespierre obtained passage of a law designed not only to speed up these trials but also to meet new aristocratic conspiracies, of which the attempted assassination of members of the Committee of Public Safety was a sign. The procedure of the revolutionary tribunal was changed to take away the few safeguards which the accused enjoyed, in particular by abolishing the use of defense lawyers. Whereas 1,251 persons had been executed in Paris in the fifteen months between March 1793 and June 1794, 1,376 were guillotined in the seven weeks beginning June 10. This recrudescence of the Terror at the very moment when victories at the frontiers seemed to make it less necessary sharpened the divisions between the Committee of Public Safety and the Committee of General Security, as well as the divisions among the members of the Committee of Public Safety itself. The military victories also caused a relaxation of the solidarity which had held the Jacobin bourgeoisie and the sans-culottes together for a year. The economic liberalism of the Jacobins again came into conflict with the economic interventionism of the sans-culottes.

After the victories at the frontiers, the immense majority of Frenchmen no longer saw any reason to prolong the Terror. Their hostility to it and to Robespierre, who seemed most responsible for it, began to come out into the open. At the same time the Parisian sans-culottes began to turn their backs on the revolutionary government, which had guillotined their leaders in March. They were also angered by the ceiling on wages decreed by the Commune of Paris on July 23, which in practice meant an arbitrary reduction of real wages at the very time when the last of the old crop had been almost all consumed, the new harvest had not yet begun, and prices soared despite the "maximum" law.

The "Great Committee" of Public Safety was deprived of its popular base and lost all support within the Convention as the result of an alliance between the provincial terrorists, who were threatened by Robespierre, and the moderates of the Plain. It was overthrown by the assembly on 9 Thermidor (July 27, 1794). After a vain attempt at resistance, Robespierre and his friends were outlawed, arrested, and guillotined (July 28). With them vanished the prospect of an egalitarian and democratic republic which they had attempted to establish.

The first consequence of the fall of Robespierre was immediate halting of the Terror. It was not long before the "maximum" on prices and wages was abolished (December 1794). The social legislation of Year II collapsed almost before it had begun to be applied.

The surviving Girondins were recalled to their seats in the Convention, which received the name of "Thermidorean" because Robespierre was toppled during the month of Thermidor. The majority of the assembly had followed the Robespierrists for a year only under the spur of necessity, victory being the indispensable condition for the survival of the principles of 1789. They now returned to their liberal and individualist ideas. There was no question of putting into effect the constitution of 1793, which was considered to be too democratic. The revolutionary government was maintained but its authority was greatly reduced. Power was shared among three governmental committees instead of two, a Committee on Legislation being given many of the duties of the Committee of Public Safety. The number of revolutionary committees was cut and their functions limited.

Under the leadership of the moderates (the democrats having split into neo-Hébertists and Jacobins) and under the pressure of bands of rebellious youths, deserters, and released suspects, the Convention slowly turned to a policy of reaction. It restricted the activity of the clubs and popular societies; on November 12 it ordered the closing of the Jacobin club in Paris. In economic affairs it repealed the "maximum" law on December 24, 1794, and reestablished economic liberalism. This measure caused prices to increase even more rapidly, followed by massive issues of assignats, which lost 68 percent of their value in May 1795, and 97 percent in July. What was later to be termed the "infernal cycle" had begun. Bondholders were ruined; the workers, who were paid in assignats, were reduced to the blackest destitution; but the newly rich—the "Marvels" and the "Incredibles" as they were called—flaunted boundless luxury and flung themselves into a life of pleasure. The condition of the popular classes was worsened by the unemployment resulting from the closing of most of the arms factories established during the previous year, and by the severity of the winter of Year III (1794–1795), one of the coldest of the century, the rivers being frozen over for several weeks.

In Germinal Year III (March 1795), popular despair turned into wrath. On 12 Germinal (April 1), a disorderly crowd invaded the Convention and demanded the application of the Constitution of 1793 and measures against the famine. National guard units from the wealthy quarters dispersed the demonstrators without difficulty; twenty members of the assembly who belonged to the Mountain were arrested, and former sans-culotte leaders were disarmed. These measures did not break the revolutionary movement in Paris but further excited the spirit of revolt. On 1 Prairial (May 20), the sans-culottes invaded the Convention again and even murdered a deputy on the floor, but they were unable to impose their program. The "committees of government," which were now in the hands of the moderates, organized a counterattack. They ordered the arrest of an additional fourteen deputies of the Mountain and forced the capitulation of the Saint-Antoine quarter with the aid of the army; this was the first time that the revolutionaries appealed to the regular army against a popular movement. Many sans-culottes were arrested; some forty were sentenced to death and were executed. The reaction extended to every part of France, and became a "White Terror." The popular movement was broken and the revolution in France remained in the hands of the bourgeoisie. The constitution of 1793 was definitely set aside and the Convention began drafting another fundamental law, the constitution of 1795 (Year III).

The royalists tried to profit by the White Terror to seize power. However, an émigré corps which attempted a landing at Quiberon on the Brittany peninsula was defeated with heavy losses (June 27–July 21), and an insurrection of royalists in Paris on 13 Vendémiaire Year IV (October 5, 1795), was crushed by government troops under the command of Napoleon Bonaparte, a young general who had distinguished himself at the siege of Tóulon in 1793.

These political vicissitudes should not cause the work done by the Thermidorean Convention in the fields of religion and intellectual life to be forgotten. In certain respects it was a remarkable achievement. To bring to an end the religious crisis which had begun in 1790, the Convention enacted the separation of church and state. This experiment did not bring a halt to the religious struggles, but it was a precursor which lasted for a longer time than the innovations attempted in the economic and social fields, and it had major repercussions in the world. If the principle of free and compulsory primary education was not applied in practice, secondary education was renovated by the establishment of "central schools" which broke with tradition by placing the sciences, drawing, and modern languages in the forefront of the curriculum, instead of Latin. Higher education was improved by creation of the Polytechnical School and the first venture at a Normal School; by establishment of the Institute of France, which was designed to bring scientists together and to direct scientific research; by foundation of the national and departmental archives, the Conservatory of Music, the Louvre museum, the Museum of Natural History, and the Conservatory of Arts and Crafts.

The intellectuals who guided France were proud of their work, which made their country the "Great Nation." However, France became the Great Nation not only because of its new institutions, but also because of the victories of its armies.

The Revolutionary Victory

The French victory of Fleurus was followed by occupation of Belgium during the summer of 1794. The next winter the United Provinces were invaded; French troops were able to cross the arms of the Rhine and Meuse rivers in the delta when extreme cold caused the waterways to freeze over. The Rhineland, with the exception of Mainz, again fell to the power of French republican armies. At both ends of the Pyrenees French troops crossed into Spain. These blows shook the coalition, which had never been very solid. No single general treaty bound the various participants. Spain was distrustful of England. Even more important, the Polish problem continued to set Prussia, Austria, and Russia at odds. At the end of 1792, after the battle of Valmy, Poland was partitioned a second time by Prussia and Russia, which seized two huge fragments of Polish territory. The Austrian government was indignant at having been cheated of its share. Furthermore, as we have already seen, the Polish Patriots grouped around Kosciuszko and led by their most ardent element, the Jacobins, attempted in 1794 to drive out the Russian invaders and to make Poland over into a democratic republic in the image of France. We have seen too why this outpouring of national and revolutionary ardor failed to bring victory to the war of independence. Austria and Russia used it as a pretext for renewed intervention. the Russians captured Kosciuszko in October 1794, and Warsaw capitulated on November 6.

It was evident that the little remnant of Poland that remained independent was also going to suffer partition. To reinforce her demand for an important share of Polish territory, Prussia had to shift all her troops to the east, and therefore had to come to terms with France. In any case, the grand duke of Tuscany, the emperor's own brother, by making peace with France on February 9, 1795, had just given the example of a prince negotiating with the revolutionaries. But the Thermidorean Convention, which still governed France, turned to the policy of "natural frontiers" which had been initiated by the Girondins. This policy required the annexation of Belgium and the Rhineland and therefore greatly complicated negotiations with the German states. Nevertheless Prussia became the first German power to sign a treaty with revolutionary France, at Basel on April 6. Prussia recognized the French republic, accepted the neutralization of all north Germany, and promised to cede its own Rhenish territories if and when France proceeded to annexation of the entire Rhineland; but in that event Prussia was to receive a compensation on the right bank of the Rhine. The Franco-Prussian treaty isolated the stadholder in the United Provinces, and he lost all hope of assistance. The new Batavian republic took the place of the old United Provinces, and it signed a peace treaty with France on May 16. The new Dutch government ceded Maastricht and Venlo to France (foreshadowing French annexation of Belgium) and promised to pay a huge indemnity of 100 million guilders. The Batavian and French republics also signed a treaty of offensive and defensive alliance. Spain concluded a peace in its turn at Basel on July 22, ceding the Spanish part of the island of Santo Domingo. As for Poland, the third partition was sealed on October 24, 1795.

The annexationist designs of France caused the anxieties of England and Austria to redouble. They tightened their alliance in order to continue the war against France, and the Italian states remained bound to Austria. The war therefore went on. Meanwhile the French armies, ill supplied, ill equipped, and ill clothed as a result of the inflation, lost half of their effectives by desertion during 1795. Nonetheless the Thermidorians continued faithful to the program of the Girondins' foreign policy—France's "natural frontiers" and assistance to all peoples wishing to recover their liberty and set up independent republics. The annexation of Nice and Savoy was not called into question, but the annexation of Belgium caused very vigorous debate. A party favoring "the lesser limits," composed primarily of the right wing of the Convention, was hostile to the incorporation of Belgium, but it was unable to prevent the passage of an annexation law on October 1, 1795, during one of the last sittings of the assembly. On the other hand, there was no vote on the annexation of the Rhineland; the Austrians still held Mainz, the Rhineland remained a battlefield, and it seemed premature, even to advocates of the "natural frontiers," to make a decision in such circumstances.

Establishment of a Batavian republic led by the Dutch Patriots reawakened the hopes of Patriots in Germany, Switzerland, and Italy. They hoped more ardently than ever for the victory of France, so that they too would be able to destroy the old regime and build democratic republics in their homelands. But the Convention terminated its existence on October 24, 1795. It was upon the successor regime, the Directory, that the heavy responsibility of building a republican Europe fell.

chapter seven

THE BOURGEOIS REPUBLIC IN FRANCE

The Constitution of the Year III

We have seen that after the riots of Germinal, the Convention had decided to set aside the constitution of 1793 and draft another. This "Constitution of Year III" was adopted by the Convention on August 17, 1795, and accepted by the French people in a referendum. There were more than a million "yes" and not quite 50,000 "no" votes out of a total electorate of six million—a majority of voters had abstained. The constitution of Year III fell very short of the constitution of 1793, and in some respects even of the constitution of 1791. It created the regime of the Directory, a republican government based upon a suffrage limited to taxpayers which has been characterized as "the republic of the bourgeoisie."

In the place of the Declaration of the Rights of Man and the Citizen of 1789, the constitution of Year III had a declaration of rights *and duties*. One of the most significant articles of the original document, "men are born free and equal in rights," was eliminated. Instead the constitution of 1795 declared: "Equality consists in the law being the same for all." "If you say that all men remain equal in rights," deputy Lanjuinais told the Convention, "you incite to rebellion against the constitution those whose exercise of the rights of citizens you have refused or suspended for the sake of the safety of all." The declaration made no mention of a right to education, a right to work, a right to assistance, or a right of insurrection, such as had been included in the declaration of 1793, but it did retain its definition of the right of property, "the right to enjoy and dispose of one's goods, income, the fruit of one's labor and industry." It therefore gave unambiguous reaffirmation of the principle of economic liberty.

Although the constitution of Year III maintained the republican regime created in 1792, it abolished universal suffrage, which had been coeval with the birth of the republic. Only Frenchmen who paid a direct tax were citizens and had the right to vote. The suffrage therefore was broader than in 1791, when payment of taxes equal to three days' work had been required to be an elector. Nonetheless it is not certain that there were any more voters in 1795 than in 1791, at least in the countryside. The two-stage electoral system was maintained; to vote in the second stage, one had to be twenty-five years of age and either own property producing a revenue equal to 200 workdays or be the tenant of a home or lands paying a rental of 150 to 200 workdays, according to the locality. There were about 30,000 members of the electoral assemblies in the entire country.

The legislative power was confided not to a single assembly, as had been done since 1789, but to two assemblies. This was the first instance of bicameralism in France. The two assemblies were the Council of Five Hundred and the Council of Ancients; the latter was composed of 250 members, who had to be more than 40 years of age and married or widowers. There was no requirement that deputies had to be taxpayers. One-third of each council was reelected each year.

The executive power was exercised by a Directory (whence the name of the regime) of five members. The Directors were elected for five-year terms by the legislative councils, with one term expiring each year. They possessed much more extensive powers than those which the king had been given in 1791. They named the ministers, who were no more than their clerks. They directed the administration, the army, the police, and the diplomatic service. Only finances were not under their control; these were entrusted to five treasury commissioners and five commissioners of national accounts, who were elected under the same conditions as the Directors.

The administrative organization of France created in 1790 was maintained in its broad lines. The departments were not touched. Each department was governed by a central administration of five elected members under the supervision of a central commissioner named by the Directory; he was a forerunner of the imperial prefect. The districts of 1790, which had played a major role in the revolutionary government, were abolished. The constitution placed a cantonal municipality at the head of each canton, but this interesting experiment did not survive the Directory. On the other hand, communes of less than five thousand inhabitants lost their municipal council, which was replaced by a municipal agent and a deputy, both elected. All told, centralization was less extreme than in Year II but much greater than in 1791. An article of the constitution gave to the Directory the important power to void the actions of administrators, to suspend and dismiss administrators from office, and to provide for their replacement until the following year.

Little change was made in the organization of the law courts. Although one justice of the peace remained in each canton, the civil tribunals were reduced to one in each department.

The constitution of Year III endeavored to restrict the activity of clubs and popular societies. The press was placed under regulation, and newspapers could be suspended for a year by enactment of a law. Nonetheless the press was much freer under the Directory than it had been under the Convention.

Although the constitution of Year III recognized the separation of church and state, new attempts were made to implant an official religion under the Directory, as had been done under the previous regimes. Theophilanthropy, which was deist in character, was followed by the Decadary cult, which was rationalist. Both failed lamentably.

The authors of the constitution did their best to prevent either a return to the regime of Year II, the dictatorship of an assembly or a committee, or a military dictatorship. The powers of the different branches of government were therefore separated to the greatest degree possible, and councils and administrators were renewed annually. Nonetheless no provision was made in the constitution either for resolving an always possible conflict between the executive and the legislature, or for assuring government under exceptional circumstances, particularly in wartime. But these were precisely the circumstances in which the new constitution was introduced.

The Internal Evolution of France (1795–1797)

The economic situation continued to get worse. In November 1795, when the Directory came to power, the index of the cost of living in Paris, taking the year 1790 as the base 100, apparently reached 5,340. The poorest classes were in destitution. The democrats sought to regain the support of the popular classes by criticizing the Directory. Babeuf, the most original of the democratic spokesmen, wrote in the *Tribune of the People* on November 6: "What is a political revolution in general? What is the French revolution in particular? A war declared between the patricians and the plebeians, the rich and the poor." On the opposite side, the royalists also attempted to exploit the situation. Although the last bands of Chouan counterrevolutionaries in the West had been beaten and their chiefs captured and shot, the royalists had at least 200 deputies in the legislative councils, and they hoped to win over an equal number of indecisive moderates. The royalists therefore decided to change their tactics and to seek to gain power legally, by obtaining a majority in the legislature. But if this plan did not succeed, they would call upon a general for help. They had Pichegru, commander of the army in Alsace, in mind. The Directory itself had a very narrow political base. It could count only upon that section of the wealthy bourgeoisie to whom the revolution had given high posts and who had been able to acquire national property or make a fortune in war supplies; they were called the "gentlemen" (*honnêtes gens*) or the "notables." As the excessive separation of powers made it difficult for the Directory to influence the legislative councils, or for the councils to influence the Directory, the history of the Directory was marked by one coup d'état after another. The first occurred on 18 Fructidor Year V (September 14, 1797), and put an end to the "First Directory."

The "First Directory," which for two years tried to govern France constitutionally, was composed of Barras, Reubell, La Revellière-Lépeaux, Carnot, and Letourneur, all former regicide members of the Convention. They first tried to rally the sincere republicans, especially the Jacobins, to their side. But Babeuf remained intractable. When an order for his arrest was issued on December 5, he went underground. Together with the Italian Buonarroti and former members of the Convention, including Drouet, who had arrested Louis XVI at Varennes, Babeuf organized a conspiracy against the Directory with the object of replacing it by a communist régime. Babeuf was therefore the first political figure of the revolution who sought to put into practice what until then had been considered only a utopian theory of the philosophes. He also abandoned the method of mass insurrection which had been customary in France; instead he organized a "Conspiracy of the Equals," a small group who kept their ultimate aims secret and upon whom he believed he could count. An economic crisis favored the agitation of the Babouvists. The value of the assignat dropped to nothing; when it was replaced by the "territorial warrant," this new paper money lost 70 percent of its value as soon as it was issued and rapidly declined even further. A return to metal currency became necessary, and the severe deflation which resulted made the hardships of the laboring classes even worse. The Directory, divided within itself, hesitated for some time before undertaking direct action against the Babouvists; but finally, at Carnot's insistence, it came to a decision. The Babouvist leaders, betrayed by a double agent, were arrested on May 10, 1796, and brought to trial before the High Court of Justice. Two, including Babeuf, were sentenced to death and executed. The Conspiracy of the Equals, which was to have immense repercussions during the nineteenth century, had as its immediate result a rapprochement between the Directory and the moderates. During the elections of Year V (Spring 1797) to replace one third of the membership of the legislative councils, the moderates won handsomely; one of their own, Barthélemy, who had negotiated the treaties of Basel, was elected to the Directory in place of Letourneur. Carnot, more and more mistrustful of the democrats since the Babeuf conspiracy, was also considered an ally of the moderates. A conflict arose between Reubell and La Revellière-Lépeaux, the republican Directors, and the councils, where the moderates were in control. Under the pressure of the moderates, among whom the royalists had organized numerous secret cells, the councils advocated quick peace without further annexations. The royalists hoped that peace would make possible prompt establishment of Louis XVIII.[1] But they remained divided among themselves on the character of a restored monarchy; some were constitutional royalists, the others partisans of absolute monarchy. But peace was not quite what the Directory sought. More than ever it was counting on the German, Swiss, and Italian Patriots to support the offensives of the French armies. The delegates of these Patriots in Paris assured the Directory of their good will and urged it to act. The Italians were especially active; some of them were already dreaming of achieving national unity and independence with the aid of France.

Two of the three main French armies, the army of Sambre-and-Meuse and the army of Italy, in which Jaco-

1. "Louis XVII," the last surviving son of Louis XVI, had died in prison.—*Trans.*

bins were strong, favored continuation of the revolutionary character of the war in order to free the peoples ruled by "tyrants." Only the army of Rhine-and-Moselle, under the command first of Pichegru and later of Moreau, was reluctant to follow this revolutionary policy; it was more disposed to support the counterrevolutionaries within France.

The campaign of 1796 sharpened these conflicts and finally consolidated the position of the republicans. On the Rhine the army of Sambre-and-Meuse, led by General Jourdan, won important initial successes and reached the upper valley of the Main. But the army of Rhine-and-Moselle under Moreau was beaten on the Danube; its retreat compelled the army of Sambre-and-Meuse to withdraw as well. These events highlighted the brilliant successes won by the army of Italy under the leadership of Bonaparte, though it had only been expected to play a secondary role in the plan of campaign. In a few weeks it occupied Piedmont, Lombardy, and Emilia and compelled the kings of Naples and Sardinia to sign treaties of peace (October 10, 1796, and April 5, 1797). The campaign of 1797 in Italy was even more decisive. After imposing peace upon the pope at Tolentino (February 19, 1797), Bonaparte's army drove to within a few leagues of Vienna. Austria, the last continental power at war with France, was compelled to conclude the armistice of Leoben on April 18, 1797. Since the contributions which Bonaparte raised in the regions conquered by his troops served to meet part of the French budget and permitted the Directory to abandon the use of paper money, it became more and more difficult for any party, or even for the government, to oppose Bonaparte's political views.

The economic situation in France remained difficult. The return to metal currency caused a severe deflation;

the abundant harvests of 1796 and 1797 made the fall of prices even worse, and agricultural prices collapsed. To be sure, the poorest classes in the cities benefited, but the conditions of the peasantry became worse, and taxes continued to reach the treasury very slowly. The royalists and moderates, who had formed a club at Clichy (hence their name of "Clichyans"), took advantage of the economic situation to increase their own political activity. They obtained repeal of a whole series of laws directed against émigrés, their families, and refractory priests. With two of their friends already in the Directory, they expected that it would adopt their program when Director Barras joined them. If Barras allied himself with Reubell and La Revellière–Lépeaux, the other directors, they counted upon General Pichegru, who had been elected president of the Council of Five Hundred, to carry through a coup d'état.

Barras, however, received from Bonaparte papers seized in Italy from a royalist agent, the Count of Antraigues, which proved that Pichegru was guilty of treason. Barras thereupon joined forces with Reubell and La Revellière–Lépeaux, making a clear republican majority in the Directory. They decided to forestall the Clichyans by appealing for protection to the general from whom they thought they had least to fear, Hoche, commander of the army of Sambre-and-Meuse. It was planned that Hoche's troops, under the pretext of crossing Paris in order to march to the west coast, where they were to prepare for a landing in Great Britain, would enter the capital and arrest the Clichyan ringleaders. The ministry was then reorganized by expulsion of the Clichyans, and Hoche himself was named minister of war. But the opponents of the republican majority in the Directory got wind of these preparations and denounced them as violations of the constitution. The troops of the Sambre-and-Meuse army could not enter the "constitutional radius"—that is, the Paris region—without authorization of the legislative councils; and it transpired that Hoche, the new minister of war, had not reached the legally required age. The Directory had to give way, and the coup failed (July 1797).

The royalists and the moderates prepared to exploit their victory. They began reorganization of the national guard by expelling the republicans, and demanded that the "constitutional clubs" authorized by the Directory be closed. But they were neither bold nor quick enough. Pichegru could not bring himself to act. Again the royalist-moderate coalition was forestalled by the Directory. In view of the impossibility of appealing to the sans-culottes, who had been eliminated politically after Prairial Year III, the Directory had to turn to Bonaparte. His Italian policy had been violently attacked in the legislative councils, and he replied by having units of his army send "addresses" to Paris, fulminating against the royalists and demanding the elimination of the Clichyans. One of his subordinates, General Augereau, happened to be opportunely at Paris, along with numerous soldiers on leave from the army of Italy. Barras, Reubell, and La Revellière–Lépeaux, the "triumvirate," called upon Augereau and Bonaparte's soldiers for help. During the night of September 3–4, 1797 (17–18 Fructidor Year V), the triumvirate ordered the arrest of Barthélemy, their fellow-director, and the leaders of the Clichyans. Carnot, forewarned, was able to escape. The councils, meeting in legal forms although only republicans were present, invalidated the election of 198 deputies; thirty-three deputies and twelve other "individuals," including Barthélemy, were sentenced to deportation. All the reactionary laws voted after the royalist victory in the elections of Year V were repealed and the previous laws against émigrés and refractory priests were put back into force. A press law placed newspapers under police supervision for one year, as was authorized by the constitution.

Neither the constitution nor the institutions were changed. Two republicans, François of Neufchâteau and Merlin of Douai, were added to the Directory, which confined itself to replacing with republicans government officials suspected of moderate opinions.

Actually neither the Directory nor the legislative councils were free to act as they pleased. They depended upon the army of Italy and its commander, Bonaparte, who had rescued them. Bonaparte was free to impose his own policy. It was a program that favored neither the "lesser limits" nor the natural frontiers; instead, under the appearance of supporting—we shall see later how far—the Italian patriots, its real purpose was to establish in Italy a state in which Bonaparte could exercise his omnipotence. While the negotiations with England which had been under way for several months were broken off, Bonaparte, who in his negotiations with Austria after the armistice of Leoben, had been torn between the orders of the Directory, the claims of Austria, and his own personal views, was at last free to follow his own bent. He demanded that Austria concede what was closest to his own heart—recognition of the "Cisalpine republic" which he had created in the plain of the Po, comprising Lombardy, the duchies of Modena and Massa-Carrara, the Romagna, and the Valtellina. Utilizing the most discredited procedures of the monarchy of the old regime, he divided the old republic of Venice—in the same way that Poland had just been partitioned—among the Cisalpine republic, which annexed most of the Terra Firma, Austria, which seized the city of Venice, Venetia and Istria, and France, which acquired the Ionian islands. Austria ceded Belgium to France in exchange for Venice, but Bonaparte did not obtain the Rhineland from Austria despite the explicit instructions of the Directory, and in this region he had to be content with a vague promise. The problem of the Rhineland was deferred to a Franco-German conference to be held at Rastadt. In any case the treaty, dated at Campo Formio on October 18, 1797, brought the continental war to an end. But hostilities between France and England continued at sea with even greater ferocity. Nonetheless, for the first time since 1792, it appeared possible that France could work out her domestic politics without the pressure of war upon her land frontiers.

The Second Directory in France (1797–1799)

The coup d'état of 18 Fructidor made the government more unified and enabled it to give its attention to the improvement of institutions. In this field it performed useful though often unappreciated work, which was a forerunner of the accomplishments of the Consulate and the Empire. It took up finances first. On 24 Fructidor (September 10), six days after the coup d'état, minister of finances Ramel proposed to the councils a reduction of the debt by means which amounted to bankruptcy; the Directory would then be able to free itself from the financial tutelage exercised over it by the generals. The law requested by Ramel was voted on September 30; it reduced the debt by two-thirds, from 250 million to 83 million francs; one-third of the value of each government bond or pension remained inscribed in the register of public debts and was called the "consolidated third." The other two thirds were reimbursed by warrants, which could be utilized as part payment for national property. Bondholders therefore suffered a partial spoliation, but government finances were in a healthier state. Revenues were increased by new taxes. A tax on doors and windows was added to the three direct taxes already established by the Constituent Assembly; together these formed what came to be called the "four old taxes," which remained the basis of the French fiscal system until 1914. An indirect tax upon road traffic was a failure and did not outlive the Directory. Taxes began to be collected more effectively as the result of the work of an agency of direct taxes composed of civil servants; the deficit was reduced and the financial situation became better than it had ever been since 1778.

Another major reform was army recruitment. The Legislative Assembly and the Convention had obtained reinforcements for the army by appeals for volunteers and by the levy *en masse* of August 1793, in which young men between eighteen and twenty-five years of age were called up. But since that date no more recruits had been ordered into military service. A conscription law proposed by General Jourdan and deputy Delbrel was adopted by the legislative council. It established obligatory universal military service in France in clear-cut fashion: "Every Frenchman is a soldier and must serve in the defense of the fatherland." Citizens reaching the age of twenty years were to be inscribed at the same time (hence the term "conscript") in the army rolls of recruits. The length of service in peacetime was to be five years, but the government was permitted to call up only a part of the conscripts, as selected by lot. With this law universal obligatory military service became one of the permanent fundamental institutions of France.

Although the coup d'état of 18 Fructidor permitted the passage of a number of major organic laws, it did not restore political stability. The coup d'état apparently brought the Jacobins back to power, and it was indeed followed by a violent repression, which has been called the "Directorial Terror." Its principal victims were émigrés who had come back to France and refractory priests. One hundred and sixty returned émigrés were shot. Two hundred and sixty-three priests were deported to French Guiana, whose deadly climate gave it the name of the "dry guillotine," and another 1,500 were interned on the islands of Ré and Oléron, off the western coast of France. But the Directory was composed of moderate republicans who really feared the sans-culottes, whom they called "anarchists," as much as the royalists. The Directors were afraid that they would be overwhelmed by the anarchists, who were linked to the Patriots of the new sister republics and the countries occupied by the French army. The "Second Directory" therefore treated the Jacobins as suspects. Nevertheless the elections of Year VI (April 1798), although carefully prepared by the government, gave a majority to the Jacobins. The electoral assemblies were frequently divided and minority candidates proclaimed elected. By virtue of a law voted on January 31, 1798, it was the function of the legislative councils to decide the validity of deputies' credentials. By a law of 22 Floréal (May 11), the councils eliminated 106 newly elected deputies, including 104 Jacobins or "Excluders" and two royalists. Fifty-three minority candidates were admitted, and fifty-three seats were left empty. Numerous regularly elected judges and other officials were similarly invalidated. This was the so-called coup d'état of 22 Floréal.

The "Second Directory" might have been able to count upon the majority which it had established, had not its foreign policy laid it open to the sharpest criticism. To be sure, the Directory accepted the treaty of Campo

Formio only because it was impossible to resist the will of Bonaparte, but it hoped to obtain at the Congress of Rastadt the cession of the Rhineland, which it had had to renounce at Campo Formio. Bonaparte was named the plenipotentiary of France at Rastadt, but he quickly renounced duties which in his opinion were more likely to bring him trouble than glory. Instead he accepted the command of the "Army of England," the French expeditionary force that had been given the task of invading Great Britain and so ending the war. The Directory accused the English of wanting the war to go on because it was a source of wealth for them; England, they charged, "stored in its treasury the tears and the blood of the peoples and grew fat by robbing them." The "Army of England" would "go to London to dictate peace."

While waiting for peace to be concluded at Rastadt and victory to be won over England, the Directory resumed the program of republican propaganda and continental expansion which the Girondins had followed in 1792. This policy no longer faced opposition from the Clichyans in the legislative councils, for they had been expelled. In response to an appeal of the Patriots of Switzerland, especially of Basel and the Vaud, French troops entered Swiss territory at the end of January 1798. The Patriots then seized power with the help of the French army, and transformed the political system of Switzerland. A "Helvetic Republic, one and indivisible," was created, but Mülhausen and Geneva, which formerly had been allied to the Swiss cantons, were annexed to France. These changes met the resistance of the peasants of the four "Original" cantons and the Valais, who rose in rebellion at the call of their priests. They were defeated by the French troops, who remained in Switzerland in order to maintain calm and collected heavy war contributions on the orders of the Directory.

Meanwhile diplomatic relations between France and the Holy See were ruptured as a result of the assassination of General Duphot in Rome. Duphot was the fiancé of Désirée Clary, sister-in-law of the French ambassador, Joseph Bonaparte. His assassination especially angered the Directory because it followed the murder of another French diplomat, Hugo de Bassville, in similar circumstances on January 13, 1793. The Directory which was at that moment under the domination of La Revellière-Lépeaux, one of the fiercest adversaries of Catholicism, ordered an invasion of the Papal States. A Roman republic was established on February 15, 1798, and the Pope took refuge in Tuscany. With the Cisalpine republic and the Genoese republic, which Bonaparte democratized under the name of the "Ligurian Republic" in May 1797, there were now three "sister republics" in Italy, in addition to the Batavian republic and the Helvetic republic to the north. This policy of revolutionary expansion coincided with a stiffening of French diplomacy; at Rastadt the French negotiators refused to grant Austria compensations in Italy in exchange for French annexation of the Rhineland. The European governments were stirred by renewed fears. In Vienna, during a demonstration on April 13, 1798, which does not seem to have been spontaneous, the tricolor flag was torn from the embassy of France; General Bernadotte, the new ambassador, thereupon quit the Austrian capital. The Rastadt negotiations became more and more difficult.

Nevertheless the Directory took decisions which could only result in worsening the situation and make renewal of general war vastly more probable. Bonaparte, after rapidly inspecting the "Army of England," returned to Paris and told the Directory that the chance of a successful landing was very small, as he did not possess mastery of the sea. He proposed an attack upon England in the East, which would strike at the very source of her economic power; Egypt, a province of the Ottoman Empire, should be occupied as the first step. Seizure of Egypt was a widely held idea among the French public. France had had continuous relations with Egypt for a long time; numerous French merchants resided in Egypt. The writer Volney wrote a best-selling description of the country a few years before the revolution. As early as 1796 Magallon, the French consul at Alexandria, proposed occupation of the country. The Directory accepted Bonaparte's plans upon the advice of Talleyrand, the minister of foreign affairs, who undertook to go in person to Constantinople on order to keep Turkey neutral. In any event, the Directors were happy to send to a place far from France a general whose glory and popularity worried them.

The expedition for Egypt was prepared in the greatest secrecy and sailed in May 1798. It anchored off Malta on June 11, and easily seized the most powerful naval base in the Mediterranean. The Knights of Malta were expelled and the island was declared a part of France. On July 1 the French army landed in Egypt. It occupied Alexandria, defeated the Mameluks—the quasi-feudal lords who ruled Egypt under the suzerainty of the Porte—and entered Cairo on July 23. But unfortunately the squadron of Admiral Brueys, which had protected the march of the expeditionary force along the coast, neither entered the port of Alexandria nor began the return voyage to Toulon. While still in the open roadstead of Abukir, it was completely destroyed by Nelson on August 1. Bonaparte and his army were the prisoners of their conquest.

The disaster of Abukir had important repercussions. It caused a hesitant Turkey to decide to take up arms against France. The king of Naples, at the urging of England and Austria, attacked the Roman republic in November. However, General Macdonald, the French commander in Rome, anticipating this eventuality, had evacuated the city in order to regroup his forces. He returned to the offensive early in December and reentered Rome in triumph on the 13th. Fearing a Piedmontese attack like that of the king of Naples, French troops occupied the northern Italian kingdom on December 5, and its sovereign was compelled to take refuge in Sardinia. The French continued to expand their control in Italy. General Championnet, who took over command from Macdonald, pursued the routed Neapolitan troops, entered Naples, and proclaimed a "Parthenopean" (Neapolitan) republic on January 26, 1799. In setting up this new "sister republic," Championnet was acting at the request of the local Patriots, but he was also violating the instructions of the Directory, which had at last become concerned about further angering the European governments and wished besides to keep Naples as a bargaining token. Tuscany, the last state where the old regime existed in peninsular Italy, was similarly occupied and "democratized" in March 1799.

The Directory could no longer hold revolutionary expansion in bounds. The spread of the revolution, when accompanied by the accession of Patriots to power in the sister republics and the democratization of their institutions, made renewal of general war even more inevitable. The powers hostile to the revolution, Austria and Russia most of all, were encouraged to resume the struggle by the neutralization of the best French army and its commander, General Bonaparte, in Egypt.

England was therefore able to form a "Second Coalition" with Austria, Russia, the king of Naples, and Turkey late in December 1798. However, as during the first counterrevolutionary alliance, the members of the Second Coalition were not bound to each other by any general treaty and their interests diverged very widely. Russia, England, and Turkey had distinct interests in the Mediterranean, as did Russia and Austria in Italy. When Russia demanded and received the right of passage for its troops from Austria, France took it as a pretext for declaring war on Austria on March 12, 1799. The Congress of Rastadt, which had been dragging on for six months, was cut short when Austrian hussars attacked three French plenipotentiaries, Bonnier, Roberjot, and Jean Debry, on April 28; only Debry survived his wounds. "It is not only the cause of freedom which we must defend; it is the cause of humanity itself," the Directory proclaimed. The war which began anew in Germany, in Italy, and within France and the occupied countries once more became revolutionary in character. In Germany Jourdan was defeated at Stokach on March 21, and his troops fell back on the Rhine. In Italy Schérer was beaten on the Adige on March 20 and April 5; his successor, Moreau, was unable to protect the line of the Adda, which was forced on April 25, and he evacuated the Cisalpine republic and Piedmont. General Macdonald, who had resumed the command of the army of Naples after the Directory recalled Championnet, was forced to fall back to the north. He made a junction with Moreau's troops in Liguria late in June. The French troops in Italy then held only Genoa and the shore of the Riviera, where they faced the Austro-Russian troops commanded by the famed Russian general, Suvorov.

In France a Jacobin majority had been reconstituted

in the councils after the elections of Year VII (April 1799). The Jacobin deputies held the Directory and its ministers responsible for the military disasters. They were supported in their opposition by the generals whom the Directory had ousted from their commands or otherwise given a rough time, such as Championnet, and by the Patriots of the sister republics who had taken refuge in France after the occupation of their homelands by the troops of the counterrevolution. On June 5, 1799, the Council of Five Hundred called upon the Directory to provide an explanation of its policy. The next day it showed its aggressiveness by annulling as unconstitutional the election of Treilhard to the Directory a year before. The Directory gave its response only on June 18 (30 Prairial), and then very vaguely. The opponents of the Directory, led by Lucien Bonaparte, a brother of Napoleon, the general, declared that statement of the Directory inadequate, and they harshly demanded the resignation of La Revellière-Lépeaux and Merlin of Douai. The two accused Directors, who were held responsible for the coup d'état of 22 Floreal Year VI, when the Jacobin candidates had been disqualified, now yielded. Although legal forms were respected, the overthrow of La Revellière-Lépeaux and Merlin has been called the coup d'état of 30 Prairial Year VII (June 18, 1799). The directors who resigned were replaced by Roger Ducos and General Moulin, unobtrusive men who had the reputation of being Jacobins. They joined Barras, Sieyès, and Gohier to form the "Third Directory." It chose ministers who also had the reputation of being Jacobins, particularly Fouché at the head of the police, Robert Lindet at the ministry of finances, Cambacérès at the ministry of justice, and Bernadotte, soon replaced by Dubois-Crancé, at the ministry of war.

Apparently the Jacobins had regained leadership of the French state. But the enemy was at the frontiers and all the sister republics had been attacked and some invaded. Two questions arose: How had this happened? How would the revolution reply?

chapter eight

THE GREAT NATION AND THE ATLANTIC WORLD

The revolution gave way before the assault of the counterrevolutionary forces in the spring of 1799 and then rallied with such energy in the fall, because it possessed elements of both weakness and strength. We can identify these elements by examining the way in which the Atlantic world reacted to the revolutionary expansion. The essential agent of this expansion was France, the "Great Nation." This was what she came to be called both by admirers, who saw her as the great liberator of the peoples, and—in irony—by her deprecators, who thought she was driving the world to ruin. The Great Nation did not spread revolutionary ideas and institutions to the same extent everywhere. In the regions which France annexed, an attempt was made to implant them as strongly as at home. In the countries which were occupied but not annexed, the revolution developed in varying depths. The sister republics adopted constitutions and institutions which, though modeled on the French, nonetheless retained their originality. The other countries of Europe reacted to the revolution in diverse ways, depending on their social structure, their political position, and their geographical situation. Nor was the revolution confined to Europe. It was Atlantic in scope—Atlantic in the colonies of France, situated principally in the Antilles, which were thrown into confusion by the revolution; Atlantic too because of the interest which not only the United States but also the Spanish and Portuguese colonies gave to the revolution in France. On the other hand, the revolution touched Africa only lightly, in the French occupation of Egypt, and Asia hardly at all, in the ephemeral French invasion of Syria and the agitation in the Mascarene islands and the French trading stations in India.

The Revolution in the Annexed Countries

France annexed the imperial principalities in Alsace and Lorraine (notably the principality of Salm), Avignon and Comtat-Venaissin, Nice, Savoy, the principality of Montbéliard, and the district of Porrentruy, by virtue of the "right of the peoples to self-determination." Some of these regions had been enclaves in French territory, and the existence of territories within France under foreign sovereignty shocked the rationality of those who had proclaimed the unity of the republic. It is beyond debate that the population in the enclaves were almost unanimous in their desire to join France. In all these districts the French language was spoken either by the entire population or at least by the bourgeoisie, so that revolutionary ideas had penetrated easily. Unlike the little enclaves, which not only did not offer any resistance to annexation but even welcomed it enthusiastically, Belgium reacted quite differently to this prospect. In 1792 Dumouriez, on the advice of Vonckist Patriots, had considered creating a Belgian republic similar to that which had been projected by the Belgians themselves in 1789. But at that time the Convention happened to be supporting the policy of "natural frontiers." On December 15 it ordered the generals commanding the French forces in all the conquered countries to destroy the old regime, to replace the princely administrations by provisional governments "from which enemies of the republic shall be excluded," and then to have new governments elected, with all candidates required to take an oath "to be loyal to freedom and equality and to renounce privileges." In Belgium new communal and provincial assemblies were elected between January and March 1793. The majority were favorable to Belgian autonomy, and Dumouriez, who vaguely hoped to become the head of the new Belgian state, encouraged them to demonstrate these sentiments. He was going against the inclinations of the Convention, where Danton declared on January 31: "The limits of France are marked by nature. We shall attain them at the four corners of the horizon, at the Rhine, the ocean, and the Alps. That is where the boundaries of our republic must be." This implied the annexation of Belgium. Nonetheless, in the face of Belgian reluctance, it was felt to be too dangerous to hold either a general referendum or an assembly, as had been done in Savoy. Danton was sent on mission with other commissioners to obtain requests for annexation from local and provincial assemblies. The Convention decreed annexation of the different parts of Belgian territory by fifteen separate decrees between March 1 and 30, 1793. But by March 18 Dumouriez' army had been defeated and Belgium evacuated.

The Mountain, which came to power on June 2, 1793, did not favor the system of "natural frontiers." In any case it was not an immediate question, since France itself was being invaded. When after the victory of Fleurus French troops again penetrated into Belgium the Committee of Public Safety acted as if the annexations voted the previous year were null and void. Belgium was treated as a "conquered country" and given a provisional administration, which exploited it for the profit of France and the French armies, as if it would soon have to be abandoned.

The "natural frontiers" was proposed anew by the Girondin deputies who returned to the Convention in 1794 and gained increasing influence. The fate of Belgium was discussed during the first nine months of 1795. The partisans of the "lesser limits" policy opposed annexation, fearing that it would delay peace by making negotiations more difficult. Carnot advocated annexation only of a few fortresses. The supporters of the "natural frontiers" policy, after finally winning a majority in the Committee of Public Safety, triumphed in the Convention on October 1, 1795. There is a question nonetheless whether this vote was legally adequate to make Belgium a part of France, for the constitution of Year III specified that any annexation had to be ratified by the "French people." But the French people had already given their judgment upon the territorial limits of France by ratifying the constitution of Year III, which included the other annexations, but not that of Belgium which was never put to a specific referendum.

Even before the vote of October 1, 1795, Belgium was divided into nine departments, as well as cantons and communes, on August 31. After the annexation, a French commissioner, Bouteville-Dumetz, was instructed to promulgate the laws of France, which were introduced in Belgium between November 22, 1795, and January 20, 1797.

The adaptation of Belgium to the new regime was difficult, especially in the area of religion. The country was profoundly Catholic. Confiscation and sale of church property and the vexatious measures inflicted on the clergy angered the inhabitants. After the coup d'état of 18 Fructidor, the Directory ordered deportation of priests who refused the oath of "hatred for royalty and anarchy"; these included almost all the 8,200 Catholic priests in Belgium. Most went into hiding and escaped arrest, but two hundred were transported to French Guiana, where many died; several were sentenced to death and shot. The Belgian church became an unyielding enemy of the Directory.

Universal compulsory military service also met vigorous resistance. After the passage of the conscription law, which applied to Belgium, the peasants of Flanders and the Ardennes rose in rebellion, as the Vendeans had done in 1793. Lacking outside help, they were rapidly defeated.

It seems probable nonetheless that the petty bourgeoisie, who had profited by the sale of "national property" and obtained the majority of public offices, became satisfied with the new regime. Perhaps it was thanks to them that Belgium remained calm when the great counter-revolutionary thrust occurred in 1799. But this calm should not deceive us. Although many Belgians accepted the revolution, annexation to France was approved only by a minority. However, Austria officially ceded Belgium to France by the treaty of Campo Formio.

This treaty also included the annexation by France of the Ionian islands of Corfu, Cephallonia, and Zante, despoiled from the former republic of Venice. With their annexation the revolution reached into the Balkans world, but the penetration was merely superficial. The Ionian islands were divided into three departments, but the introduction of French institutions met resistance by the population, a majority of whom were Greeks in nationality and Orthodox in religion. In most cases it was not possible to hold elections; administrators and judges had to be named by the general who represented the French government. The French troops which landed at the end of June 1797 immediately began to levy requisitions and contributions. A general insurrection broke out when the Russian and Turkish ships appeared before the archipelago in October 1799. Yet it was through the Ionian islands that the revolutionary ideas penetrated into the Balkans. They were seeds that sprouted slowly, until they burst forth in the insurrection of Serbia in 1810 and Greece after 1820.

The last annexations accomplished by the Directory were those of Mülhausen on March 1, 1798, and Geneva, on April 15, 1799. Mülhausen was incorporated into the department of Haut-Rhin, within which it had enclaved. Geneva became the capital of a new department, Léman, formed from the territory of Geneva and part of Savoy. Mülhausen easily adopted French institutions, but not Geneva. The Genevans had been very proud of the independence of their little republic. They accepted incorporation into the Great Nation only with reluctance, and continued to miss their independence.

The Conquered Lands

There were also regions which were occupied by the French armies but not annexed. Their fate continued uncertain, but revolutionary ideas and institutions were introduced nonetheless. This occurred in the Rhineland, the island of Malta, and Egypt.

The French had broken into the Rhineland in the autumn of 1792, at the same time as into Belgium. The abolition of the old regime had been proclaimed but in general was not carried out in practice. The Patriots formed clubs, especially at Mainz. In March 1793, when the doctrine of the "natural frontiers" was approved by the Convention, the French government decided to have the local population vote upon annexation. As in Belgium, the vote was held in numerous local assemblies. A Rhenish Convention, elected by a tiny majority of the population, met at Mainz on March 21, 1793, and sent to Paris a request that France annex the Rhineland. But when the French troops were defeated in Belgium, they also withdrew from the Rhineland; Mainz soon came under siege and capitulated on July 23. The French did not return to the Rhineland until the summer of 1794, but they were not able to recapture Mainz; the Austrians held it until after the treaty of Campo Formio in December 1797.

Meanwhile those in the Convention who favored a "natural limits" policy demanded annexation of the Rhineland as well as of Belgium. Reubell, an Alsatian, was a particularly ardent advocate of annexation. The fact that the Rhinelanders spoke German would be no obstacle, he argued. The Alsatians spoke German too, and hadn't they been as good Frenchmen as any for a century and a half? He told the Convention how wealthy the Rhineland was—it was a major producer of coal, iron, and wool, it was well provided with modern ironworks and textile mills, and the best navigable waterway in Europe, the Rhine, ran along its eastern boundary. During the summer of 1795 a magazine at Reubell's suggestion instituted a prize competition on the question, "Is it in the interest of the French republic to extend its frontiers to the Rhine?" The supporters of annexation talked a great deal about prestige and power, but none of them mentioned the desires of the local population. Perhaps this is why the Convention decided not to take up the proposed annexation. When Reubell became a member of the Directory, he continued to push this policy. At his urging, Bonaparte was instructed to compel Austria to cede its territories in the Rhineland. We have seen that the general was satisfied with a vague promise by Austria, and that the Directory had to go along with him. The Congress of Rastadt was no more successful than Bonaparte in settling the question of the Rhineland.

The Rhenish Patriots and revolutionaries, fearing that French annexation of the Rhineland would not be achieved, still sought some way to avoid a return to the old regime. They proposed that an independent Cisrhenan republic be established in the Rhineland, on the model of the Cisalpine republic. General Hoche, who commanded the army of occupation, gave this proposal his approval and encouragement. After he died suddenly on September 19, 1797, the Directory, in which Reubell's influence had gone up after the coup d'état of 18 Fructidor, continued to take measures aimed at eventual annexation. Reubell obtained the appointment of his fellow-Alsatian Rudler to a position of control in the Rhineland in November 1797. Rudler divided the territory into four departments and gradually introduced French institutions. His measures against the feudal regime were even more radical than those adopted in France. All feudal dues and tithes were abolished without compensation. Land held on rental could also be acquired by the tenant on the basis of paying its worth—but he was required to reimburse the landowner only if the latter could show an original deed of leasehold untainted by any feudal dues. The abolition of feudalism proved to be permanent. None of the governments which ruled the Rhineland after 1798 dared to reverse these measures. They made the peasants a satisfied class, which generally remained calm during the great offensive of the allies against France in 1799. Juridically, however, the Rhineland remained a part of the Holy Roman (German) Empire.

Malta at this period also was an occupied but not annexed country. The island's strategic position was of the first importance in the Mediterranean. As soon as French forces occupied the Ionian islands, Bonaparte planned to seize Malta from the Knights of St. John of Jerusalem. The island was poorly defended and it was easily taken by the French on June 12, 1798. Before leaving for Egypt, Bonaparte organized Malta "in the French manner," with municipalities, cantons, and a top administration of nine members. But the question of annexation by France was submitted neither to the French legislative councils nor to the population of the island. In any case the inhabitants, angry over the requisitions and the taxation which rained down on them, revolted on September 2. The English and the Sicilians, who were the masters of the sea after the disaster of the French fleet at Abukir (August 1), supported the rebels, who drove out the French. Nonetheless, the French occupation left its traces in Malta. Return of the Order of St. John became impossible, and the idea of independence remained to ferment.

The temporary French occupation of Egypt was of enduring importance, for it was through Egypt that the revolution reached Africa and the borders of Asia. After destroying the feudal regime of the Mameluks, who had ruled the country, Bonaparte was in a position to liberate the Egyptian people. Instead he continued the harsh subjugation of the *fellahin* to the traditional hierarchies, which he brought under French control. But in breaking the bond that united Egypt to the Ottoman Empire for three hundred years without interruption, Bonaparte—and with him revolutionary France—acted as precursors of Egyptian independence. The principal French effort was to modernize and rationalize the administration of Egypt. At the head of each of the provinces were placed an *aga,* the chief police, and an intendant, who directed the financial services: they were assisted by a *divan,* or council of seven members, which remained closely supervised by a French general and a French commissioner. At the head of the administration of the country Bonaparte placed a general divan of thirty Egyptian notables, which had only a consultative role. This organization of the Egyptian government was an innovation of fundamental significance. It meant the penetration of the Enlightenment into the Near East, the crossroads of Africa and Asia, where for three centuries there had seemed to be no change. Yet the old taxes were maintained, and in the judicial field the French confined themselves to creating two commercial tribunals. Bonaparte was insistent upon respecting freedom of religion. He proclaimed his personal sympathy for Islam. The first modern hospitals were created for the army; the doctors who accompanied the expedition began the study of tropical diseases and their cure. Did Bonaparte intend to make Egypt a French colony to replace Santo Domingo, where the plantations had been destroyed by the slave revolt? Or did he wish only to make Egypt a modern state which would awaken the Middle East under the influence of France? It is difficult to say what he really intended, but it is incontestable that the French revolution lies at the origin of the transformations which took place first in Egypt and then in all the Arab countries.

The Sister Republics

The establishment of free independent "sister republics" was part of the general conception of a great revolution to liberate all peoples. Anacharsis Cloots, a German refugee in France, and some French revolutionaries, particularly the Girondins, dreamed of a world federation of equal republics, but they had only sketchy notions of how to achieve it. The creation of new republics was the work of France, the Great Nation, thanks to its military victories. The new republics, which were small, weak, and always in danger from powerful neighboring states where the old regime still held sway, could not survive without the help of France. In fact, therefore, they were less sister republics than vassal states. Furthermore, the Directory was more interested in territorial expansion than in more control. For reasons of both domestic and foreign policy, as we shall see, the Directory opposed the formation of the unified republic in Italy, which some Patriots in the peninsula already advocated. The policy of creating sister republics, therefore, did not succeed, but it had great consequences nonetheless, for it carried the French doctrines, ideas, and institutions to the Low Countries, Italy, and Switzerland and made the revolution in these countries an integral part of the Revolution of the West.

Leaving out of consideration the ephemeral Rauracian republic, which was established in 1792 in Porrentruy and was annexed to France on March 23, 1793, there were six sister republics: the Batavian, recognized by France in the treaty of The Hague of May 16, 1795; the Cisalpine, recognized by Austria in the treaty of Campo Formio of October 18, 1797; the Ligurian, formed from the previous republic of Genoa on June 6, 1797; the Roman, proclaimed February 15, 1798; the Neapolitan (Parthenopean), created

January 26, 1799; and the Helvetic, organized in April 1798. Three other attempts at creating such regimes failed. After the entry of French troops into Venice in April 1797, the city was "democratized," but it had to be ceded to Austria six months later by the treaty of Campo Formio. After the king of Sardinia was driven out by the French in December 1798, the Piedmontese Patriots hoped to make their country a republic, but the Directory decided to hold a referendum in Piedmont on annexation by France. This vote was held on February 16, 1799, under dubious conditions, and the annexation was approved. Finally, when the French entered Tuscany after the departure of the grand duke in March 1799, they prepared to organized a republic, but they had to leave the country in late April before the new regime was proclaimed.

The first thing the sister republics did on coming to power was to write constitutions. These were all inspired by the French constitution of Year III; this is not surprising, for France was the Great Nation, the propagator of the revolution which was to bring happiness to the peoples. Nonetheless, with rare exceptions, these constitutions were not servile copies of their French model. Sometimes they took inspiration from articles in the French constitution of 1793; more often they took into account local aspirations and the reforms which their own jurists had already proposed. Holland, Switzerland, and Tuscany had all experienced important movements of study of public law reform. It should not be forgotten that Tuscany had almost been the first country in Europe to have a modern constitution. Drawn up by the philosophers Gianni, Paolini, and Tolomei, it was set aside by Grand Duke Peter Leopold only because of the formal objections of his brother, Emperor Joseph II, who feared that it would cause a revolution.

Several of the new constitutions were adopted after they had been submitted to a popular referendum. This was the case with the Batavian constitution. A first draft was rejected on August 8, 1797, by a coalition of Right and Left; the conservatives felt that it was too revolutionary and the democrats that it was too moderate. This was the second time during the eighteenth century that a constitution had been rejected by the people anywhere in the world; the first time had been in Massachusetts in 1778. Another constitution was drafted which was closer to the French constitution of Year III than its predecessor. It was adopted in the referendum of April 23, 1798, by 154,000 votes to 11,600. In Italy the constitution of the Cisalpine republic was drawn up by a committee of Italian jurists and politicians. They borrowed numerous articles from the constitutions of the ephemeral Bolognese and Cispadane republics established in late 1796 and early 1797, which had been widely discussed by fairly representative elective assemblies. The constitution of the Ligurian republic was written by a legislative committee and approved in the referendum of December 2, 1797, by 100,000 votes to 17,000. The Neapolitan constitution was also the work of local Patriots. On the other hand, the constitution of the Roman republic was written by French commissioners and reproduces the constitution of Year III, sometimes word for word. However, it gave the French institutions names borrowed from Roman antiquity; there were consuls instead of directors, praetors instead of judges, and so on.

The Helvetic constitution was drafted by the Basel patriot Peter Ochs, but was revised by the French Directors Reubell and Merlin of Douai. It was submitted to a referendum; some cantons endorsed it by large majorities, others rejected it, and some even rebelled against it. The four "Original" cantons and the Valais did not accept it until they had been defeated by French troops in bloody combat.

All these constitutions created unified and centralized states; they gave power to the bourgeoisie on a more or less wide basis of property qualification, different in each republic; suffrage was universal in the Batavian, Helvetic, and Cisalpine republics. All proclaimed freedom and equality of rights. They abolished the seignorial regime under conditions which varied according to the country. They suppressed the nobility and the privileges of the clergy; they often (but not always) abolished the guilds and their component institutions. The relations of religion and the state, which had so gravely troubled France, were the subject of careful study, and everywhere care was taken to avoid schism. The Ligurian republic recognized Catholicism as the state religion. In general, these constitutions borrowed the notion of social rights from the French constitution of 1793 to a greater degree than did the French constitution of Year III. The Batavian constitution proclaimed that the laws should provide for improvement of public health and that the state should furnish "work to the industrious and assistance to the poor." The Ligurian constitution affirmed that "society owes the means of subsistence to the indigent and education to all citizens." The Neapolitan constitution declared that a citizen has the duty of helping his fellow men, feeding the indigent, and enlightening and instructing those around him. The control of the central government over provincial administrations was better organized in Helvetia and the Roman republic, where appointed prefects directed the administration of each department, than it was in France. In the Neapolitan republic provision was made for a kind of constitutional court, an "assembly of ephors," to sit fifteen days each year for the purpose of determining whether the constitution had been violated during the preceding year. The French constitution of Year VIII was inspired by these institutions.

Although the Patriots were a minority in all these republics, the new institutions might have functioned normally if the French government had not constantly interfered in local politics through its commissioners and ambassadors. The French Directory was in fact fearful that power would be seized by the more democratic Patriots, whom it looked on as "anarchists." It suspected—with good cause—that they were in contact with Babeuf, Buonarroti, and their friends and drew inspiration from their doctrines. The Directory endeavored to destroy the influence of the advanced democrats. It was equally hostile to the moderates, whom it suspected of wishing to reestablish the old regimes. The French Directory was therefore led to maintain in power men on whom it believed it could count but who were often only puppets without influence in their own countries.

When the Batavian and Cisalpine republics were established in 1796 and 1797, the moderates who had been in control of French policy since the discovery of the Babeuf conspiracy favored as rulers in these two states men whose opinions were as neutral as possible. But the Jacobins, who returned to power in France after the coup d'état of 18 Fructidor Year V (September 4, 1797), considered it indispensable to "democratize" the sister republics. In the Batavian republic, General Joubert, helped by the Dutch general, Daendels, arrested the federalist deputies on January 22, 1798; they had opposed the introduction of a more centralized and more democratic regime, which the Patriots demanded. In the Cisalpine republic General Brune forced three Directors to resign (April 13, 1798), also at the suggestion of local Patriots. In the Helvetic republic, army commissioner Rapinat called upon two moderate Directors to resign and brought the Jacobin Peter Ochs into the Directory.

But the wind had already turned in France. The Directory, which invalidated the election of Jacobin deputies by the coup d'état of Floréal Year VI (May 11, 1798), also desired to be rid of their friends, the Jacobins in power in the sister republics. This was the source of a new series of coups d'état. In the Batavian republic, General Joubert, again with the help of Daendels, arrested a Batavian Director and several deputies upon the orders of the Directory in Paris; two other Dutch Directors had to resign and the municipal governments of Amsterdam and Rotterdam were dismissed. In the Cisalpine republic, the Jacobins who had come to power several months before were expelled on August 30 and December 10, 1798. A new constitution which repealed universal suffrage and in general was less democratic than the constitution which had been in force was introduced by the French minister at Milan, Trouvé.

The formation of the Second Coalition and the sharpening of the counterrevolutionary threat led to election of numerous Jacobin candidates in the French elections of early 1799. They gave their support to the Batavian and Neapolitan Jacobins, whose influence rose. However, the successes of the coalition prevented any further increase in the power of the Jacobins in the sister republics. In fact, the Cisalpine republic, invaded by the Austrians and Russians, collapsed in April 1799. The Neapolitan and Roman republics were the prey of counterrevolutionary insurrections as soon as the French troops marched out. The governments retained no authority outside Naples and Rome, the capitals. The Batavian, Ligurian, and

Helvetic republics became the theater of major military operations. The republican institutions, which in these countries rested upon old traditions, survived, but all power passed to French generals.

The Revolution in Europe

The revolutionary movement made continuous progress in Europe until around 1793 or 1794. Thereafter it began to retreat wherever there were no French armies in occupation. The established governments had become cognizant of the revolutionary danger. The war against France strengthened their authority and their means of action. The organization of the counterrevolution improved and it acquired a doctrine. A hunt for Jacobins began. Revolutionaries were tracked down and their societies dissolved. Their plots were betrayed by informers and the members of their clubs were tried and punished.

As we have seen, it was Great Britain where the revolutionary movement undeniably had acquired the greatest breadth outside France. It was there, too, that it met its most categorical reply at the level of doctrine, in Burke's *Reflections on the Revolution in France*—a book that detached an important fraction of the British bourgeoisie from the revolution. In any case, the interests of English businessmen were threatened when the French occupied Antwerp at the end of 1792 and reopened the Scheldt river to shipping. The English bourgeoisie accepted the war against France without protest, and the war enabled the government, led by the younger Pitt, to sharpen its measures against the revolutionaries. Their clubs were closed; agitators and writers who supported the French revolution were brought to trial before carefully selected juries and given harsh sentences. After Parliament granted Pitt's request for suspension of the Habeas Corpus Act on May 16, 1794, suspects were arbitrarily arrested and enrolled as seamen in the Royal Navy.

But disorders and disturbances among the people continued. They were spurred by French victories in 1795, which inflicted serious damage on British trade, and by the short harvests of 1794 and 1795, which caused a rise in the price of food. Rioting broke out in London, Birmingham, and Dundee. When Parliament met on October 27, 1795, King George III and Pitt were violently attacked during the course of a public meeting. The government replied by sharpening its repressive measures. Meetings of more than fifty persons were forbidden except in the presence of a magistrate. Seditious publications were prosecuted. At the same time, however, steps were taken to reduce the price of bread. The crisis eased. Agitation fell off, at least in England proper, but it persisted in secret in Ireland and among the sailors of the fleet.

On April 15, 1797, a mutiny shook the Channel fleet based at Spithead. Richard Parker, a sailor, proclaimed a "floating republic" in the North Sea fleet when it also mutinied, on May 11. Negotiations between the Admiralty and the mutineers led to the capitulation of the Channel squadron; the North Sea fleet then had to give in too. Parker was tried and hung. A French landing in England might well have succeeded if the French government had taken advantage of these mutinies, which immobilized the British navy. It seems probable that the mutineers had connections with French Jacobins, but they were linked principally with the Irish secret societies, particularly the United Irishmen.

Secret agitation in Ireland had continued after 1780. In an effort to restore calm, Pitt granted the vote to Catholics, but it was inadequate—the Irish Catholics demanded complete equality with Protestants. The Whigs in Pitt's cabinet were inclined to concede such equality as well, but George III was opposed to it and Pitt accepted the king's decision. Disorders increased in Ireland, sustained by the Society of United Irishmen under the leadership of Wolfe Tone. In Ulster the United Irishmen organized an outright civil war and sought help from France and the United States. In late December 1796 the French sent an expeditionary force under the command of Hoche to land in Ireland. An error in tactics caused their fleet to be divided into two groups as soon as it left Brest. Only a few French ships reached Ireland, and the landing could not be made. Nevertheless the revolutionary agitation in Ireland continued, encouraged by the mutiny of the British fleet in the spring of 1797. A general rebellion broke out in Ireland early in 1798. It was a vast peasant insurrection, similar to the revolt of the Vendée in France. But the French were not then ready to send help to the Irish. They did send a small squadron in August 1798, but more to create a diversion for the sake of their own Egyptian expedition than to support the Irish rebels. General Humbert, who landed with a French half-brigade on August 22 at Killala Bay, was able to rally only a few peasants. He ventured nonetheless to within sixty miles of Dublin, but his force was trapped and he had to surrender to the British on September 8. Wolfe Tone was captured aboard a French ship and committed suicide while in prison. The suppression of the Irish rebellion was very harsh; more than 30,000 victims were reported. England treated Ireland as a conquered country. The Act of Union of 1800 proclaimed that Ireland was indissolubly tied to Great Britain; it lost its own parliament, and the Catholics were deprived of the few rights they had possessed.

The revolution in Great Britain was defeated for a

long time—but it had been a close call. In recalling these events, we can understand the stubbornness of the English government in its war with France. In struggling against revolutionary France, it was also combating the development of the revolution in Great Britain itself.

These revolutionary troubles also explain both the peace initiatives of the English government and their failure. Pitt wished to negotiate only with a French government that would repudiate all revolutionary propaganda. He consented to enter negotiations through Lord Malmesbury in October 1796, when, after the discovery of the Babeuf plot, the moderates were in power in France. These negotiations failed as the result of the demands of the English, who were willing to recognize only France's boundaries of 1792 plus Nice and Savoy, and demanded for themselves cession of the Dutch overseas possessions of the Cape Colony and Ceylon. The negotiations resumed at Lille on July 7, 1797, still with Lord Malmesbury as intermediary; the partial elections for the legislative councils in France (one-third of the membership had to be renewed annually) brought a triumph of the Clichyans. The negotiations were broken off immediately after the coup d'état of 18 Fructidor, which returned Jacobins to power. It was feared that establishment of peace and the resulting easy communications with France would greatly increase the peril from the revolutionary danger in Ireland, then growing rapidly. The need to combat the revolution within its own territory held a top priority in the entire policy of Great Britain from 1793 to 1799. In forming the second coalition cabinet against France late in 1798, Great Britain proved that it was the soul of the counterrevolution.

In Germany the revolution caused less serious problems than in England. By 1794 the conspiracies of the Austrian and Hungarian Jacobins had been uncovered and their leaders condemned to death and executed. The policy of the Hapsburgs became one of violent reaction. All partisans of the Enlightenment were dismissed from public office—although the two predecessors of Francis II had chosen their principal councilors from among them. All societies were put under close surveillance and student associations were dissolved. The police became all-powerful, opening letters, raiding homes, and controlling the press. Sale of the works of the philosopher Kant was banned. Still the liberals continued to have some supporters at court; under their pressure Thugut, the minister of foreign affairs, began preliminary negotiations with France at Basel in June and July 1796. These were broken off for a while when the Austrian troops won some victories in Germany. But, after Bonaparte won his triumphs in Italy, the liberals compelled Thugut to sign the preliminary peace of Leoben on April 18, 1797. The counter-revolutionary action bore fruit when, on April 15, 1798, a popular riot took place against the embassy of France in Vienna because the republican shield had been attached to the balcony and the tricolor flag had been raised.

In the other states of Germany a reaction modeled upon the repression in Austria raged. In Bavaria Jacobins were accused of treason and brought to trial. In the small states of central Germany, writers ceased to publish work favorable to the revolution; Goethe and Schiller kept silence. In Prussia Sieyès, who had been sent by the Directory as the ambassador of France, was given a glacial reception in June 1798.

Eastern Europe was shut off more tightly than ever from revolutionary influences. Police terror reigned in Poland after the third partition (1795). In Russia a number of peasant insurrections broke out between 1796 and

1798; the nobility blamed the rebellions—without justification—upon the influence of the French revolution, and abandoned whatever sympathy they had shown for it. Tsarina Catherine II, who died on November 7, 1796, was succeeded by her son Paul I, a person of impulsive and abnormal character. He was so opposed to the French revolution that he forbade use of the words "citizen," "fatherland," "freedom," and "constitution." Paul I was one of the principal animators of the second coalition and the Russian army and navy took an active part in the war against France.

In Scandinavia, the kingdoms of Sweden and Denmark endeavored to maintain their neutrality. King Gustavus IV Adolphus, who succeeded the assassinated Gustavus III in Sweden, had difficulty in establishing his authority and did not summon the Riksdag until 1800. In Denmark the leading minister Bernstorff attempted to mediate in 1797 between France and England to restore peace. After he failed, he became the most zealous defender of the neutrality of the Scandinavian states.

In the Balkans, after Turkey declared war on France in 1798, it resisted the penetration of revolutionary ideas with increased vigor. Rhigas and eight of his friends who were turned over to the Turks by the Austrians were strangled in a Belgrade prison. Spain and Portugal, which were at peace with France, could not show as much severity, but the still powerful Inquisition prevented the importation of French books and newspapers; even French priests who had emigrated to Spain were subjected to very strict conditions of residence. The revolutionary propaganda had no success in the Iberian peninsula.

By the beginning of 1799 the revolution had found its limits in Europe—the Rhine, the Alps, and the eastern coast of the Adriatic. It affected primarily the Atlantic countries, with the exception of Spain and Portugal. But the revolution did not halt at the shores of the Atlantic; it crossed the ocean and had a profound effect in America.

The Revolution and America

The revolution reached across the Atlantic into the French colonies of the Antilles. It also penetrated to the French colonies in the Indian Ocean—the Mascarene Islands and the trading posts in India—but there it found few echoes. The Jacobins confined themselves to forming clubs; when the clubs of Île de France and Île Bourbon "joined" in 1793, the name of La Réunion—"union" or "joining"—was given to Île Bourbon. In the Antilles, on the contrary, the revolution was violent and had important results. We have seen that the "colored people" and the white planters came into conflict in 1789; the Constituent Assembly believed that it had ended this struggle by its ambiguous declaration of September 24, 1791, which left the colonial assemblies, composed primarily of representatives of the white colonists, free to determine the condition of freedmen and mulattos. But, instead of stopping, disorders became worse. First the freedmen and then the slaves rose in rebellion. The white planters, in terror and without hope of any assistance from France, where the democrats were in control, asked the British fleet and army to help them after war began between France and England. Late in 1793 English troops landed at Santo Domingo and Tobago; in March 1794 Jervis's fleet conquered Martinique and Guadeloupe. But commissioners sent by the Convention organized resistance to the English. At Santo Domingo, Victor Hugues proclaimed the abolition of slavery; his decree was approved by the Convention of February 4, 1794. France thereby became the first state in the world to forbid slavery. This measure rallied the Negroes to the French side. They hurled the English into the sea at Guadeloupe; in Santo Domingo, under the leadership of the Haitian Negro Toussaint L'ouverture, they drove the English back to the ports and attacked the Spanish part of the island, which was ceded to France by Spain on July 22, 1795. Toussaint L'ouverture did not succeed in effectively occupying this Spanish region, but he was soon master of all the former French colony. The planters emigrated in mass to the United States, where they campaigned vigorously against French democracy as it was being practiced by the Convention in Paris; they also strongly opposed those who favored emancipation of the Negroes. In Martinique and Tobago, on the other hand, where the English were still in occupation, slavery was maintained and most of the French planters stayed on.

The revolution thus came near to the United States, where it had first appeared thirty years before. But the Americans had not waited for the troubles in the Antilles to show their interest in the French revolution. In 1789 a majority of citizens of the United States were enthusiastic supporters of the new revolution, which they looked upon as a continuation of their own. Lafayette presented to Jefferson, the ambassador of the United States in Paris, one of the keys of the Bastille to bring to Washington, the newly elected president of the American republic. In an accompanying letter, Lafayette declared "that it is beyond doubt that the principles of the United States opened the gates of the Bastille, and consequently it is in America that the key to the Bastille must find its rightful place." Frenchmen living in the United States formed clubs and published journals, which came to reflect the various shades of opinion in their homeland. The Americans also split in their attitude towards events in France. The Federalists, who controlled the new government of the United States, were critical of the turn taken by the revolution in France after 1792, but the Democrats continued to applaud everything that happened there. The anti-Federalists had the principal speeches before the revolutionary assemblies in Paris translated into English and distributed in numerous copies. In reply the Federalists printed accounts—sometimes enlarged and exaggerated—of the massacres, the peasant revolts, and the burning of manor houses. They republished the pamphlet *Publicola* written by John Quincy Adams, son of John Adams, which was similar in tone and ideas to Burke's *Reflections.*

When war broke out between France and England, the increasing importance attached in the United States to international relations was reflected in political debate. The Democrats held that the alliance concluded with France in 1778 placed a moral obligation on the United States to support the French republic; the Federalists urged that the country keep out of this entangling alliance. Genêt, the new representative of the French Republic in the United States, believed that he could count upon the support of the Democrats and public opinion in order to bring the United States into the war against England. He sponsored Jacobin-style demonstrations. Democrats wore the red bonnet and the tricolor cockade, and called each other "Citizen." An innkeeper near Philadelphia went so far as to name his place "The Guillotined Queen of France." Political clubs increased in number, and more Liberty Trees were planted. Genêt even distributed letters of marque to American privateers. But President Washington solemnly proclaimed neutrality on April 22, 1793, and he was determined to maintain it. Jefferson, Madison, and Monroe, the Democratic leaders, did not dare to oppose the policy of neutrality. Washington finally demanded that the Convention recall Genêt. His letter arrived after the insurrection of June 2, 1793; the Mountain complied all the more willingly with his demand because they looked with suspicion upon Genêt, who had close ties to the Girondins. Fauchet was sent to replace him, but until his arrival Genêt continued his propaganda, not without some success. The orator who spoke at Boston on July 4, 1793, on the occasion of the anniversary of the independence of the United States, attempted to explain and excuse the Terror. New England ministers lauded in lyrical terms France's destruction of the Catholic church and its attacks upon the papacy.

But the Federalists continued to gain ground. Washington sent Chief Justice Jay, a Federalist, to London with the mission of establishing the closest possible political, economic, and cultural relations between the United States and Great Britain. A treaty was signed in 1795, which in practice terminated the French-American treaty of 1778 and gave England extremely favorable terms of trade. The Jay treaty was ratified by the Senate over very strong opposition. From this time American opinion became increasingly wary of the revolution in France. In his State of the Union address of 1795, Washington denounced the Jacobin clubs as anti-American. The Federalists organized a violent campaign against France, and antirevolutionary pamphlets were printed in thousands of copies.

Nevertheless the government of the United States dispatched a mission to France in 1797 to seek a rapprochement between the two countries. It failed miserably due to the mistake of Talleyrand, the skillful but corrupt foreign minister of the Directory, who attempted to extort enormous bribes from the American negotiators. This "XYZ affair" led to the rupture of diplomatic relations between the two countries and even to quasi-war. President John Adams, who followed Washington in 1797, obtained enactment of an Alien Act permitting the expulsion of Frenchmen under suspicion for their revolutionary ideas, and a Sedition Act which authorized punishment of those who slandered officials of the American government in the press or conspired against them. American newspapers began to show greater interest in the movements of Nelson's fleet and Suvorov's armies than in the vicissitudes of the French revolution. The American government even refused passports to Pierre Du Pont de Nemours, the economist, and a delegation from the Institute of France which wanted to visit the United States. Although not actually expelled, many Frenchmen left the United States because they were harassed or threatened. The New England clergymen who had greeted the revolution as an anti-papist movement now preached against the revolution, even after the French drove the pope out of Rome.

But revolutionary France had not lost all of its supporters in the United States. In 1798 James Sullivan, a Massachusetts publicist, in a book published at Boston, put the revolutionary events in France in a favorable light. When Jefferson was elected president of the United States some months later and the Democrats came to power there was another shift of public opinion. But by that time Bonaparte had become the master in France. In any case it must be recognized that the policy of neutrality followed by Washington was profitable to the United States. It permitted the new country to consolidate and organize itself. Who knows what would have happened if he had followed the advice of the Democrats and entered the war against Great Britain?

The revolution had less effect in other parts of America. In Canada, it consolidated the French character of the province of Quebec. The British government followed through with the policy of the Quebec Act of 1774 by a law of 1791 organizing separate and autonomous administrations for Upper Canada, which had been settled by English, and Lower Canada, which had been settled by French. The French Catholic Canadians showed their gratitude as well as their feelings of strong hostility to the anti-Christianizing revolution in France by their loyalty to the British crown.

In South America, on the other hand, the ideas of liberty and independence which had been evident since 1793 in the activities of Nariño, Espejo, and Belgrano were strengthened under the influence of Miranda. After participating in the battles of Valmy and Jemmapes, Miranda fell under the suspicion of the Mountain because of his friendship with Dumouriez. He was imprisoned during the Terror but was able to reach England in 1797. There he actively prepared the rising of the American colonies of Spain, which at that time was an ally of France and hence an enemy of Great Britain. Miranda sent agents to propagandize New Granada. They organized a conspiracy at Guayra to win the independence of Venezuela. The plot was discovered and more than fifty conspirators were sentenced to death and executed. Among the papers seized were numerous republican pamphlets and a Spanish translation of the "Carmagnole," a famous French revolutionary song. Although Miranda was residing in England, he cited the example of the French revolution in calling upon his compatriots to win their freedom and independence. The Venezuelan plotters who were able to escape the repression made their way to Europe. Among them was young Simón Bolívar, who revived his faith by the study of the principles of the French revolution, and learned his strategic ideas by study of the campaigns of

Bonaparte. Ten years passed nevertheless before the revolutionary movement again flowed across the Atlantic to shake the Spanish colonies of America to their depths and to lead them after long struggle to independence. By that time the revolution in Europe had profoundly changed character, for late in 1799 Bonaparte "terminated" the revolution in France. But for another fifteen years he also spread its fundamental principles throughout Europe, from the Moskova to the Guadalquivir.

chapter nine
CONCLUSION: BRUMAIRE

The coup d'état of 18 Brumaire Year VIII (November 9, 1799) brought the bourgeois republic in France to an end. It was therefore a phase of the Revolution of the West. Like the Terror, the coup d'état which brought General Bonaparte to power was a consequence of the war and the grave dangers which hung over France. The second coalition made a major effort during the spring and summer of 1799 to strike down the revolutionary movement everywhere in Europe. The allies combined the thrusts of their armies and peasant insurrections, and succeeded in shaking the revolution. In order to repulse this counter-revolutionary threat, the government of the Directory might have called upon all the forces of the people and adopted measures of public safety, as the Convention had done in Year II. For a moment it considered such a policy. But the wealthy bourgeois who had been in power for four years feared the revival of the Terror. They preferred to put their trust in the army to resist the forces of counterrevolution within France and abroad. By a set of extraordinary and unforeseen circumstances, the most prestigious of all the French generals happened to be in Paris at just the right moment. Thus Bonaparte was able to seize power with little difficulty, in order to "terminate the revolution" while preserving the principal "conquests" of 1789.

The Counterrevolutionary Assault of the Spring of 1799

The second coalition, formed at the end of 1798 by England, Austria, Russia, Turkey, the king of Naples, and all other European adversaries of the revolution, made a gigantic assault upon revolutionary France in the spring of 1799, comparable in scope to the offensive of 1793. While Austrian, Russian, Turkish, and British armies attacked the French in Italy, Switzerland, the Rhineland, and Holland, native counterrevolutionaries organized vast peasant uprisings in Italy, Switzerland, and France.

Immediately after the resumption of hostilities the Austrians and Russians won victories—at Stokach on the Danube on March 21; in Italy at Magnano on April 5, and Cassano on April 27. The French troops in Germany and Switzerland were driven back upon the line of the Rhine, while in Italy they had to evacuate the Cisalpine republic and Piedmont. Simultaneously the frail governments of the other sister republics of Italy were swept away by counterrevolutionary uprisings. In the Neapolitan republic, Cardinal Ruffo organized a peasant insurrection early in 1799. He took advantage of the animosity of the peasants towards the bourgeois, who were not only republicans but were very often also stewards, farmers-general, and collectors of manorial dues and taxes for the great estate owners. The insurrection spread rapidly, especially after May 5, when Macdonald's army evacuated Naples to fall back toward north Italy, where it joined the local army, which was also in retreat.

On June 9, Ruffo's adherents, called the "Army of the Holy Faith" or Sanfedists, entered Naples and restored the old regime. The Patriots who took refuge in the forts together with several French military units which had remained in Naples, capitulated on condition that their lives would be spared and they would receive the honors of war. But Nelson, who blockaded the port with his squadron, annulled the capitulation agreement and delivered the Neapolitan Jacobins to the atrocious vengeance of their Sanfedist foes.

At the same time the peasants of Umbria, in the Roman republic, and adjacent Tuscany, rose to the cry of "Long Live Mary!" On June 28, the "Viva Marias," as they were called, seized Siena, where they burned thirteen Jews, including three women and two children, on the great square, claiming that they were "Jacobins." In July, Bishop Scipione de Ricci, who had been considered the leader of the Italian Jansenists before the revolution, was arrested at Pistoia. The republican government meanwhile held on in Rome until September 30, and the French garrison at Ancona capitulated only on November 13.

In north Italy, especially in Emilia, there were several peasant uprisings similar to those of the Sanfedists and the Viva Marias. But in Piedmont it was the Jacobins themselves who organized an insurrection against the French. We have seen the discontent of the Italian Patriots with the policy of the Directory, which constantly endeavored to keep the most patriotic Italians—those who advocated unification of the peninsula—out of power, because it suspected them of being "exclusive Jacobins" or "anarchists," who shared the ideas of Babeuf and Buonarroti. The Piedmontese patriots replied by forming a secret society of the "Rays," on the model of the conspiracy of the Equals. When the Directory ordered a referendum on February 16, 1799, under very dubious conditions, for the purpose of approving annexation of Piedmont to France, the society of the "Rays" organized a broad insurrection. The rising was bloodily suppressed by General Grouchy, commander of the French forces. Later when the Russian army under Suvorov invaded Piedmont, the democratic forces offered no resistance. In July 1799 the French army in Italy still occupied only the Ligurian Riviera, with Genoa as their principal base.

The Attempt at a Regime of "Public Safety"

The defeats in Italy caused serious anxiety among the French Patriots. Military men placed responsibility upon the civilian government. It was also opposed by the Jacobins, because it had annulled the elections of 22 Floreal Year VI (May 11, 1798). We have seen how the Jacobins, supported by the military, "overthrew" the "Second Directory" on 30 Prairial Year VII (June 18, 1799). The new government was a coalition of Jacobins and generals; two former regicide members of the Convention, Fouché and Robert Lindet, became the ministers of police and finances, General Moulin was named a Director and General Bernadotte minister of war. The new rulers attempted to galvanize the country by employing measures of "public safety," as during Year II. The law of hostages (July 12, 1799) authorized officials in the departments troubled by political assassinations or rioting to arrest as hostages nobles, parents of émigrés, and the relatives of suspects. These hostages were also made civilly responsible for compensation to victims and for payment of the wages of the repressive forces. A forced progressive loan of 100 million francs on the wealthy to be repaid in "national property" was instituted on August 6 in order to obtain the funds necessary for national defense without reestablishing the hated paper money. Measures were taken for rapid application of the Jourdan-Delbrel conscription law without any exemptions. Commissions of inquiry were set up to determine the responsibility for the defeats and to investigate the conduct of three former Directors, Reubell, La Revellière-Lépeaux, and Merlin of Douai. Freedom of the press was restored and political clubs were allowed to reopen; the Jacobins again began to meet in the Riding Club in Paris. Italian Patriots who took refuge in France were warmly greeted, and on August 1 the legislative councils heard with interest and sympathy a petition in which Italian refugees asked the Directory to proclaim the "Republic of Italy" without delay, in spite of foreign occupation of their country.

But these measures of "public safety" met with extreme resistance. The law of hostages was not equally enforced everywhere. The forced loan aroused the wrath of the entire wealthy bourgeoisie, that is, the ruling class. They accused the Jacobins of wishing to introduce the principle of equality of wealth, which they charged had already been the slogan of Robespierre and Babeuf. Directors and ministers dared not alienate the bourgeoisie, who had brought them to power. Sieyès and Fouché decided on August 13 to close the Jacobin Club, which had already been compelled to leave the Riding Club on July 27 and had been meeting since in the church of St. Thomas Aquinas. Once the government lost the support of the Jacobins, it had no choice but to seek the backing of the military. Meanwhile the measures of public safety began to produce results in midsummer.

The allies attempted to set off vast insurrections in west and southwest France in early August, to coincide with a landing and a popular uprising in Holland and a powerful offensive in Switzerland. In southwest France a rebellion began, which was especially serious around Toulouse. The city itself almost fell into the hands of the insurgents, but they were repulsed thanks to the vigorous attitude of the local authorities, who were Jacobins. On August 9 bands of rebel peasants under the command of royalist officers were beaten under the walls of Toulouse; on August 20 their final defeat was accomplished at Montréjeau. A revolt was supposed to begin in west France, in Vendée and Brittany, at the same time as the rising in the southwest. Due to a failure in coordination, the revolt in the west started only in September. But by then the offensives of the allied armies had failed. The Anglo-Russians who landed in Holland on August 27 succeeded in capturing the Dutch fleet anchored in the Texel without firing a shot, but were defeated by Franco-Dutch troops under General Brune on September 19 and October 6. On October 18 the Duke of York, commander of the landing force, signed a convention with Brune, permitting him to evacuate his troops. In Italy the Russian troops under Suvorov defeated the French army at Novi on August 15. The Austrians became fearful that control over Italy would pass out of their hands; they therefore made an arrangement to take over in Italy from the Russian troops, who went to Switzerland to replace the Austrians there. Masséna took advantage of the enemy movements to defeat the Russians on September 25 and 26 near Zurich. Thus the grand enterprise of the second coalition against the revolution failed by early October. Yet the task of defeating the counterrevolution in France still remained. Now that the Directory was deprived of the support of the Jacobins, was it strong enough to crush the counterrevolution without putting itself into the hands of the military? Could it crush the counterrevolution within the framework of the constitution of Year III, which had been designed for peacetime and provided no exceptional methods for time of war. The constitution actually created instability by the provision for annual renewal of a third of the legislative councils, and it prompted the executive power to resort to coups d'état in order to apply long-term policies. After the coup d'état of 18 Fructidor, a number of politicians and intellectuals began to consider revising the constitution. But under the terms of the constitution, it required at least nine years for an amendment to be adopted—a delay incompatible with the urgency of the immediate needs. Another coup d'état became necessary in order to amend the constitution. The technique was by now familiar to the statesmen of the Directory. In addition to the French coups d'état of 18 Fructidor Year V, 22 Floréal Year VI, and 30 Prairial Year VII, they had repeatedly arranged them in the sister republics; there were coups d'état in the Cisalpine republic on April 13, August 30, October 19, and December 10, 1798, in the Roman republic on September 15, 1798, in the Ligurian republic on August 31, 1798, in the Batavian republic on January 22 and June 12, 1798, in the Helvetic republic on June 16, 1798. Most of these coups had been carried through by generals, by Brune and Joubert in particular. It was inevitable therefore that the ruling bourgeoisie should call upon a general to enable them to amend the French constitution, to stabilize the government, and to defeat the counterrevolution by guaranteeing the "conquests of 1789" without frightening property owners by a return to the regime of Year II. "I'm looking for a saber," Director Sieyès remarked during the summer of 1799. Sieyès seems to have sounded out Moreau, although his past was suspicious; Moreau had been very close to Pichegru, whose treason was notorious. In any case Moreau, who was hesitant by nature, refused. Joubert was asked next. He had experience with coups d'état but lacked military prestige. He was appointed the commanding general of the army in Italy so that he could acquire some glory; but he was killed in his first battle at Novi on August 15, 1799. There was Bernadotte, the minister of war, but the problem in his case was that he was rumored to be very close to the Jacobins.

This was how things stood when events suddenly took a sensational turn. Bonaparte landed at the little French Mediterranean port of Fréjus on October 9, 1799. Until this unexpected return, Bonaparte had been thought to be in Egypt, although an order to come back had already been sent to him. Now he was received as a savior. Nothing was known in France of his defeats in the East; the people still thought of him as the prestigious conqueror of Italy and the pacifier of Europe. They hoped that he would provide France with both peace and victory in 1799, as he had done two years before. As for the projected coup d'état, once Bonaparte was back, what other general could be called on to carry it out?

Sieyès and his friends besieged Bonaparte as soon as he reached Paris on October 14. It was not hard to persuade him. Sieyès thought that everything would go as it had in the previous coups and that Bonaparte would step aside when the new constitution came into force. Bonaparte, however, saw in the proposals which were made to him an opportunity to obtain supreme power in France, such as he had already wielded in Italy and Egypt.

The coup d'état was prepared during the first week of November. The plan was that the Council of Ancients, in which a majority had been won over to the coup, was to order the transfer of the legislative councils to Saint-Cloud, outside Paris, on the pretext of an "anarchist" plot, as was its right under the constitution. At the same time it would give command of the army of Paris to Bonaparte. Act One ran off without difficulty on 18 Brumaire (November 9). Act Two—which required that the councils amend the constitution in violation of legal procedure—almost failed. A minority in the Council of Ancients protested, and a large majority in the Council of Five Hundred was violently hostile; some deputies went so far as to demand that General Bonaparte be declared an outlaw. Fortunately for Napoleon, his brother Lucien was presiding over the assembly of the Five Hundred. At the decisive moment Lucien suspended the meeting. Lucien and Napoleon called to their aid the soldiers stationed around the château of Saint-Cloud. The soldiers obeyed the president of the assembly and the general and rushed into the meeting hall to "protect the deputies"—but the deputies fled through the windows. At the same moment the Directory was disorganized by the resignation of Sieyès, Roger Ducos, and Barras, while the two other Directors were held under arrest in the palace of Luxembourg by General Moreau.

A provisional government became necessary. Sieyès and Bonaparte brought together a number of deputies whom they knew to be on their side during the evening of 18 Brumaire. The deputies decided to entrust the government to a "executive consular commission," composed of two former Directors, Sieyès and Roger Ducos, with

General Bonaparte as the third member. This provisional Consulate was instructed to prepare a new constitution with the aid of two legislative commissions, one composed of twenty-five deputies of the Ancients, the other of twenty-five deputies of the Five Hundred. Actually the Consulate held all power, and in the Consulate it was Bonaparte who at once took command, contrary to Sieyès's plans.

Though it was chance that gave power to Bonaparte, the coup d'état of 18 Brumaire was a logical outcome of the revolution. On the one hand, ever since 1789 the revolution had been marked by a succession of dictatorships exercised by groups which seized power by means of violence—the Patriots in the Constituent Assembly, with the help of the peasantry and the people of Paris; the Girondins in the Legislative Assembly; the Commune of Paris, after August 10, 1792; the Committee of Public Safety in Year II; and then the Directory. Why shouldn't a victorious general become the chief of state in turn? Robespierre had foreseen such a development in 1792. Furthermore, only a minority truly accepted the republic in 1799, although those who wanted a return of the old regime were also a minority. The majority, although sincerely devoted to the "conquests of 1789," were indifferent to the form of government; what they wanted from government was above all a guarantee of the "conquests of 1789" and peace. They would probably have accepted Louis XVIII had he accepted the abolition of feudalism, privileges, and absolute monarchy. But in his most recent declarations Louis XVIII proclaimed his intention of restoring the old regime "minus its abuses." A return to the regime of Year II in order to defend and perpetuate the "conquests of 1789" was not possible either, since the bourgeoisie did not want such a regime; only one way out remained—military dictatorship. It was an accident that dictatorial power was given to Bonaparte. He at once reassured the French by proclaiming his desire to "terminate the revolution," by establishing the principles with which it began and by restoring peace abroad.

Can it be said that Bonaparte did in fact bring the revolution to a close? The answer depends on the meaning one gives to the word "revolution." If by it we mean the violent movement which tended to give power to the popular classes, the revolution had been over since the defeat of the last insurrections of the sans-culottes in Germinal and Prairial of Year III. If, on the contrary, we use the word for the inevitably slower transformation of the society and the economy of the old regime—that is, a society characterized by privilege, division in orders, the corporative system, and the handicraft economy—into a modern society, marked by equality of rights and economic liberalism, then the revolution did not end in 1799. Bonaparte was called upon to consolidate this revolution and especially to extend it more than any other Frenchman. Where in 1799 the revolution in this latter sense encompassed a geographical area limited to the East by the Rhine and the west coast of the Adriatic, and to the West by the Allegheny mountains and the Caribbean, it was Napoleon who carried the fundamental principles of the revolution beyond the Rhine, the Danube, and even the Vistula by his military campaigns. It was he too who expanded the revolution in America—in North America by reannexing the immense colony of Louisiana from Spain and then ceding it to the United States; in South America by spurring the American colonies of Spain and Portugal to declare their independence and to organize themselves in conformity with the revolutionary principles after his occupation of their mother countries. The revolution which had begun upon the American shores of the Atlantic, after reaching a height in the French revolution, in which it clarified its principles and consolidated its doctrine, continued upon the American shores of the Atlantic even after the fall of Napoleon.

SELECT BIBLIOGRAPHY

Prepared by John M. Cammett

Bibliographic Aids

The American Historical Association's Guide to Historical Literature. New York, 1961. *Cf.* especially pp. 464–497.

Caron, P. *Manuel pratique pour l'étude de la Révolution française.* Paris, 1947. The principal guide to research on the French Revolution.

Godechot, J. *Les Révolutions, 1770–1799.* ("Nouvelle Clio," 36). Paris, 1963. There is a detailed bibliography of the subject, with considerable emphasis on the revolutions outside France, on pp. 11–75.

Palmer, R. R. "The Impact of the French Revolution: Recent Interpretations," in *The Nineteenth Century World,* pp. 44–85. New York, 1963.* A critical bibliography originally written in 1954, with an appendix of 1962.

Walter, G. *Répertoire de l'histoire de la Révolution française (Travaux publiés de 1800 à 1940).* 2 vols. Paris, 1941–1951.

Some Essays on the Historiography of the Period

Farmer, P. *France Reviews Its Revolutionary Origins: Social Politics and Historical Opinion in the Third Republic.*

* An asterisk after a title denotes that a paperback edition is available.

New York, 1944. A survey of the relationship between the historiography of the Revolution and changing political ideas in France.

Geyl, P. *Encounters in History*. New York, 1961.* Pp. 87–142. The dean of Dutch historians examines the various schools of French Revolutionary historiography. Mainly devoted to the earlier writers.

Rudé, G. *Interpretations of the French Revolution* ("Historical Association Pamphlets," G.47). London, 1961. A succinct yet comprehensive essay on the subject.

General Works on the French Revolution

Classic Works of the Era Itself and of the Nineteenth Century

Although many of these books are tendentious and dated, they retain considerable historical and literary interest (most of the originally French works have been translated into English):

Lord Acton (from his lectures of 1895, but published posthumously,* Barnave (first published, 1842), Abbé de Barruel (1797–1799), Blanc (1847–1862), Burke (1790),* Carlyle (1837), Croker (1857), Mallet du Pan (1793), Michelet (1847–53), Mignet (1824), Quinet (1865), Mme. de Staël (1818), Taine (1876), Thiers (1823–27), Tocqueville (1856).*

Twentieth-Century Works

Aulard, A. *Histoire politique de la Révolution française*. 4 vols. Paris, 1901. Eng. trans., *The French Revolution, a Political History, 1798–1804*. 4 vols. London, 1910. The first historian of the Revolution to use scientific methods of analysis and criticism, though greatly influenced by his position as a Radical of the Third Republic. Danton was the central figure of his narrative.

Belloc, H. *The French Revolution*. London, 1911. A Roman Catholic especially concerned with the conflict of Church and state. Still, he was one of the first historians to take a charitable view of Robespierre.

Brinton, C. *A Decade of Revolution, 1789–1799.* New York, 1934. A volume in the Langer series. A fine introduction which is somewhat critical of the Revolution.

Cobban, A. *A History of Modern France. Volume I: 1715–1799.* Revised ed., 1961.* An excellent shorter history with most of the volume devoted to the revolutionary period. *Cf.* also his *Myth of the French Revolution* (London, 1955) and *The Social Interpretation of the French Revolution* (Cambridge, 1964). These lectures contain some interesting criticism of the "social" school of Lefebvre, Soboul, Rudé, and Cobb.

Gaxotte, P. *La Révolution Française.* Paris, 1928. Eng. trans., *The French Revolution.* London, 1932. A thoroughly negative view of the Revolution from the position of a French ultraconservative.

Gershoy, L. *The French Revolution and Napoleon.* New York, 1933. A standard narrative. *Cf.* also his *Era of the French Revolution, 1789–1799: Ten Years that Shook the World.** Princeton, 1957.

Godechot, J. "The French Revolution," in *Chapters in Western Civilization.* 3rd ed. New York, 1962. Pp. 1–54. A good summary of Godechot's theses.

Goodwin, A. *The French Revolution, 1789–1794.* Revised ed. London, 1956.* A fine survey relying in part on the work of Mathiez and Lefebvre.

Gottschalk, L. *The Era of the French Revolution, 1715–1815.* Boston, 1929. There are many later editions of this standard account.

Guérin, D. *La Lutte de classes sous la première République: Bourgeois et "bras-nus"* (1793–1797). 2 vols. Paris, 1946. A Trotskyist interpretation which attacks Robespierre from the Left. *Cf.* also Guérin's "D'une nouvelle interprétation de la Révolution française," *Annales: économies-sociétés-civilisations,* xx (January–February, 1964).

Hampson, N. *A Social History of the French Revolution.* Toronto, 1963. A balanced survey of the political and class alignments in the revolutionary process.

Hobsbawm, E. *The Age of Revolution: Europe, 1789–1848.* Cleveland and New York, 1962.* The material on the French

Revolution and its background is highly stimulating and original.

Jaurès, J. *Histoire socialiste de la Révolution française.* 4 vols. Paris, 1901–1904. New edition by A. Mathiez, Paris, 1922–1924. A pioneering work for the study of the Revolution as a class struggle.

Lefebvre, G. *Études sur la Révolution française.* Paris, 1954. A collection of many of Lefebvre's best articles.

Lefebvre, G. *The French Revolution.* 2 vols. New York, 1962–1964. Trans. from the 1957 edition of *La Révolution française.* The standard history of the Revolution. The material relating to developments outside of France was greatly expanded in the 1957 edition of this work. There is a large and very good working bibliography at the end of each volume.

Madelin, L. *The French Revolution.* London, 1916. The original French edition appeared in 1911. As a Bonapartist, Madelin saw the high points of the Revolution in 1789 and in Napoleon's coup d'état of the 18th Brumaire.

Mathiez, A. *La Révolution française.* Paris, 1922–1927. Eng. trans., *The French Revolution.* London, 1928.* Albert Mathiez and Georges Lefebvre were the most important historians of the Revolution working before World War II. Mathiez' great tasks were to establish the reputation of Robespierre as the most important statesman of the period and to ensure that studies on the Revolution would be approached from a primarily "social" perspective.

Mousnier, R. and Labrousse, C-E. *Le XVIIIe siècle: Révolution intellectuelle, technique et politique.* Paris, 1953. 3rd ed., 1959. This general work in the "Histoire générale des civilisations" series takes account of the "Atlantic" interpretation of the Revolution.

Rudé, G. *Revolutionary Europe, 1783–1815.* Cleveland and New York, 1964.* A fine survey insisting—in opposition to Palmer and Godechot—on the peculiarity and uniqueness of the French Revolution as compared to other movements of the period.

Salvemini, G. *The French Revolution, 1788–1792.* New York.* This book, first published in 1905 and inspired by Aulard's work, ends with the fall of the monarchy.

Soboul, A. *Précis d'histoire de la Révolution française*. Paris, 1962. Albert Soboul is the leading French Marxist historian of the Revolution. The Italian edition (Bari, 1964) of this important synthesis has a very large and well organized scholarly bibliography. *Cf.* also Soboul's "Classes and Class Struggles During the French Revolution," *Science and Society*, XVII (Summer, 1953), 238–257.

Thompson, J. M. *The French Revolution*. New York, 1945. The author is the founder of modern British studies of the French Revolution.

The Political, Economic, and Social Background to the French Revolution and Its Causes

Barber, E. *The Bourgeoisie in Eighteenth Century France*. Princeton, N.J., 1955. A stimulating if somewhat controversial marriage of sociological methodology and historical enquiry.

Cobban, A. *Historians and the Causes of the French Revolution*. London: Historical Association Pamphlet, 1958. In this survey, Prof. Cobban argues that the "social" causes of the Revolution have been exaggerated: "the substitution of a capitalist-bourgeois order for feudalism is a myth."

Cochin, A. *Les Sociétés de pensée et la démocratie*. Paris, 1921. The "conspiracy" thesis of the origins of the Revolution.

Dakin, D. *Turgot and the Ancient Régime in France*. London, 1939. A study of Turgot's economic policies.

Faÿ, B. *La Grande Révolution (1715–1815)*. Paris, 1959. A revival of the conspiracy thesis as the origin of the Revolution.

Ford, F. L. *Robe and Sword: the Regrouping of the French Aristocracy After Louis XIV*. Cambridge, Mass., 1953. Perhaps the most important study of the French nobility on the eve of the Revolution.

Forster, R. *The Nobility of Toulouse in the Eighteenth Century: A Social and Economic Study*. Baltimore, 1960. Based on a thorough examination of the local archives.

Funck-Brentano, F. *The Old Régime in France*. London, 1929. The French edition appeared in 1926. The author calls the legitimacy of the Revolution into question by idealizing the Old Régime.

Gershoy, L. *From Despotism to Revolution, 1763–1789.* New York, 1944.* An important volume in the Langer series. The paperback edition has a revised bibliography.

Greenlaw, R. *The Economic Origins of the French Revolution—Poverty or Prosperity?* Boston, 1958.* A good selection of articles dealing with the economic background to the Revolution by authors from Michelet and Tocqueville to Labrousse and Lefebvre.

Labrousse, C-E. *Esquisse du mouvement des prix et des revenus en France au XVIIIe siècle.* 2 vols. Paris, 1933. *Cf.* also his *La Crise de l'économie française à la fin de l'ancien régime et au début de la Révolution.* Paris, 1944. Labrousse's work throws new light on the dynamics of prosperity and poverty in eighteenth-century France.

Lefebvre, G. *The Coming of the French Revolution.* Paris, 1939.* The best introduction to the economic and social background of the Revolution and to early events in the Revolution itself. *Cf.* also his *La Grande Peur de 1789.* Paris, 1932.

Levasseur, E. *Histoire des classes ouvrières et de l'industrie en France avant 1789.* 2nd ed. 2 vols. Paris, 1900–1901. An older but still valuable work on a much neglected subject.

Lough, J. *An Introduction to Eighteenth Century France.* London and New York, 1960. A general work attempting to relate political, economic, and social conditions to contemporary French literature.

Martin, G. *La Franc-Maçonnerie française et la préparation de la Révolution française.* Paris, 1926. A solid study of Freemasonry and the origins of the Revolution.

Sée, H. *Economic and Social Conditions in France during the Eighteenth Century.* New York, 1927. Still of great importance for its information on industry and trade, workers, and peasants.

Young, A. *Travels in France During the Years 1787, 1788, 1789.* Cambridge, 1929. The best eye-witness account of conditions in France, especially in rural areas, on the eve of the Revolution.

The Philosophes and the French Revolution

Becker, C. *The Heavenly City of the Eighteenth-Century Philosophers.* New Haven, 1932.* In this by-now classic work, Becker attempted to show that the philosophes were much closer to the medieval world than commonly thought.

Church, W. F., ed. *The Influence of the Enlightenment on the French Revolution: Creative, Disastrous, or Non-existent?* Boston, 1964.* A collection of writings on the subject.

Cobban, A. *In Search of Humanity: The Role of the Enlightenment in Modern History.* New York, 1960. A survey of the political and ethical thought of the Enlightenment stressing its relevance to modern issues. Compare with Becker.

Hazard, P. *The European Mind, 1680–1715* and *European Thought in the Eighteenth Century.* New Haven, 1952–1954. 2 vols. An essential and detailed study of European intellectual history in the period.

Martin, K. *French Liberal Thought in the Eighteenth Century: A Study of Political Ideas from Bayle to Condorcet.* 2nd ed. London, 1954.* An important survey.

Mornet, D. *Les Origines intellectuelles de la Révolution française, 1715–1787.* Paris, 1933. A study of the interaction of ideas and economic conditions.

Peyre, H. "The Influence of Eighteenth Century Ideas on the French Revolution," *Journal of the History of Ideas.* X (1949), 63–87. Asserts that the ideas of the philosophes were an important cause of the Revolution.

Rockwood, R. O., ed. *Carl Becker's Heavenly City Revisited.* Ithaca, 1958. *Cf.* especially the critical essays by Gay, Guerlac, and Dorn.

Some Special Studies on Various Aspects of the French Revolution

WORKS DEALING WITH PARTICULAR PERIODS OR EVENTS OF THE REVOLUTION

1. The Aristocratic Reaction

Carré, H. *La Fin des parlements, 1788–1790.* Paris, 1912. A description of the parlements and a discussion of their end during the aristocratic reaction.

Egret, J. *La Pré-Révolution française, 1787–1788.* Paris, 1962. A fine study by the leading French historian working on this problem.

Egret, J. *La Révolution des notables: Mounier et les monarchiens, 1789.* Paris, 1950. On Mounier's attempt to force a compromise between the bourgeoisie and the nobility.

Goodwin, A. "Calonne, the Assembly of Notables and the Origins of the *Révolte nobiliaire*," *English Historical Review* (1946), 203–234, 329–377. Shows that the Assembly of Notables was the beginning of the Aristocratic reaction.

Renouvin, P. *L'Assemblée des notables: la conférence du 2 mars.* Paris, 1921. Describes the attack on Calonne's budget.

2. The Estates General and the Constituent Assembly

Braesch, F. *1789, l'année cruciale.* Paris, 1941. Controversial work arguing that violence could have been avoided in reforming the state.

Chauvet, P. *1789: L'Insurrection parisienne et la prise de la Bastille.* Paris, 1946. Considers the question of whether the Parisian artisans might have taken over the leadership of the Revolution.

Herbert, S. *The Fall of Feudalism in France.* London, 1921. The effect of the reforms on the peasantry.

Sagnac, P. *La Législation civile de la Révolution française.* Paris, 1898. Good summary of the work of the Constituent Assembly.

Thompson, E. *Popular Sovereignty and the French Constituent Assembly.* Manchester, 1952. The problem of political theory and legislative practice in the Constituent Assembly.

3. 1792–1794

Caron, P. *Les Massacres de septembre.* Paris, 1935. The standard work on the September Massacres.

Clapham, J. *The Causes of the War of 1792.* Cambridge, 1899. A balanced assessment of the responsibilities for the origins of the war.

Cobb, R. *Les Armées révolutionnaires: Instrument de la terreur dans les départements, avril 1793–Floréal an II.* 2 vols. Paris, 1961–1963. A work of great importance for evaluating the work of these paramilitary armies of sans-culottes in carrying out the directives of the National Convention.

Greer, D. *The Incidence of the Terror During the French Revolution.* Cambridge, Mass., 1935. On the number and social composition of the victims of the Terror.

Mathiez, A. *Le Dix Août.* Paris, 1931. An important work on the Revolution of August 10, 1792. *Cf.* also his *The Fall of Robespierre and Other Essays* (London, 1927) and his *La Vie chère et le mouvement social sous la Terreur* (Paris, 1929), which shows the social meaning behind mob actions in Paris.

Michon, G. *Robespierre et la guerre révolutionnaire, 1791–92.* Paris, 1937. On the outbreak of the Revolutionary wars.

Palmer, R. R. *Twelve Who Ruled: The Committee of Public Safety During the Terror.* Princeton, 1941.* The only detailed study devoted exclusively to the Committee of Public Safety.

Sirich, J. B. *Revolutionary Committees in the Departments of France, 1793–94.* Cambridge, Mass., 1943. On the methods used by Paris to assert its rule over the country during the Terror.

Soboul, A. *The Parisian Sans-culottes and the French Revolution.* Oxford, 1964. The original French edition appeared in 1958. The first complete study of the ideas, institutions, and activities of the Parisian sans-culottes during the Terror.

4. The Post-Thermidorian Period

Dejoint, G. *La Politique économique du Directoire.* Paris, 1951. Emphasizes the economic doctrines of the Directory.

Godechot, J. *Les Commissaires aux armées sous le Directoire.* Paris, 1941. Especially important for the story of relations between the French generals and commissaries and the population of occupied countries.

Guyot, R. *Le Directoire et la paix de l'Europe.* Paris, 1912. Still a basic work on the diplomatic history of this period.

Lefebvre, G. *Les Thermidoriens.* Paris, 1937 (4th ed., 1960). And *Le Directoire.* Paris, 1946 (2nd ed., 1950). Shorter summaries intended to complete Mathiez' *La Révolution française.*

Mathiez, A. *After Robespierre: The Thermidorian Re-*

action. New York, 1931.* The French original, *La Réaction thermidorienne,* appeared in 1929.

Mathiez, A. *Le Directoire*. Paris, 1934. The story ends at 18 Fructidor. This is a posthumous work edited by Godechot, who assembled Mathiez' previously published articles on the subject.

Tönnesson, K. *La Défaite des sans-culottes: mouvement populaire et réaction bourgeoise en l'an III*. Oslo and Paris, 1959. A study of the popular movements of Germinal-Prairial.

Vandal, A. *L'Avènement de Bonaparte*. 2 vols. Paris, 1902–1907. An important work, which emphasizes the defects of the Directory.

Works Dealing with Particular Areas or Problems of the Revolution

1. Institutions

Duguit, L. and Monnier, H. *Les Constitutions et les principales lois politiques de la France*. Paris, 1898 *Cf.* the introduction for what Cobban says is "the best short survey of the constitutional history of the Revolution."

Duverger, M. *Les Constitutions de la France* ("Que sais-je?" no. 162). Paris, 1964. *Cf.* pp. 38–61 for a brief introduction to the constitutional history of the Revolution.

Godechot, J. *Histoire des institutions de la France sous la Révolution et l'Empire*. Paris, 1951. An indispensable modern survey with a good bibliography.

2. Political Movements

Brace, R. M. *Bordeaux and the Gironde, 1789–1794*. Ithaca, 1947. The extent to which the bourgeoisie was involved in the Girondist movement.

Brinton, C. *The Jacobins*. New York, 1930. Shows the bourgeois origin of the Jacobins.

Colloque International de Stockholm. *Babeuf et les problèmes du Babouvisme*. Paris, 1963. Essays by Dommanget, Daline, Soboul, Lehming, Markov, etc.

Godechot, J. *La Contre-révolution, doctrine et action, 1789–1804*. Paris, 1961. Sees the counterrevolution as an international movement culminating in the counteroffensive of 1799.

Greer, D. *The Incidence of the Emigration during the French Revolution*. Cambridge, Mass., 1951. On the number and social composition of the emigrés.

Hyslop, B. *French Nationalism in 1789 according to the General Cahiers*. New York, 1934. Thesis that French nationalism was evident from the beginnings of the Revolution.

Martin, Gaston, *Les Jacobins* ("Que sais-je?" no. 190). Paris, 1945. The Jacobins as a petty-bourgeois group which imposed moderate solutions by extreme means.

Mazauric, C. *Babeuf et la Conspiration pour l'égalité*. Paris, 1962. Contains a good resume of the movement itself as well as biographies of the principals and an analysis of the doctrine.

Onnis, Pia. "Filippo Buonarroti, la congiura di Babeuf e il babuvismo," *Nuova Rivista storica* (1952), pp. 489–504. An important review article. *Cf.* also J. Godechot, "Les travaux récents sur Babeuf et le babouvisme," *Annales historiques de la Révolution française* (1960), pp. 368–387.

Sydenham, M. J. *The Girondins*. London, 1961. A study in the style of Namier which asserts the similarity in background of Girondins and Jacobins.

3. Economics and Finance

Bouchary, J. *Les Manieurs d'argent à Paris à la fin du XVIIIe siècle*. 3 vols. Paris, 1939–1943. On the role of banking and finance in the Revolution.

Clough, S. B. *France: A History of National Economics, 1789–1939*. New York, 1939. A good survey with much bibliography.

Festy, O. *L'Agriculture pendant la Révolution française: l'utilisation des jachères*. Paris, 1947. Deals with the technical problems of agriculture, especially with the question of fallow land.

Harris, S. E. *The Assignats*. Cambridge, Mass., 1930. On the utility of the assignats as a new method of state financing.

Marion, M. *La Vente des biens nationaux pendant la Révolution avec étude spéciale des ventes dans les départe-*

ments de la Gironde et du Cher. Paris, 1908. *Cf.* also his *Histoire financière de la France depuis 1715* (volumes II–IV). Paris, 1919–1925. Still works of great importance.

Nussbaum, F. L. *Commercial Policy in the French Revolution: A Study of the Career of G. J. A. Ducher*. Washington, 1923. On the movement from economic liberalism to mercantilism under the Committee of Public Safety.

4. Church and State

Aulard, F. V. A. *Christianity and the French Revolution*. Boston, 1927. The French edition appeared in 1924.

Hales, E. E. Y. *Revolution and Papacy, 1769–1846*. New York, 1960. A survey by the Catholic biographer of Pius IX.

Latreille, A. *L'Église catholique et la Révolution*. 2 vols. Paris, 1946–1950. A Catholic view and a standard work on relations between Church and state during the Revolution.

McManners, J. *French Ecclesiastical Society under the Ancien Régime: A Study of Angers in the Eighteenth Century*. New York, 1960. A study of the religious life of a French community throughout the century and the impact upon it of the Revolution.

Mathiez, A. *Les Origines des cultes révolutionnaires, 1789–1792*. Paris, 1910. *Rome et le clergé français sous la Constituante*. Paris, 1907. *La Question religieuse sous la Révolution*. Paris, 1930. *La Révolution et l'Eglise*. Paris, 1910. *La Théophilanthropie et le culte décadaire, 1796–1802*. Paris, 1904. A whole series of works on the problem by the prolific French historian.

5. Other Problems

Lefebvre, G. *Les Paysans du Nord pendant la Révolution française*. Lille, 1924. 2 vols. (New ed. in French, Bari, 1959.) A pioneering work showing the complexities of the social and economic positions of the peasantry. *Cf.* also his *Questions agraires au temps de la Terreur*. Paris, 1932.

Mahan, A. T. *The Influence of Sea Power upon the French Revolution and Empire, 1793–1812*. 2 vols. Boston, 1893. Admiral Mahan was the classic historian of the role of sea power in history.

Mathiez, A. *La Révolution et les Étrangers.* Paris, 1918. On the activities of foreign agents in Paris.

Phipps, R. W. *The Armies of the First French Republic and the Rise of the Marshals of Napoleon I.* 5 vols. London, 1926–1939. A detailed military history of the whole period.

Rudé, G. *The Crowd in the French Revolution.* Oxford, 1959. An important work centered on the problem of the class origins of Revolutionary crowds and the causes and motives for their agitations. *Cf.* also his *The Crowd in History, 1730–1848.* New York, 1964. Chapters Six through Eight deal with "riots" of the French Revolution.

Sorel, A. *L'Europe et la Révolution française.* 8 vols. Paris, 1885–1904. Though now badly out of date, this is still an important work on international relations.

Some Biographies of Revolutionary Figures

Barthou, L. *Danton.* Paris, 1932.

Brinton, C. *The Lives of Talleyrand.* New York, 1936.*

Clapham, L. *The Abbé Sieyès: An Essay in the Politics of the French Revolution.* London, 1912.

Cooper, D. *Talleyrand.* London, 1932.

Curtis, E. N. *Saint-Just, Colleague of Robespierre.* New York, 1935.

Dawson, J. C. *Lakanal, the Regicide.* New York, 1948.

Dowd, D. L. *Pageant-Master of the Republic: Jacques-Louis David and the French Revolution.* Lincoln, Nebraska, 1948.

Dupré, H. *Lazare Carnot, Republican Patriot.* Oxford, Ohio, 1940.

Eagan, J. M. *Maximilien Robespierre, Nationalist Dictator.* New York, 1938.

Eisenstein, E. *Filippo Michele Buonarroti: The First Professional Revolutionary.* Cambridge, Mass., 1959.

Ellery, E. *Brissot de Warville: A Study in the History of the French Revolution.* Boston, 1915.

Gershoy, L. *Bertrand Barère, a Reluctant Terrorist.* Princeton, 1962.

Gottschalk, L. R. *Lafayette.* 4 vols. Chicago, 1935–1950.

Gottschalk, L. R. *Jean-Paul Marat: A Study in Radicalism.* New York, 1927.

Korngold, R. *Robespierre, The First Modern Dictator.* London, 1937.

Loménie, L., and C. de. *Les Mirabeau.* 5 vols. Paris, 1878–1890.

Madelin, L. *Fouché.* 2 vols. Paris, 1900.

Reinhard, M. *Le Grand Carnot.* 2 vols. Paris, 1950–1952.

Scudder, E. S. *Prince of the Blood.* London, 1937. A biography of Philippe Egalité.

Sieburg, F. *Robespierre, the Incorruptible.* New York, 1938.

Thompson, J. M. *Leaders of the French Revolution.* Oxford, 1929.

Thompson, J. M. *Robespierre.* 2 vols. Oxford, 1935. *Cf.* also his *Robespierre and the French Revolution.* New York, 1952.*

Van Deusen, G. C. *Sieyès: His Life and His Nationalism.* New York, 1932.

Walter, G. *Hébert.* Paris, 1930.

Ward, R. S. *Maximilien Robespierre: A Study in Deterioration.* London, 1934.

Welch, O. J. G. *Mirabeau: A Study of a Democratic Monarchist.* London, 1951.

Wendel, H. *Danton.* New Haven, 1935.

The Atlantic Revolution: Some General Works

Amann, P., ed. *The Eighteenth-Century Revolution—French or Western?* Boston, 1963. A collection of articles for and against the Palmer-Godechot thesis as well as some on the non-French Revolutions of the time.

Anderson, M. S. *Europe in the Eighteenth Century, 1713–1783.* New York, 1961. Provides an excellent up-to-date background to the various revolutions.

Brinton, C. *The Anatomy of Revolution.* New York, 1938. Rev. ed. 1952.* A comparative study of the English, American, French, and Russian Revolutions.

Echeverria, D. *Mirage in the West: A History of the French Image of American Society to 1815*. Princeton, 1957.

Gentz, F. *Three Revolutions: The French and American Revolutions Compared.* Trans. by John Quincy Adams (n.d.) Chicago, 1959.* Gentz, who was Metternich's secretary, regarded the American Revolution as legitimate because it, unlike the French, took cognizance of tradition.

Godechot, J. *La Grande nation: L'expansion révolutionnaire de la France dans le monde de 1789 à 1799*. 2 vols. Paris, 1956. Set within the framework of the "Western Revolution" idea, but dealing mainly with the expansion of France.

Gottschalk, L. "The Place of the American Revolution in the Causal Pattern of the French Revolution," *Publications of the American Friends of Lafayette,* No. 2 (1948). Stresses the importance of the American Revolution in bringing about the French Revolution.

Hill, H. B. "The Constitutions of Continental Europe, 1789–1813," *Journal of Modern History,* VIII (1936), 82–94. Shows that nearly all those constitutions were products of French intervention.

Markov, W., ed. *Maximilien Robespierre 1758–1794: Beiträge zu seinem 200 Geburstag*. Berlin, 1958. The prȍblem of Jacobinism in a number of European countries and in America.

Palmer, R. R. *The Age of the Democratic Revolution. A Political History of Europe and America, 1760–1800*. 2 vols. Princeton, 1958–1964. The most detailed exposition of the Palmer-Godechot thesis that all the movements for change in this period were fundamentally interrelated and grew out of similar needs and ideas. For Palmer, this does not mean that the French Revolution did not have particular and original features.

Palmer, R. R., and Godechot, J. "Le problème de l'Atlantique du XVIIIè au XXè siècle," *Relazioni del X° Congresso Internazionale di Scienze Storiche,* V, pp. 175–239. Rome, 1955. Asserts the unity of an Atlantic civilization in the eighteenth century.

Rudé, G. "The Outbreak of the French Revolution," *Past and Present,* No. 8 (1955), 28–42. In opposition to the Palmer-Godechot thesis.

Works on Individual Countries During the Eighteenth Century and the Age of the Democratic Revolution

The Balkans and Greece

Dascalakis, A. *Rhigas Velestinlis: La Révolution française et les préludes de l'indépendance hellênique.* Paris, 1937.

Demos, R. "The Neo-Hellenic Enlightenment (1750–1821)," *Journal of the History of Ideas,* XIX (1958), 523–541. On the connections between French and Greek thought.

Jelavich, C., ed. *The Balkans in Transition since the Eighteenth Century.* Berkeley, 1963. *Cf.* the articles by Shaw, Stavrianos, and Stoianovich.

Stavrianos, L. *The Balkans Since 1453.* New York, 1958. The standard history.

Stoianovich, T. "The Conquering Balkan Orthodox Merchant," *Journal of Economic History* (1960), pp. 234–313. The role of these merchants in disseminating ideas in the Balkans. A pioneering study.

Belgium

Gorman, T. K. *America and Belgium: A Study of the Influence of the United States on the Belgian Revolution of 1789–1790.* London, 1925.

Harsin, P. *La Révolution liégeoise de 1789.* Brussels, 1958.

Tassier, S. *Les démocrates belges de 1789: Étude sur le Vonckisme et la révolution brabançonne.* Brussels, 1930. *Cf.* also her *Histoire de la Belgique sous l'occupation française en 1792 et 1793.* Brussels, 1934.

Canada

Burt, A. L. *The Old Province of Quebec.* Minneapolis, 1933. On the establishment of British rule in what is now Quebec and Ontario.

Christie, R. *History of the Late Province of Lower Canada.* 6 vols. Quebec and Montreal, 1848–1855. A political history of the years 1791–1840 by a participant in the events.

Wade, M. "Quebec and the French Revolution of 1789; the Missions of Henri Mezière," *Canadian Historical Review*

(1950), pp. 345–368. The role of emigré priests to French Canada in establishing the negative image of the Revolution.

Germany

Biro, S. S. *The German Policy of Revolutionary France.* 2 vols. Cambridge, Mass., 1957. A massive study of French policy in Germany from 1792 to 1797.

Bruford, W. H. *Germany in the Eighteenth Century.* Cambridge, Mass., 1935. With Holborn, the only detailed work on Germany in this period.

Droz, J. *L'Allemagne et la Révolution française.* Paris, 1949. Shows that pro-revolutionary sentiment in Germany was primarily intellectualistic and abstract.

Gooch, G. P. *Germany and the French Revolution.* London, 1920. Especially on the impact of the Revolution on intellectual movements.

Holborn, H. *A History of Modern Germany: 1648–1840.* New York, 1964. The revolutionary era as one in which German politics and intellectual movements cooperated.

Rosenberg, H. *Bureaucracy, Aristocracy and Autocracy: The Prussian Experience, 1660–1815.* Cambridge, Mass., 1958. The impact of the French Revolution as a "revolution from above."

Valjavec, F. *Die Entstehung der politischen Strömungen in Deutschland, 1770–1815.* Munich, 1951. On the origins of democratic thought in Germany.

Voegt, H. *Die deutsche jakobinische Literatur und Publizistik, 1789–1800.* Berlin, 1955. Contains important documents on German Jacobinism.

Great Britain and Ireland

Birley, R. *The English Jacobins from 1789 to 1802.* London, 1924.

Brown, P. A. *The French Revolution in English History.* London, 1918. Sympathetic to the English Jacobins.

Calkin, H. L. "La propagande en Irlande des idées de la Révolution française," *Annales historiques de la Révolution française* (1955), pp. 143–160.

Cobb, R. "Les Jacobins anglais et la Révolution française,"

Bulletin de la Société d'Histoire Moderne, 14 (1960), 2–5. Thesis that the English Jacobins were "strangers in their own country," a view which is not shared by many of these other writers.

Cobban, A., ed. *The Debate on the French Revolution, 1789–1800.* 2nd ed. London, 1950.

Cobban, A. *Edmund Burke and the Revolt Against the Eighteenth Century: A Study of the Political and Social Thinking of Burke, Wordsworth, Coleridge, and Southey.* London, 1929.

Cole, G. D. H., and Postgate, R. *The British Common People, 1746–1946.* New York and London, 1961.* *Cf.* especially Chapters X through XIV.

Davies, A. "La Révolution française et le Pays de Galles," *Annales Historiques de la Révolution française,* XXVII (1955), 202–212. On revolutionary forces in Wales.

Dechamps, J. *Les îles britanniques et la Révolution française, 1789–1803.* Brussels, 1949. Emphasizes the importance of radical discontent in Great Britain.

Hall, W. P. *British Radicalism, 1791–97.* New York, 1912.

Hayes, R. *Ireland and Irishmen in the French Revolution.* London, 1932. The background to the uprising of 1798.

Jacob, R. *Rise of the United Irishmen, 1791–1794.* London, 1937. A study of the United Irish Club to its suppression in 1794.

Laprade, W. T. *England and the French Revolution, 1789–97.* Baltimore, 1909.

Maccoby, S. *English Radicalism, 1762–1785: The Origins.* New York, 1955. On the beginnings of the reform and revolutionary movements in England.

Meikle, H. W. *Scotland and the French Revolution.* Glasgow, 1912. Sympathetic to Jacobinism in Scotland.

Rose, J. H. *William Pitt and the Great War.* London, 1911.

Rudé, G. *Wilkes and Liberty.* Oxford, 1962. On the reform movement preceding the revolutionary era.

Stuart Jones, E. H. *An Invasion that Failed: The French Expedition to Ireland, 1796.* Oxford, 1950.

Stuart Jones, E. H. *The Last Invasion of Britain.* Cardiff, 1950. On Colonel Tate's invasion of 1797 and its consequences.

Thompson, E. P. *The Making of the English Working*

Class. London, 1963. *Cf.* the preface and pp. 9–185 of this great work.

Western, J. R. "The Volunteer Movement as an Anti-Revolutionary Force, 1793–1801," *English Historical Review* (1956), pp. 603–614. On an attempt by the British government to counteract revolutionary propaganda among the workers.

THE HAPSBURG EMPIRE

Benda, K. "Les Jacobins hongrois," *Annales historiques de la Révolution française,* XXXI (1959), 38–60. Benda is the leading authority on the Jacobins in Hungary. He has also published the writings of the Hungarian Jacobins: *A Magyar Jakubinusok Iratai.* 3 vols. Budapest, 1952–1957.

Bödy, P. "The Hungarian Jacobin Conspiracy of 1794–95," *Journal of Central European Affairs,* XXII (1962), 3–26.

Eszarly, C. d': "Les Jacobin hongrois et leurs conceptions juridico-politiques," *Revue d'histoire moderne et contemporaine* (1960), pp. 291–307.

Fejtö, F. *Un Habsbourg révolutionnaire, Joseph II: Portrait d'un despote éclairé.* Paris, 1953.

Kerner, R. J. *Bohemia in the Eighteenth Century: A Study in Political, Economic and Social History with Special Reference to the Reign of Leopold II, 1790–92.* New York, 1932. *Cf.* especially for land tenure and class relations in Bohemia on the eve of the Revolution.

Kutnar, F. "La critique de la Révolution française dans les brochures tchèques d'alors," *Le Monde slave* (1935), pp. 131–158. Important for the counterrevolutionary literature.

Mejdricka, K. "Les Paysans tchèques et la Révolution française," *Annales historiques de la Révolution française* (1958), pp. 64–74. Attempts to show that the lower classes in Bohemia were well aware of events in France.

Palmer, R. R., and Kenez, P. "Two Documents of the Hungarian Revolutionary Movement of 1794," *Journal of Central European Affairs,* XX (1960), 423–444. "Catechisms" of the Hungarian Jacobins.

Sugar, P. F. "The Influence of the Englightenment and the French Revolution in Eighteenth-Century Hungary," *Journal of Central European Affairs,* XVII (1958), 331–355.

Wangermann, E. *From Joseph II to the Jacobin Trials: Government Policy and Public Opinion in the Hapsburg Dominions in the Period of the French Revolution.* London, 1959. An important study of popular discontent and radicalism.

Italy

Candeloro, G. *Storia dell'Italia moderna.* Vol. 1. Milan, 1956. The best synthesis of Italian history from 1700 to 1815. Contains a fine critical bibliography.

Canzio, S. *La prima repubblica cisalpina e il sentimento nazionale.* Modena, 1944. A study of the democratic press of the time.

Cingari, G. *Giacobini e Sanfedisti in Calabria nel 1799.* Messina, 1957.

Codignola, E. *Illuministi, giansenisti e giacobini nell'Italia del settecento.* Florence, 1947. Asserts that Jansenism was an essential element in the later reforms and radicalism.

Croce, B. *La Rivoluzione napoletana del 1799.* 3rd ed. Bari, 1912. A major work on the so-called "Parthenopean" Republic.

Cuoco, V. *Saggio storico sulla Rivoluzione napoletana.* Bari, 1913. First published in 1800, this famous work by a participant in the Revolution established the distinction between "passive" and "active" revolutions.

Felice, R. de. "Richerche storiche sul 'Giacobonismo' italiano," *Rassegna storica del Risorgimento* (1958 and 1960), pp. 1–19 and 1–32. On Pasquale Matera and Giuseppe Ceracchi.

Ghisalberti, C. *Le costituzioni "Giacobine" 1796–1799.* Milan, 1954. Emphasizes Italian rather than French contributions.

Giuntella, V. "L'esperienza rivoluzionaria," in *Nuove questioni di storia del Risorgimento e dell'unità d'Italia.* Milan, 1961. Pp. 311–343. A careful summary of the latest scholarship with an annotated bibliography of recent work. *Cf.* also his *La crisi del potere temporale alla fine del settecento.* Bologna, 1954.

Godechot, J. "Les Français et l'unité italienne sous le

Directoire," *Revue internationale d'histoire politique et constitutionnelle* (1952), pp. 96–110, 193–204. Shows how the Directory did not encourage the unification of Italy for fear of reviving Jacobinism in France itself.

Luraghi, R. "Politica, economia e amministrazione nell'Italia napoleonica," *Nuove questioni di storia del Risorgimento e dell'unità d'Italia*. Milan, 1961. Pp. 345–386. A good summary.

Morandi, C. *Idee e formazioni politiche in Lombardia dal 1748 al 1814*. Turin, 1927. On relations between the Lombard liberals and the Austrians.

Peroni, B. "La passione dell'indipendenza nella Lombardia occupata dai Francesci, 1796–97," *Nuova rivista storica* (1931), pp. 60–102. *Cf.* also his "Gli italiani alla vigilia della dominazione francese, 1793–96," *Nuova rivista storica* (1951), pp. 227–242.

Reinhard, M. *Avec Bonaparte en Italie*. Paris, 1946.

Roberti, M. *Milano capitale napoleonica: La formazione di uno stato moderno, 1796–1814*. 3 vols. Milan, 1947. Especially important on administration and legislation.

Rota, E. *Le origini del Risorgimento (1700–1800)*. 2 vols. Milan, 1938. Considers the whole eighteenth century, not just the revolutionary period, as the "premise" of the Risorgimento.

Saitta, A. *Filippo Buonarroti: Contributo alla storia della sua vita e del suo pensiero*. 2 vols. Rome, 1950–1951. Contains many important texts and documents on Franco-Italian relations from 1793 to 1796.

Vaccarino, G. *I Patrioti "anarchistes" e l'idea dell'unità italiana, 1796–99*. Turin, 1955. The Italian Jacobins as the originators of the idea of Italian unification.

Valsecchi, F. *L'Italia nel settecento, dal 1714 al 1788*. Milan, 1959. The most up-to-date summary on a large scale of eighteenth-century Italy. *Cf.* also his "Dispotismo illuminato," in *Nuove questioni di storia del Risorgimento e dell'unità d'Italia*. Milan, 1961. Pp. 189–240.

Zaghi, C. *Bonaparte e il Direttorio dopo Campoformio: Il problema italiano nella diplomazia europea 1797–98*. Naples, 1956. Shows the inability or unwillingness of the Directory to give sufficient support to revolutionary forces in Italy.

Zangheri, R. *Prime ricerche sulla distribuzione della pro-*

prietà fondiaria nella pianura bolognese, 1789–1835. Bologna, 1957. Demonstrates that the Italian peasantry received fewer benefits than the French from land distribution in the revolutionary period.

Latin America and the Caribbean

Barbagelata, H. D. *La Révolution francaise et l'Amerique latine*. Paris, 1936.

Caillet-Bois, R. *Ensayo sobre el Rio de la Plata y la Revolución francesa*. Buenos Aires, 1929.

Humphreys, R. A., and Lynch, J., eds. *The Origins of the Latin American Revolutions, 1809–1830: European Influences or American Nationalism?* New York, 1964.* A series of essays evaluating the influence of the French Revolution on Spanish and Portuguese America.

James, C. L. R. *The Black Jacobins: Toussaint l'Ouverture and the San Domingo Revolution*. New York, 1938. The effects of the French Revolution on the Negroes of the Caribbean.

Korngold, R. *Citizen Toussaint*. Boston, 1944.

Ruy, A. *A primeira revoluçao social brasileira, 1798*. Rio de Janeiro, 1942.

Whitaker, A. R., ed. *Latin America and the Enlightenment*. New York, 1942. A collection of essays.

Poland

Bain, R. N. *The Last King of Poland and His Contemporaries*. London, 1909.

Grossbart, J. "La Presse polonaise et la Révolution française," *Annales historiques de la Révolution française* (1937), pp. 127–150, 241–256, and (1938), pp. 234–266.

Lesnodorski, B. "Les Facteurs intellectuels de la formation de la société polonaise moderne au siècle des lumières," in *La Pologne au Xe Congrès International des Sciences Historiques à Rome*. Warsaw, 1955. *Cf.* also his bibliography of recent works on "Le Siècle des lumières en Pologne," *Acta Poloniae Historica*, Vol. 4, 1961.

Montfort, H. de. *Le Drame de la Pologne: Kosciuszko, 1746–1817*. Paris, 1945.

Przeglad Historyczny [Historical Review]. Warsaw, 1951.

Issue devoted to Poland in the late eighteenth century, especially on the peasant question and on the role of the Jacobin Kollontai. Summaries of each article in French.

Russia

Larivière, C. de. *Cathérine II et la Révolution française.* Paris, 1895.

Mazour, A. *The First Russian Revolution: The Decembrist Movement, its Origins, Development and Significance.* Stanford, 1937.

Strange, M. N. *La Société russe et la Révolution française.* Moscow, 1961. By a Soviet historian.

Vernadsky, G. "Reforms Under Czar Alexander I: French and American influences," *Review of Politics* (1947), pp. 47–64.

Scandinavia

Bain, R. N. "The Hats and Caps and Gustavus III," in *The Cambridge Modern History,* Vol. VI (1900).

Hovde, B. J. *The Scandinavian Countries, 1720–1865: The Rise of the Middle Classes.* 2 vols. Boston, 1943.

Petiet, R. *Gustave IV Adolphe et la Révolution française.* Paris, 1914.

Söderhjelm, A. *Sverige och den franska Revolutionen.* 2 vols. Stockholm, 1920.

Spain

Herr, R. *The Eighteenth-Century Revolution in Spain.* Princeton, 1958. Emphasizes the great importance of the Enlightenment and the French Revolution in the creation of modern Spain.

Hyslop, B. "French Jacobin Nationalism and Spain," in *Nationalism and Internationalism: Essays Inscribed to Carlton J. H. Hayes.* New York, 1950.

Ossorio y Gallardo, A. *El Pensiamiento político catalán en la guerra de España con le República francesa, 1793–95.* Madrid, 1913. Shows that nationalistic appeals of the French type (*levée en masse,* etc.) were used in Catalonia for conservative purposes.

Sarrailh, J. *L'Espagne éclairée de la seconde moitié du XVIIIè siècle.* Paris, 1954.

SWITZERLAND

Chapuisat, E. *La Suisse et la Révolution française.* Geneva, 1945. *Cf.* also his *La Prise d'armes de 1782 à Genève.* Geneva, 1932.

Custer, A. *Die zürcher Untertanen und die französische Revolution.* Zurich, 1942. A study of the attitudes of the rural population outside of Zurich.

Feldman, J. *Propaganda und Diplomatie: Eine Studie über die Beziehungen Frankreichs zu den eidgenössischen Orten von Beginn der französischen Revolution bis zum Sturz der Girondisten.* Zurich, 1957. Argues that the Swiss revolutionaries in France had little effect on French policy in Switzerland.

Gasser, A. "Der Irrweg der Helvetik," *Zeitschrift für schweizerische Geschichte* (1947), pp. 425–455. Stresses the foreign inspiration of the Helvetic Republic.

Rufer, A. "La République helvétique," in the *Dictionnaire historique et biographique de la Suisse.* 1928. According to Palmer and Godechot, a very good and sympathetic summary of the history of the Helvetic Republic.

Weber, E. *Pestalozzi, der revolutionäre Patriot.* Zurich, 1946. *Cf.* also M. Bächlin, *Pestalozzi als Socialrevolutionär.* Zurich, 1946.

TURKEY

Gibb, H. A. R., and Bowen, H. *Islamic Society and the West.* 2 vols. Vol. 1: *Islamic Society in the Eighteenth Century.* New York, 1950–1957. A survey of the Ottoman Empire in the mid-eighteenth century.

Lewis, B. "The Impact of the French Revolution on Turkey," *Journal of World History* (1953), pp. 105–115. The French Revolution as the origin of Ottoman reformism.

THE UNITED PROVINCES

Colenbrander, H. T. *Die bataafsche Republiek.* Amsterdam, 1908. Critical of the Batavians.

Geyl, P. "The Batavian Revolution: 1795–1798," in *Encounters in History,* pp. 226–241. New York, 1961.* An essay of 1956 emphasizing the "moderate" character of the revolution.

Geyl, P. *Geschiedenis van de Nederlandsche stam.* Vol. III. Amsterdam, 1959. Contains a detailed discussion of the Batavian Republic. *Cf.* also his "Noord-Nederlandse patriotten-beweging en Brabantse revolutie," *Nieuw Vlaams Tijdschrift* (1953), pp. 3–20. A critique of Colenbrander's views on the Batavians.

Palmer, R. R. "Much in Little: The Dutch Revolution of 1795," *Journal of Modern History,* XXVI (1954), 15–35. "A typical revolution of the era."

The United States

Alden, J. R. *The American Revolution, 1775–83.* New York, 1954.*

Clauder, A. C. *American Commerce as Affected by the Wars of the French Revolution and Napoleon, 1793–1812.* New York, 1932.

Gipson, L. H. *The Coming of the Revolution, 1763–1775.* New York, 1954.* By a leading authority on British imperial policy.

Hazen, C. D. *Contemporary American Opinion of the French Revolution.* Baltimore, 1897. Hostile to the influence of the Revolution in America.

Jameson, J. F. *The American Revolution Considered as a Social Movement.* Princeton, 1926.* *Cf.* the critique of this classic work by F. B. Tolles, "The American Revolution Considered as a Social Movement: A Reevaluation," *The American Historical Review,* LX (1954), 1–12.

Knollenberg, B. *The Origins of the American Revolution, 1759–1766.* New York, 1960.* Especially on British imperial policy of the 1760s.

Link, E. P. *Democratic-Republican Societies.* New York, 1942. A study on the American equivalent of the Jacobin Clubs.

Lyon, E. W. "The Directory and the United States," *The American Historical Review,* XLIII (1938), 514–532.

Miller, J. C. *Crisis in Freedom: The Alien and Sedition Acts*. Boston, 1951. A strong critique of the acts.

Morgan, E. S. *The Birth of the Republic, 1763–1789*. Chicago, 1956.*

Ritcheson, C. R. *British Politics and the American Revolution*. Norman, 1954. Especially on the effects of the revolution on British political thought.

Schlesinger, A. M. *The Colonial Merchants and the American Revolution, 1763–1776*. New York, 1918. On the merchants' attempts to guide the movement in their interests.

Vossler, O. *Die amerikanischen Revolutionsideale in ihrem Verhältnis zu den europäischen*. Munich, 1929. The French Revolution as the catalyst for the American sense of a mission for freedom in the entire world.

Wahlke, J. C., ed. *The Causes of the American Revolution*. Boston, 1962. Rev. ed.* Contains writings by Hacker, Andrews, Dickerson, Gipson, Knollenberg, Rossiter, Jensen, Becker, J. T. Adams, and P. Smith.

INDEX